D0204088

IRAQ AND THE INTERNATIONAL OIL SYSTEM

James Kistler

IRAQ AND THE INTERNATIONAL OIL SYSTEM

Why America Went to War in the Gulf

Stephen Pelletière

PRAEGER

Westport, Connecticut
London

Library of Congress Cataloging-in-Publication Data

Pelletière, Stephen C.
Iraq and the international oil system : why America went to war in the Gulf / Stephen Pelletière.
p. cm.
Includes bibliographical references and index.
ISBN 0-275-94562-6 (alk. paper)
1. Persian Gulf War, 1991—Causes. 2. Petroleum industry and trade—Political aspects—United States. 3. Petroleum industry and trade—Political aspects—Middle East. 4. United States relations—Iraq. 5. Iraq relations—United States. I. Title.
DS79.719P45 2001
956.7044'2—dc21 00-042773

British Library Cataloguing in Publication Data is available.

Library of Congress Catalog Card Number: 00-042773
ISBN: 0-275-94562-6

First published in 2001

Praeger Publishers, 88 Post Road West, Westport, CT 06881
An imprint of Greenwood Publishing Group, Inc.
www.praeger.com

Printed in the United States of America

The paper used in this book complies with the Permanent Paper Standard issued by the National Information Standards Organization (Z39.48-1984).

10 9 8 7 6 5 4 3 2

To Neelo, for
All the Help

You don't have to prove it.
You just have to know how it's done.

—Old political saying

Contents

Introduction

The fight of the Iraqis against, primarily, the United States has rarely been viewed as having much to do with oil. This book contends that this is natural, given that the activities of the oil industry both inside and outside the United States are little understood by Americans.

The author first became aware of this situation while researching this book. All of the conventional explanations as to why the Gulf War occurred seemed untenable. It was fought with such ferocity, and so many resources were expended, that there had to have been some great stake.

Since Iraq has oil and took over Kuwait, which also has oil, and since oil is so important to the smooth functioning of the world's economy, it appeared natural that oil would have had something, if not everything, to do with why the war took place.

The contradiction, which soon proved difficult to rationalize, was why Iraq with so much oil would have thought it necessary to take over Kuwait.[1] To get *more* oil? There is no economic justification for such a move.

After considerable research a much more believable explanation began to emerge. There is such a thing as an oil system, using the word "system" in the sense of a setup to achieve control of something (in this case, oil). That system was put in place in the 1920s by three large oil companies that joined together in a cartel. The cartel's history is well chronicled, thanks to a 1952 Senate Investigation Committee report.[2] However, it is generally presumed that the cartel and the system that it supported went out of business sometime after 1952, certainly by 1973, the date of the Organization of Petroleum Exporting Countries (OPEC) revolution.

The author's research, however, showed that this was not the case. The cartel ceased to be; the system limped along. In regard to the cartel, several attempts were made to revive it, and all proved unsuccessful.

Then in 1988, Iraq emerged from the Iran–Iraq War as a victor, and it began to appear that it would seek to capitalize on its win by, among other things, making itself the head of OPEC. That would have given it a great say—if not a determining one—over how oil was produced, and that, of course, would have translated into control over pricing.

This was a situation repugnant to many, and thus forces inimical to Iraq started a media campaign, the effect of which was to so polarize conditions between the Iraqis and the United States that, at a certain point, war became inevitable.

This book examines the campaign in all of its phases because it was quite complex and not at all simple, as the conspiracy theorists would make it out to be.

This book then speculates about the future of Iraq–U.S. relations. It concludes that America's present policy toward Iraq—the so-called Dual Containment policy—is ruinous. Unless it is amended, there is every chance that the United States will have to go to war, perhaps not against Iraq but against some other oil-producing country whose situation is analogous to that of Iraq. In other words, the finding of this book is that the plight of Iraq, vis-à-vis oil, is matched in other lands, and therefore it would be foolish for American policymakers to dismiss the 1991 war as an aberration.

The book is divided into six chapters. The first has to do with the rise of the oil industry in the United States and its subsequent move overseas. Chapter 2 takes up the formation of the great cartel and begins to examine the system that the oil magnates created.

In Chapter 3, attempts by the U.S. government to check the power of the cartel are examined. We see how the cartel was able to turn these aside. We also begin to deal with the issue of exploitation by the cartel of the Iranians and Iraqis.

Chapter 4 is devoted totally to the clash—actually a series of clashes—between successive regimes in Iraq with the oil cartel. Here we first encounter the Iraqi Ba'th Party of the present leader, Saddam Hussein.

Chapter 5 is about OPEC and its coup in 1973, in which it effectively pushed the cartel to one side as it attempted to take control of production and pricing of oil.

Chapter 6 explores the media campaign against Iraq that eventually produced the war. This book ends with an assessment of America's current involvement in the Middle East in general and the Gulf in particular.

One more word about systems before we proceed. Along with everything else, they are coercive arrangements. Based on force, they depend for their success on the ability of the operators to get their way. The idea is to gain control over something (as we said above) with the intent of benefiting, and since the aim is to achieve the greatest benefits possible, the whole operation of system building tends to be pretty heedless.[3]

Systems, as the author defines them, are setups designed to guarantee benefits to the few by denying them to the generality. We begin our investigation with a look at the growth of the oil industry in the United States.

NOTES

1. Iraq is believed to have the second largest reserves of oil in the world, and by some, it is regarded as having more oil than the world leader, Saudi Arabia.

2. U.S. Senate, *The International Petroleum Cartel, Staff Report to the Federal Trade Commission, Submitted to the Subcommittee on Monopoly of the Select Committee on Small Business* (Washington, DC: Government Printing Office, 1952).

3. In other words, a system, in the sense we are construing it, is something illicit, and like all illicit combinations it depends for its successful operation on force. As we will see, who applies the force is crucial.

CHAPTER 1

The Birth of the U.S. Oil Industry and Its Movement Overseas

THE ECONOMICS OF OIL

Col. Edwin Drake unleashed a great revolution when in 1859 he drilled his first successful well in Pennsylvania. Until then Seneca Oil, as it was known to the natives around Titusville, was used mainly as a medicine.[1] The firm that patented the oil did well. However, in order to make a profit, it had to price the oil fairly high; a bottle went for $1.50.[2]

Some businessmen in the East had been looking into oil as an illuminant. In those days, lighting was supplied mainly by whale oil or paraffin or gas, all of which were not very efficient means. In addition, whales, having been hunted almost to extinction, were about to disappear as a source.

The businessmen wanted to use Seneca Oil as a lighting substance, but they knew that to do so successfully, it must be mass-marketed, and that meant ensuring a large and dependable supply.

Drake's innovation of drilling was a real breakthrough, considering the way oil exists in nature. Oil stands in pockets of porous rock that spread out under the ground in a broad stratum. By digging down and tapping into the chambers where the oil is secreted, one can cause it to rise to the surface. Sometimes the oil will rise at tremendous speed, and then it bursts into the air as a gusher. A gusher can yield hundreds of thousands of barrels of oil a day. Once Drake succeeded in extracting oil in such large quantities, the product could then be developed on a grand scale.

As soon as Drake sank his first successful well, his employers circulated oil specimens to potential investors on the East Coast of America and in Europe for the purpose of having them analyzed.[3] On the basis of these, contracts were let, which showed that a market did exist for the product. This, in turn, triggered a kind of gold rush, in which thousands of prospectors converged on Titusville, seeking to make their fortunes. Production of oil rose rapidly, going from 450,000 barrels in 1860 to 3 million barrels in 1862; oil sold in January 1861 for $10 a barrel.[4]

There was, however, an unfortunate side effect of the oil industry—it tended toward glut. This came about because of the way the law operated. In the United States, the owner of a piece of property may claim not only what is on the surface but what is underneath as well. This is almost unique; few other countries permit this.[5] In addition, American law provides for "the rule of capture," whereby one may claim whatever strays onto one's property from a neighbor's land, including oil.[6]

Once the oil underground has been tapped for extraction, it can be withdrawn without letup, until the field is exhausted. In the process, oil from neighboring claims will be captured, since the law allows for this. Unless the owners of those nearby claims want to be pillaged, they have to sink wells of their own and commence to drill. Thus, one can see that, within a relatively short space, hundreds of thousands of barrels of oil will be thrown onto the market, and that will make the price plunge.[7]

This is what happened. In January 1861 oil stood at $10 a barrel, by June it was down to 50 cents, and by the end of 1861 it was down to 10 cents.[8] At that, those prospectors who could no longer cover their costs packed up and left the fields. This made the whole industry come to a halt. Refiners had to shut their plants (having nothing to refine), and railroads, which had dedicated cars to transporting oil to market, had to leave them standing in the yards with nothing to ship.

This situation took the heart out of many who were involved with oil. The tendency of the industry toward glut seemed an insuperable barrier to making a success. Of course, as it turned out, this was not a correct assessment; ultimately, all obstacles were overcome, but the means whereby this was done were ruthless.

BIRTH OF THE SYSTEM

What was required was that somewhere along the line the oil flow should be interdicted. The logical place to apply the cutoff was at the refinery stage. The refineries had storage capacity and thus could hold onto the oil until such time as the price recovered. The problem with this solution, however, was that the refiners, like the prospectors, were difficult men to control. Not impossible; the *prospectors* were impossible. The refiners—because there were fewer of them—could be brought into line.[9]

The question was, By what means? What was the mechanism that could accomplish this? Effectively, it was the "drawback." Drawbacks were a form of coercion levied by the railroads on the refiners. By distinguishing a category of refiners whom they chose to aggrandize and another lot that they effectively meant to destroy, the railroads created conditions whereby the industry could be brought into line, that is, made to behave as a disciplined unit, which is the way that regulation was achieved.[10]

The railroaders singled out for preferential treatment a group of refineries associated with John D. Rockefeller.[11] Rockefeller seems to have been selected because he already had initiated a plan to rationalize the refining end of the oil business.

Rockefeller set up his first refinery in Cleveland in 1865 and shortly afterward induced two other refineries to combine with him, so they could pool their oil and in this way win rebates from the railroads.[12] Rebates were standard practice in those days. Whenever a shipper could assure the railroads of regular large consignments, he would be rewarded with a rebate.

Rockefeller, after first getting two other firms to combine, then went after others. This appears to be what brought him to the attention of the railroaders. An approach was made (by whom is not certain), and a meeting was arranged between Rockefeller and three of the largest railroads serving Pennsylvania at that time—the New York Central, the Pennsylvania, and the Erie. The meeting was held in November 1871 in New York City.[13]

The scheme, as it was put forward, was that the railroads would charge Rockefeller's combine a preferential rate for shipping its oil and charge all those not associated with it extra. A percentage of the extra (i.e., the drawback) would then be paid over to Rockefeller to use as he determined, but it appears, in fact, that he was meant to wield it as a club against his rivals.[14]

Rockefeller went to those refiners who were competing against him and urged them to join what he called the South Improvement Association.[15] This was a misnomer. The South Improvement group was not a civic organization; it was not even a volunteer outfit. Rockefeller was offering to buy his rivals out, and the cash for this came from the drawbacks. If the rivals refused, Rockefeller proceeded to "crush them"[16]; that is, he signaled the railroads to raise his rivals' rates so they could not make a profit. While the rivals floundered about trying to determine what was happening to them (because, of course, all this was being carried on in secret), Rockefeller shipped his oil at the railroads' reduced rate.

Ironically, looked at in retrospect, this was not a bad deal that Rockefeller was offering his rivals—provided they accepted his terms. The oilmen slated for buyout were expected to take their remuneration in Standard Oil Co. stock (this was the name that Rockefeller had given his firm). Those who did and who held onto the stock became extraordinarily wealthy men. However, those who went along became employees of Rockefeller. He sweetened his offer by allowing them to retain management control of their businesses (in that way they could remain active).[17] Still, there was no mistaking the fact that, under the new setup, Rockefeller ran the show.[18]

Obviously, the drawback scheme was crooked, which the schemers knew, as could be seen from how they operated. Refineries that accepted Rockefeller's buyout offer were made to sign secrecy oaths; they were not to mention that their firms had been taken over—even to their wives.[19] Ultimately, however—as might have been imagined—the word got out, and then there was a great uproar.

The refiners who had been excluded from Rockefeller's association formed a combine of their own and invited independent oil producers to join. The inclusion of the producers made sense since they, too, feared Rockefeller. It became obvious fairly quickly that the Standard combine was trying to gain control of the refinery business nationwide, and, of course, if that happened, it would be able to set prices, something no producer could relish.

Under ordinary conditions, refiner–producer unions would be too unstable to prove effective. The members of this particular front, however, were able to hold together long enough to force the railroads into capitulating. The railroads announced the dissolution of their deal with Rockefeller.

From the standpoint of the independents, this was a good thing. However, in the lead-up to this result, Rockefeller had moved with surprising speed to buy out 20 of the 26 refineries in Cleveland.[20] (At this time Cleveland was *the* oil refining center of the nation.) This gave him control over the largest "pool" of oil in the United States, and that, in turn, increased his leverage with the railroads. Even though they swore to the independents (as the opponents of Rockefeller came to be called) that they would eschew the rebate, the roads, in secret, reinstituted it for Rockefeller, and for him alone.[21]

Rockefeller through all of this period behaved like a man who was driven. He seems to have appreciated that, unless great gains were made quickly, his forward march would bog down. Hence, with barely a misstep, he would no sooner pull off one coup than he was on to another. After Cleveland, he moved quickly to cajole or coerce refiners in Pittsburgh and Philadelphia and in the oil regions to sell out to him. By 1875 it was estimated that he controlled 95 percent of the nation's refining capacity.[22]

Rockefeller and the railroad men, when they hatched the drawback scheme, operated on a simple principle: to control price and keep the industry profitable, one had to keep output of refined oil down.[23] In the 1870s, the refining end of the business was dominated by one set of interests—Rockefeller's. One would have assumed, therefore, that Rockefeller was safely positioned, the crucial maneuver whereby control was to be gained having been successfully completed.

It is a feature of the oil industry that vigilance can *never* be relaxed. Because of the way the industry is set up, *at any time* arrangements holding destructive forces in check may give way. This is what threatened in the last years of the nineteenth century—Rockefeller's position of dominance was about to be tested, and a serious attempt would be made to shake his control.

THE TRANSPORTATION END

The threat developed in the oil regions. The independent producers and refiners there hit upon a plan of transporting their oil to market via pipeline.[24] Pipelines for transporting oil had existed from the first days of the industry. However, two things were thought to militate against their extensive use. One, the shipment of oil by pipe is cost-effective only if one has enormous quantities to transport.[25] Two, it was deemed impossible to move large quantities of oil over difficult stretches of terrain, such as mountains. Since the independents were essaying to move their oil to tidewater, this encompassed a great deal of difficult terrain.

The first consideration did not apply to the independents. Rockefeller's practices confronted them with the prospect of extinction. They had to find a way to get their oil to market, any way that they could.

As for the second constraint, the engineering art had progressed sufficiently by this date so that this, too, was not a problem. In 1876 the independents formed a company for transporting oil by pipe, and an engineer was found to build the line.

If this book were solely a study of Rockefeller, we would now want to see how he thwarted the pipeline venture; indeed, it makes for fascinating reading. For anyone interested, it is all in Ida Tarbell's classic work, *The History of the Standard Oil Co*. Here, it is enough to say that the scheme did not work; the independents, although they got the pipeline built, could not keep it from being taken over by Rockefeller. But Rockefeller's victory proved costly—it put another powerful figure in the business, Joseph D. Potts, on his guard.

Potts owned the Empire Transit Co., the biggest pipeline organization in the country. He now came to fear that Rockefeller, having whipped the independents, would next turn his sights on him.[26] Potts therefore set about to buttress his position by negotiating contracts for oil shipments through his lines with as many independent refiners and producers as he could. He wanted to be sure that, if Rockefeller tried to shut off his supply, he would have alternative sources to draw upon.

When Rockefeller and Potts commenced their fight, it was taken for granted that it would be a long, vicious struggle. Potts was associated with the Pennsylvania Railroad, and therefore it was anticipated that, in this affair, he could draw on the road's resources.

So he would have been able to do, except for an unexpected development. Coincidentally with the initiation of the fight, the Pennsylvania was hit with a bitter strike, which went on for many months.[27] At the end, the road was hurt badly and had to skip its dividend, the first time that it had done so since it was founded.

Because of this reverse, Pennsylvania was not in a position to support Potts, and thus, by 1888, the line was forced to meet with Rockefeller in New York, where it capitulated to his demand that all of the facilities of Empire be sold to him.[28] With that, Rockefeller and his associates had gained control of the second crucial area of the oil industry, transportation. This put Standard in a position to dispense with the railroads, having a pipeline system that could transport oil more efficiently than the railroads were able to do.

Looking back, then, what was accomplished in the period from 1865 to 1888? Effectively, the oil business was rationalized. Who initiated the process—whether it was the railroads or Rockefeller—is not certain.[29] Nor is this important. All we need know is that a system was developed whereby rationalization was effected, and first the railroads and Rockefeller and then Rockefeller alone carried through on it.

The basis of the system was to keep down the output of refined, so prices could be manipulated at will. The method for achieving control was to cow the producers and, once they were whipped, to maintain discipline over them. The guiding force in the conspiracy was Rockefeller. However, in time, the system was modified so that it could be directed not only by men of genius (of the Rockefeller stamp) but also by institutions. Still, the basic principle remained the same—control was achieved by reducing the number of significant players, creating a hierarchy of controllers, and keeping the control group small enough to be manageable.[30] We see this scheme adhered to throughout all of the subsequent stages of the industry's phenomenal growth.

One other point needs to be made. Rockefeller never was an oil producer; he stayed out of that end of the business. Production is extremely risky. For every 10 wells drilled, it is estimated that only 1 pays off.[31] Thus, by staying clear of this department, Rockefeller spared himself great potential loss. Along with that, given the peculiar economics of oil, it isn't necessary to be a producer if one wants control. To control the business, one only has to take over the refineries and, after that, see to transportation. Whoever has charge in these two areas rules.

Summing up, the Standard Oil Co., under Rockefeller's direction, succeeded in converting oil production into a mass-marketing operation. It did this by first smoothing out the boom-and-bust cycle in production and afterward by devising a means of conveying the oil to market in large quantities, which meant that the costs of production could be brought down and profits raised, but not unreasonably so. Consumers might gripe about prices, but they would pay, because the price was set so that they could just afford to.

One can gain an appreciation of what this meant by considering the following statistics—by 1872 oil was the fourth largest export of the United States and the first among man-made products.[32] By 1877 millions of gallons were being sold by the Rockefeller Trust, and the partners were making 25 cents on the gallon. Obviously, their profits ran into the multimillions. In 1877 Standard was able to pay a dividend of 50 percent, and, according to one of Standard's directors, there was so much money being made that the dividend could have been paid out twice over, and the company would still have made a profit.[33]

We now want to look at what happened when Rockefeller's methods created such widespread hostility in the United States that, to offset this, the trust was driven to go overseas.

THE OHIO LITIGATION

Because of the ruthless manner in which he operated, Rockefeller had few friends in the United States. Moreover, the oil business generally had developed a taint thanks to swindlers peddling stocks for which claims were inflated. Americans who wanted to get rich quickly would buy stocks for supposititious oil finds. In some cases the claims were legitimate, but more often they were not. Soon worthless oil stocks became a byword in the United States, and there was a tendency to ascribe a shady character to oil dealings generally.

Along with this went public awareness of the enormous power of Standard Oil and the capability that this gave the company to set prices. Standard always maintained that it strove to bring prices down, and it could, when confronted, produce statistics to show that this, in fact, was occurring. But the claims were generally false, as Tarbell has shown in her book.[34]

In any event, whether the price rose or fell depended on Standard's requirements; once Standard had gained a monopoly, it could manipulate economic forces as it pleased—or, at least, this was the attitude that it took.[35] The public did not like this, but, having once become used to lighting with kerosene, it was motivated to suffer price swings, as long as they did not get too far out of hand.

Eventually, however, urged on by the mounting public hostility toward Standard, various governments moved against it.[36] Most notable were investigations in the states of New York and Ohio and (ultimately) by the federal government. Since most states at this time had laws on their books that forbade control of local corporations by individuals residing out of state, it was this aspect of the trust activity that the investigations focused on.[37]

When called on to testify, the Standard trustees initially claimed that they had nothing to do with management of the separate concerns constituting the trust. They, as trustees, only received dividends from the companies; direction was entirely in the hands of the companies' managers, the trustees claimed.

This was false. In fact, Rockefeller and the trustees were constantly monitoring the companies' operations and sending down directives and ordering a change of front here, there, and everywhere. The investigators were able to prove this by producing regular forms that Rockefeller dispatched from his headquarters at 26 Broad Street, Manhattan, to managers throughout the East Coast and in the Midwest, requiring them to report on the most picayune matters.[38]

Nonetheless, until 1890, when the state of Ohio took on the trust, no progress was made against it. The Ohio investigation was significant because Standard Oil of Ohio, at the time, was *the* holding company for all the Standard concerns.[39] To get a judgment against it would seriously have damaged the trust and perhaps could have killed it.

Ohio authorities took the line that, in violation of state law, Ohio Standard had entered into an agreement whereby it transferred a large block of its shares (34,993 out of 35,000) to Rockefeller and his associates, all of whom were nonresidents of Ohio, and these out-of-staters directed the company's affairs.[40]

In responding to this charge, Rockefeller and the other trustees claimed that it was not Standard Oil of Ohio that had entered into the agreement; rather, this was done by the individual stockholders.[41] The state declared that this was not true, that, in fact, the transfer of such a large block of stocks was a corporate decision, and therefore what was done was illegal, and the illegality had to be corrected. Ohio Standard was ordered to disassociate itself from the trust.

When the company pleaded for time to carry out the court's decree, this was granted. However, it soon developed that Rockefeller had no intention of complying; he was merely temporizing, letting things go on as they always had. Therefore, in 1892 Ohio went back into court, with the result that the trust moved—lock, stock, and barrel—to New Jersey, where the laws were more amenable to its type of operation.[42] There, Standard Oil of New Jersey took over the functions formerly performed by the Ohio group. It became the holding company, and effectively nothing changed.

Thus, the first attempt to clip the wings of Standard failed. Ohio had ruled against the company, and in that sense the oilmen lost; but no real damage had been done since, before the judgment of the court could be carried out, Standard had fled the court's jurisdiction. By pursuing this modus operandi (which essentially was to do as it wished, and the public be damned), the trust was able to maintain its autonomy.[43]

At the same time, however, Standard was, in one respect, hurt by the Ohio litigation. Its reputation, which already was bad, came to be seen as scandalous. The trust came under attack from every quarter.[44] Some states attempted to take it into the courts, where they hoped to get judgments against it; others sought to tax it to the limit on the assumption that it should be made to disgorge its wealth.

Another company might have foundered under such treatment. But the momentum built up by Standard was such that it simply kept going on the course that it had charted. Balked in one area, it changed tack but continued as it was going. In this instance the Standard directors went on stonewalling at home; however, at the same time they began focusing more of their energies on developing markets overseas.[45]

STANDARD OVERSEAS

Standard was selling oil overseas, particularly in Europe, almost from the first day that it went into business. The Europeans were drawn to consume kerosene in greater and greater quantities, and Standard—thanks to the efficiency with which Rockefeller ran the organization—could cater to their needs. Moreover, it was not only Europe that used Rockefeller's product—Asia was almost as good a customer. By 1884, it was estimated, shipments of kerosene to the Far East accounted for nearly a quarter of all Standard Oil's exports.[46]

Everywhere that Standard operated overseas, it followed the same arrangements. Oil was always supplied from the United States; long-term contracts were never entered into; and no more than three weeks' supply of product was kept in-country. By behaving in this way, the company was able to exercise the same tight control over price outside the United States as at home.[47]

Additionally, Standard made it a rule always to operate through agents. In France, for example, it worked with a group called the Cartel Dix, about which we have more to say when we discuss the development of oil in the Middle East. In Germany it developed ties to a particular German, Heinrich Riedemann. Reidemann headed the Deutsche-Amerikanische Petroleum Gesellschaft (DAPG), which ultimately became an integral component of the Standard operation.[48] As for Britain, there, too, Standard worked through an agent, although at one point it felt compelled to create a seemingly independent firm (the Anglo-American Oil Co., Ltd.), which many believed to be British; in fact, this was a dummy corporation controlled from 26 Broad Street.[49]

The Europeans, to be sure, were not pleased with having always to get oil from Standard on its terms; they would have liked to break free of the company's grip. This particularly was the case with the Germans. At this time Germany was endeavoring to become a great military power. The German high command appreciated the potential of oil in warfare; it rankled that an energy source on which it might have to depend was available only from foreigners.

In the late 1870s the Germans—and many other Europeans—became more interested than ever in breaking free of Standard. In 1879 Rockefeller inflated the price of refined.[50] Indeed, he ran it up so steeply that a tremendous furor was occasioned both in the United States and overseas.

In Europe the Germans led the charge, as it were. They called angry meetings at which they railed against the "disastrous practices" of Standard,[51] and they translated anger into action. The Germans began buying crude oil directly from the few independents that had survived Standard's campaign in the United States. They brought it to Europe and processed it through refineries that they had built.[52] This was not at all to Standard's liking.

Along with that, an even more profound development occurred. A major European banking house, the House of Rothschild in Paris, saw that, with Rockefeller's run-up of prices, the prospects for making money in oil had improved enough for them to start thinking about putting money in.[53]

Effectively, then, we have these two reactions to Rockefeller's price-rigging maneuvers. The Germans began to seek out alternative suppliers (and later on they went beyond this; they bought fields of their own and developed them[54]). In Paris the Rothschilds decided that the economics of oil were now so good that they could afford to invest.

Before we go on to discuss how these ventures turned out, we need to ask why Rockefeller did as he did; as the man exhibited such extraordinary acumen throughout his career, why did he act so apparently foolishly in this instance? After all, there are economic laws that obtain in spite of everything. One fundamental law is that if prices rise too high, a reaction occurs, the market weakens, and competition is stimulated. Did Rockefeller think that he could get around this result?

Tarbell seems to think that he did. She cites three separate instances where Rockefeller ran prices up as far as he could. In each case he made millions. She cites declared dividends for the years 1873 through 1880 (the first period in which Rockefeller pushed up prices)—1873, $347,610; 1874, $358,605; 1875, $514,230; 1876, $501,285; 1877, $3,248,650; 1878, $875,000; 1879, $3,150,000; and 1880, $1,050,000.[55]

In making her case against Rockefeller, Tarbell chides him for hubris. Had he exercised constraint (not tried to take too big a scoop, she says[56]), he might have spared himself trouble later on, chiefly, the appearance of significant competitors in Europe.

The author's feeling is that Rockefeller simply was not concerned with adverse consequences of his action. Throughout his career Rockefeller adhered to two main principles whereby he did business. One was to keep himself out of the hands of the New York City banks. To that end, he always strove to finance operations from within his company.[57] The other rule was to move as far as he could, as fast as he could. The speed with which he caused his company to grow is breathtaking.

Taking these two principles into account, it would seem that Rockefeller's method was to seek a strong position from which to defend himself, *unaided.* To achieve this, he had to accumulate tremendous profits, that is, amass a hoard. Once he had his hoard, he could defy any sort of opposition—he could finance the bribery of politicians, he could retain high-priced legal talent, and he could eliminate whichever rivals might appear against him.

At the same time it is ironic that, in pursuing this strategy, Rockefeller created conditions from which the banks could benefit. As a result of his depredations, the oil industry was stripped clean, as it were. Virtually all small-time players were wiped out. The only individuals left who could compete with Rockefeller were the very wealthy, including the biggest banking houses. These institutions originally had no desire to get involved in oil—until Rockefeller ran the price up to such heights. Then, almost immediately, the big banks came in.

OIL FROM RUSSIA

With the exception of Russia, Romania, and Galicia, there is not a lot of oil in Europe, and the Eastern European fields are off the beaten track, or were in the nineteenth century; therefore, they are not convenient to exploit. But then, in the late 1870s Rockefeller pushed up the price of oil in the United States, and what formerly were seen as insuperable obstacles were no longer perceived as such.

After 1879, individuals and governments began tentatively to get themselves involved in oil. Those who took the plunge tried at first to limit their commitment. However, with oil it is practically impossible to put one's toe in, as it were. The industry requires enormous outlays of cash at the outset; it is only after one's fields have been developed and transportation arrangements set that costs come down. (Indeed, with the economics of scale inherent to the industry the outlays become negligible.)

As a consequence, the Europeans who went into oil in the 1880s were forced, willy-nilly, to invest more and more heavily. Further, they were beset by Rockefeller, who followed his regular practice of seeking to destroy each new rival who raised his head.[58]

In short order, the Europeans became increasingly preoccupied fighting off the Americans. Many gave up, but those who hung on eventually were rewarded as circumstances came into play that benefited them. Profound changes were under way within the oil business, which the Europeans, even more than the Americans, were in a position to exploit.

In the mid-1890s it became apparent that the oil industry had, in effect, transcended itself. Whereas formerly oil was mainly used as an illuminant, now it began to be used as a motor fuel, and this was largely due to the invention of the internal combustion engine, which made it possible to convert what formerly was a waste product of the distilling process into a salable commodity.

The implications of the breakthrough were revolutionary. Oil of the type found in Pennsylvania, when made into an illuminant, leaves at most 18 percent of residue behind, whereas the Russian product contains from 60 to 70 percent of heavy components, which originally were discarded. When the internal combustion engine was perfected, this waste (or *mazut*, as it was called in Russian) became the staple of the motor fuel industry. Hence, a great drawback of Russian oil was removed, the drawback of how to dispose of the waste. Instead of burning it off or dumping it, one could now turn it into a salable product, and that was a great leg up for the Russian producers.[59] The major producers of Russian fuel at this time were the Rothschilds and the Nobels.[60]

FAMILY POWER

In the early 1870s Robert Nobel, the son of Immanuel Nobel (who pioneered the armaments industry in Russia), turned up in Azerbaijan, which then was a practically inaccessible region abutting the Caspian Sea. Robert was on a world tour looking to found a business (as his father had done), and passing through the area, he became interested in the possibilities of producing and marketing oil.[61] The czar had just then opened the fields in Azerbaijan and Grozny to private investment.[62] Robert bought several large tracts of land and commenced drilling, using Drake's steam rig apparatus.

Behind Robert were the tremendous resources of the Nobel family and also its business acumen. Robert's more sober-minded elder brother, Ludwig, took an interest in the oil field operations, and after that the venture prospered.

Once the Nobels struck oil, they were not tardy in developing a market in

Russia, but afterward they looked to expand further, into Europe. Here, they confronted a problem of transporting their oil, a difficult task since Azerbaijan is separated from Europe by the Caucasus Mountains. The Nobels, as befits a family that had made its money in dynamite, blasted a way through the Caucasus range, laying pipe as they went.

Once this was done, the prospect of developing the Russian fields became universally attractive; and now the Rothschilds, who had been hovering in the wings, came in. The Paris branch of the house in 1883 agreed to back two Russian oil concessionaires in building a railroad from the fields to Eastern Europe and in return got that portion of the Russians' oil production that could not be sold at home.[63] This was not a lot of oil, but it does not appear that the Rothschilds intended, at this point, to go heavily into the business.

The development of the Azerbaijan fields proceeded apace, and by 1891 Russian production figures were beginning to be impressive—nothing on the order of what Rockefeller was able to achieve in the United States, but not negligible either. According to Tarbell, in 1885, 50 barrels of Russian oil reached the European market. By 1890 that figure had risen to 400,000. Moreover, new fields were being opened up so fast that a promising future seemed assured.[64]

At this point the men at 26 Broad Street intervened to try to nip their foreign competition in the bud. The Americans began a price war in Europe, where both the Nobels and Rothschilds were seeking to sell their oil.[65]

The Nobels had an extensive market in Russia, which the Americans had not been able to crack. Thus, the family was able to retreat there and live off it for a while. The Rothschilds, however, had no such cushion, and thus when Rockefeller began his fight, they could not but feel the pain.

They could always, of course, have gotten out of the business, but perhaps they were too heavily invested for this, or perhaps they could read the future. For whatever reason, we see the Rothschilds looking for a market outside Europe. The family settled on Asia.

ENTER MARCUS SAMUEL

The Rothschilds in the 1880s approached a British merchant, Marcus Samuel, proposing that he, in effect, become their man in the Orient.[66] Samuel would sell Russian oil to Asian customers, something he was peculiarly well equipped to do. Samuel's family had for some time been trading in the Far East, particularly with Japan, then in the process of becoming a great commercial power. The family began its trade with curios (lacquered boxes mainly, decorated with seashells). Later it moved on to more substantial goods, like coal; it sold not only to Japan but all over the Far East.

As a consequence, by this period the Samuels had developed contacts throughout the Far East, which could be exploited for selling Rothschild oil. Along with that, the Samuels had a fleet of ships that they used to transport their wares, and these could be converted to hauling oil.[67] Finally, Samuel was a British subject of some prominence, an advantage that came into play relatively quickly.

The fact of Samuel's having ships proved crucial. At the time, oil almost uniformly was being transported in the form of stacked tins.[68] (The blue tins in which Standard Oil was retailed were famous all over the world.) Because this was the preferred means of moving such cargo, Great Britain benefited. The British dominated the carrying trade, and they even monopolized the shipment of the Americans' oil worldwide.[69]

However, under the Rothschilds' scheme, shipment of oil in tins was to be abandoned.[70] Instead, the oil would be moved in bulk, in tankers specially fitted out to accommodate such deliveries.[71] This would be more economical, since shipments by tins were not the most efficient means. Also, once the tins were eliminated, those merchants (predominantly Chinese) who sold the oil throughout the Orient could also be eliminated. The oil would be shipped to Bombay, Singapore, or wherever; it would be off-loaded into custom-built tanks onshore; and then Samuel's European contacts would take over retailing.[72]

All of these economies were necessary if the Europeans were to tackle Standard in its Eastern market. However, there was one additional economy that they planned to make—Samuel and the Rothschilds had determined to ship their oil through the Suez Canal.[73] This would shave thousands of miles off the distance to be traversed and undercut Standard's shipping costs greatly. The Americans had to send its oil to Asia clear around the Horn of Africa.[74]

Here, however, a complication arose—the canal directors were not disposed to permit oil, viewed as a dangerous cargo, to pass through the canal, a strategic asset. To get around this, Samuel (who was an alderman of the city of London and a man of influence) and the Rothschilds (who could call on the London branch of their family for assistance) began to lobby the Canal Board for permission to transit the vital waterway.[75]

Immediately, however, they ran into stiff opposition. The Tank Syndicate scheme (as it came to be known) could not but hurt the interests of the British shippers. After all, what was Standard likely to do if the scheme proved practical? It almost certainly would adopt it. Standard would start building a tanker fleet of its own, and thus the British flag carriers would lose out.[76]

As a consequence, a fierce debate developed that largely was fought out in the press.[77] In the end, the Samuel–Rothschild group won, but they had to apply extraordinary pressure to do so. They called on powerful interests in Russia (who were invested in the Rothschilds' oil business), and these individuals brought their influence to bear.[78]

What finally seems to have swung the deal was a particular tactic that the Samuel–Rothschild combine adopted. It made it known that the Shell tankers (Samuel had named his firm after the curios with which his lacquered boxes were decorated) were being reconverted by British shipyards and that British companies would be called on to manufacture the tanks that would be erected at various locations throughout the Far East. This split the native opposition, and the Canal Board refused to block the oil ships from transiting the waterway.[79]

Once the deal was done, and news of the opening of the canal was broadcast, Standard—as was expected—reacted. The company approached Samuel, offering to buy him out.[80] Had Samuel agreed, he would have become Standard's employee; this was not acceptable to him.[81] Samuel seems to have believed that he could eventually cut free of his Rothschild connection, and carry on independently, and even hold his own against the Americans.

Finding a rebuff from Samuel, Standard began a price war. However, as the fight dragged on, the Americans switched from their normal tactics (i.e., to fight to the finish) and offered to carve up their markets in Europe and the Far East.[82] This was a significant change of field, and it represented a style of behavior that not only the Americans but all the major operators in the oil business were to pursue from now on.

T.A.B. Corley, writing the history of the Burmah Oil Company, makes some interesting observations along this line.[83] He says that oil dealings throughout this period tended to be volatile. Companies had to be able to move from outright competition to collaboration with rivals. The reason for this was the "inflexibility" of oil. Once discovered and developed, the oil fields had to be kept producing, because, if the production cycle once was broken, no convenient way existed to accommodate this—the oil could not be stored (not past a certain point, anyway), and it could not be dumped.

As long as Standard was dominant in every area of the world, it could employ the price war tactic with virtual certainty of success.[84] But as its rivals found alternative markets (as, in the case of the Nobels, in Russia), the company no longer had that surety. Hence, the trust had to be ready to break off the fight and do a deal, as occurred here.[85] Effectively, what we are witnessing is the opening up of the "cartel era." Whereas in the past great trusts, like Standard, believed that they could go it alone, now more than one trust found it expedient to "cartelize."

Finally, another consideration drove Standard to compromise. The czar of Russia had announced his intention (never acted upon) of revoking the concessions that he had tendered; he wanted to reestablish the state monopoly.[86] This seems to have rattled the Russian entrepreneurs and put them in a frame of mind to accept Standard's compromise offer.[87]

Perhaps it was to offset a setback that the Rothschilds now started looking to further improve their position. It was not enough simply to have additional markets; they needed new sources of supply, and for that they turned to the East Indies. The family entered into talks with a company that was, at the time, virtually a nonentity—the Koninklijke Nederlansche Maatschappij tot exploitatie van Petroleumsbronnen in Nederlandsch Indie (the Royal Dutch Company).[88]

ROYAL DUTCH APPEARS

Samuel's original value to the Rothschilds was as an overseas agent, someone to market the product that they derived from Russia. But once the Russian market passed beneath a cloud, the Rothschilds felt compelled to find an alternative supplier.[89] In the first decade of the twentieth century, the likeliest source of oil—outside the United States and Russia—was the East Indies.

Samuel already had twigged to this and had bought up potential oil lands in North Borneo[90]; therefore, had they wished, the Rothschilds might have continued dealing with him, letting him, in effect, be their point man in opening up the East Indian territory.[91]

The Rothschilds seemed to have had reservations about the Britisher. His business methods (although in some respects inspired) were overall disorderly. The Rothschilds did not feel that they could sever their association with Samuel; however, they wanted more than one support to lean upon.[92]

The Royal Dutch Company (exactly as its name implies) was a firm that operated under patent of the Dutch government. At the time all of Java (the principal location of potentially exploitable oil in the Far East) was controlled by the Netherlands. This certainly influenced the Rothschilds to work with Royal Dutch. At any time, were the Americans to try to intervene, the Dutch could shut them out.[93]

The East Indian fields had been developed by a succession of Dutch colonials. In the 1890s, when the Rothschilds first went out to the area, Royal Dutch was headed by Jean Baptiste August Kessler.[94] Kessler had brought in his first successful well in 1892 and for a time had been able to exploit this achievement to win further support from the Hague. However, in 1898 that well went dry.[95] Fortunately for him, he brought in another producing well, so Royal Dutch was able to carry on.

Thus, the company was up and running when Samuel appeared in the region. Indeed, the Britisher's arrival had been long anticipated; the fight over opening the Suez Canal was watched from afar, and the Netherlanders drew useful pointers from it. Particularly, they were impressed by the Tank Syndicate scheme that Samuel and the Rothschilds were pursuing. All that Samuel was doing, the Netherlanders felt that they could do, and maybe improve on.[96]

For example, the Dutch could build tankers to carry their product (which they called Crown Oil) in bulk, and, since Royal Dutch was located in the Far East, they could do this more economically than the Shell people, who had to bring their product all the way from southern Russia.[97]

Further, they could build tanks in which to store their oil onshore, and what is more, since the distances to be traversed were far less, they could keep a continual circuit of the region replenishing supplies.[98] As for agents, the Dutch were not adverse to using the Chinese, many of whom were being cut out by Samuel's venture. Finally, Royal Dutch could exploit its ties to the Hague. It could call on its people at home to shut out competition, both the Americans (Standard) and the British (Shell).

The upshot was that, without meaning to, Samuel and the Rothschilds—in opening up the Far East (with specific intent of surviving Standard's price wars)—provided an unknown entity, Royal Dutch, with an opportunity to expand and become a contender in the competition.

This hurt Samuel, but, since capital is fungible, the Rothschilds were not hurt at all. They had put money into both firms (Shell and Royal Dutch). Thus, it happened that the two outfits drew on the selfsame support of the House of Rothschild.

Ultimately, it was not Kessler who reaped the rewards of all this; he died in 1901. Taking over from him was a young man, Henri Deterding, who had been entrusted by Kessler with the job of setting up the system whereby Crown Oil was to be marketed. Deterding, after getting this arranged, served as Kessler's handpicked lieutenant and then stepped into the old man's shoes when he died.

Deterding not only waged the fight against Shell but, after Shell was bested, he assumed direction of the war of Royal Dutch–Shell against Standard. However, we are getting ahead of ourselves. Before we look out how the anti-Standard fight developed, we must discuss why Samuel succumbed to the Dutch–Rothschild combination and the consequence of that.

SAMUEL LOSES

We mentioned earlier that Samuel bought a producing well in North Borneo. However, this project had not fared well. The oil was of a darkish color and had an offensive odor. Hence, the Oriental clientele did not favor it.[99] To recoup, Samuel threw himself into another, much bigger scheme. He contracted to take 100,000 gallons of oil a year at a fixed price for 21 years from the famous Spindletop well in Texas.[100] This was one of the all-time great gushers in oil history. Discovered on January 10, 1901, this well brought in 75,000 barrels a day until mid-1902, at which point it died. Samuel was badly burned when Spindletop went down. The Mellons of Pittsburgh (who owned the well as part of their Gulf Oil operation) evaded their obligation to compensate the Britisher.

Thus, Samuel lost money in Texas. In Borneo, too, he had not done well, and now—along with everything else—in the early 1900s the Boxer Rebellion erupted in China, which wiped out many of the markets that Samuel had pioneered.[101] Since Deterding was essaying to sell in China, he, along with Samuel, should have been hurt by the unrest. However, as Deterding was to maintain later in his career, "to survive in oil, it is necessary to have a long, long purse."[102] At this point, along with the Rothschilds, Deterding's backers were Dutch bankers and, in addition, the Hague.

As for Samuel, he had his own fortune, and that was considerable. Had he husbanded his resources, he might have held out. However, he seems to have squandered his opportunities. During the time when things began to go badly for him, he became involved in a round of strenuous social activities. Samuel was to become the lord mayor of London (an extraordinary accomplishment for a merchant whose family had begun selling curio boxes). Rather than cut down on banquets, stately processions, and all the rest of the panoply, he gave himself up to "partying." His behavior disturbed many of his associates (and one who particularly disapproved was Rothschilds' agent in London, Frederick Lane).[103]

Samuel had picked a particularly bad time to scant his commercial obligations. By 1910 (the period that we are approaching) the sale of gasoline worldwide had surpassed that of kerosene. The price of the former had gone from 9.5 cents in October 1911 to 17 cents in January 1913. In London and Paris motorists were paying 50 cents a gallon, and in some parts of Europe up to a dollar a gallon for motor fuel.[104]

As the craze for motorcars erupted, so did the public's enthusiasm for the oil industry. As had occurred in the United States in the 1860s, this produced a wave of stock buying.[105] Deterding took advantage of this phenomenon, providing himself with a whole new cash fund. Deterding's scheme was simple—using his basic cache of money (from the Rothschilds et al.), he bought up concessions and then advertised them on the market. When it became known that Royal Dutch was interested in a particular field, the public rushed to buy.[106] Hence, Deterding made money as his initial stock purchases rose in value, which enabled him to repeat the operation elsewhere.

In 1902 Samuel approached Deterding with an offer that they form a partnership.[107] Samuel would see to the transportation end of the business, and Deterding, the production. Deterding was interested, but only if he could control the merged entity.

As had happened with Rockefeller, Samuel turned this offer down.[108] Nonetheless, so difficult was his position that he could not completely reject Deterding's counteroffer. His firm was in trouble. He was paying a dividend of only 2.5 percent against Royal Dutch's 36 percent.[109]

Ultimately, a deal was struck—a whole new firm appeared, Asiatic Petroleum, which was set up to do business exclusively in the Far East.[110] The two men, Deterding and Samuel, each held a third interest in the firm, along with the Rothschilds, who took another third.

By 1907, as Samuel's dividends continued to slip, the Britisher renegotiated his deal with Deterding, agreeing to enter a partnership over which Deterding had management control.[111] Thus, the lineup within Royal Dutch/Shell (as the new entity was called) now became Deterding and the Dutch interest; Samuel and the British (Shell); and the French (the Rothschilds).[112]

One final point needs to be made about the revolution in oil—as soon as sales of motor fuel outstripped sales of kerosene, Rockefeller's dictum (about staying out of production) no longer made sense. The Americans had always disdained to get into production because, as stated previously, it was too risky.

Moreover, they were content to develop oil fields in one region only, basically Pennsylvania and Ohio. There were a number of reasons for this. First, Pennsylvania/Ohio oil was the highest grade available and ideal as an illuminant. But also the aim of Rockefeller was to keep the production of oil down, so as to be able to manipulate the price. Thus, he had no desire or incentive to go barnstorming around the United States—much less go overseas—prospecting for new fields.

But Deterding—alive to the changing nature of the business—was keen to get his hands on as much oil from as many sources as he could.[113] Thus, it fell out that Deterding's Royal Dutch set the pattern for the future development of the industry. It became the first truly integrated oil company. It, alone among the major companies, controlled the production of oil from wellhead to market. Today, when all of the major oil companies behave this way, we say that they are "invested in upstream and downstream operations."

At any rate, here we see the difference between the American and European oilmen—the latter were oriented toward the stock markets, but the Americans wanted nothing to do with that.[114] The attitudes of the two toward government also were at odds. The Europeans were not averse to accepting government help—indeed, they depended on it. The Americans regarded the state with suspicion.

In 1907 Deterding went to the United States to acquire oil properties, an audacious step on his part.[115] Five years earlier he probably could not have gotten away with it—Rockefeller would have crushed him. But now Standard had gotten into difficulty at home. The federal government had brought suit against it under the Sherman Anti-Trust Act. Washington meant to break up the great trust in the way that Ohio earlier had tried—and failed—to do.[116]

THE DISSOLUTION OF THE TRUST

Earlier we alluded to the makeup of the trust, saying that the principle on which it was based was deception—to keep concealed from the public that Rockefeller controlled 39 companies spread over several states. When Ohio fought Standard, it cited laws that forbade such arrangements. But then Standard relocated to another state (New Jersey), where this sort of activity was condoned.

The flagrancy of the move so outraged public opinion that Washington felt compelled to intervene. At the turn of the century (when the federal suit was brought) the legal basis for such intervention existed. The Congress had passed the Sherman Anti-Trust Act, which governed the operation of so-called common carriers. Since Standard had shifted the bulk of its oil transport to pipelines, it fell under this category.

This gave the government the opening to move against it. The suit was brought in 1905 by the administration of Theodore Roosevelt, one of the great reforming presidents of the United States. In making its case, the government concentrated on activities in restraint of trade. This was the particular behavior that galled Americans, the part that was so egregiously outside the law.

Standard's trustees, as to be expected, denied all of the charges. But so much evidence was brought out to the contrary in so many anti-trust actions in so many states that the position was not tenable. Consequently, few were surprised when the government—as had occurred in the Ohio case—found against Standard.

A problem developed, however, when it came to enforcing the breakup. In

1911, when the action was taken, few who were invested in the trust wanted to see it dissolved. According to testimony before the Congress, between 1893 and 1901 the parent company paid out more than $250 million in dividends.[117] Who would want to give up a stake like that? At the same time, however, those not benefiting looked on the trust as an obscenity.

The company was a kind of superstate, an entity more powerful than the Union itself. It was alleged to be branching out into other fields. Indeed, the fear then current was that, left to its own devices, Standard would swallow up the United States.

This was the line that the famous muckraking journalists (of whom Tarbell was one) took against it. Before the muckrakers were done with Standard, its reputation had sunk so low as to be negligible, at which point the climate of opinion in America was receptive to any punishment that the federal government might bring against it.[118]

Interestingly, however, when the government did finally succeed in breaking up the trust, it left it a number of avenues to recoup. Washington decided that restraint of trade could be "reasonable." What did that mean? Apparently, the government convinced itself that big corporations, like Standard, could not be treated as were smaller outfits.

Big corporations should be allowed to grow reasonably. A reasonable mode of growth was through merger. Strong companies should be able to "in-gather" subsidiaries as a way of strengthening their operations by making them more efficient.

Standard was quick to avail itself of this accommodative spirit. It went along with the dissolution decree, but afterward it behaved as if it were still a trust—the individual companies continued working together.

In 1911, under the decree, the bulk of the trust's assets was left in the hands of Jersey, a windfall for that company. However, at the same time, all of Jersey's crude oil suppliers were ordered to disaffiliate. Jersey was mishapen, as it were—heavily endowed with refineries and with an excellent marketing setup, but practically no product.

What Jersey did was to continue dealing with its erstwhile suppliers as if they were still attached. The whole operation (or the main elements, anyway) carried on as if the trust were intact. Moreover, Jersey, having so much of the trust's wealth, set up as a lender to the disaffiliated groups. This kept in force Rockefeller's injunction against becoming involved with the Wall Streeters. It also gave Jersey influence over the manifold entities that made up the Standard family.

Thus, a single, powerful entity survived the breakup, and it then not only took to reconstitute itself but labored to improve the condition of the affiliated groups, helping them to become viable also. In this way the trust carried on. From now on in this book, unless otherwise stipulated, when we speak of Standard, we mean Standard of New Jersey.

While all of this was going on (and the process stretched over a period of years), the Europeans moved against Standard. The attack was launched first in Mexico and then moved north into the United States.

OIL IN AMERICA—NORTH AND SOUTH

As indicated earlier, Deterding was not the first European to have tried to penetrate the North American oil market. Samuel, we already spoke about. But roughly at the same time as Samuel, a British engineer, W. D. Pearson, made the attempt. In 1901 Pearson—while building a railway along Mexico's east coast—espied standing pools of oil at Tampico, and this led him to seek concessions from the Mexican government.[119]

Standard was already active in Mexico. In the late nineteenth century the company had contracted with wealthy landowners to extract oil from their estates.[120] This oil Standard imported to the United States, where it was refined and resold to the Mexicans at a profit of sometimes up to 600 percent.[121]

The president of Mexico when Pearson came forward was Porfirio Diaz, and he was only too happy to encourage the Britisher; to Diaz, any competition to Standard was worthwhile. Pearson bought concessions in several likely areas. However, it was not until 1908 that he made a significant find. After that he lifted enormous quantities of oil, which he marketed under the brand of the Mexican Eagle.[122] The Eagle became one of the world's most prolific oil concessions.

Standard, naturally, looked on Diaz's opening to the British with distaste. The trust began agitating against the Mexican president. It threw its support to a rival candidate for the presidency, Francesco Madero. This led to an actual shooting war, with 26 Broad Street subsidizing the insurrectionists, and in 1910 Diaz was overthrown.

The role of the U.S. government in all of this is interesting—Henry Lane Wilson, the American ambassador in Mexico City, did not support Madero, Standard's handpicked man. Not because of Washington's anti-trust policy. In fact, it appears that the ambassador was a friend of the Guggenheims, who had extensive silver mining interests in Mexico. The Guggenheims did not like Madero, and this led to the unusual situation of the American ambassador's being on the side of the British and against his compatriots in the Standard company.[123]

In 1910 General Francesco Huerta overthrew Madero and then had the luckless civilian assassinated, whereupon Britain immediately recognized the new president. But, as Frank Hanighen writes in his book *The Secret War*, "Standard wasn't pumping salt water yet."[124] In 1912 Woodrow Wilson came to power in Washington, and (for reasons that had nothing to do with oil diplomacy) he removed the ambassador from his Mexico City post.[125] President Wilson then advised Huerta to resign, and when the general balked, Washington threw its support behind another general, Venustiano Carranza, who—coincidentally—was supported by Standard.

Huerta tried to make a fight of it but lost out when the British deserted him, which they felt compelled to do, as they would not risk a rupture with the United States on the eve of the Great War in Europe. As a consequence of all this, just before the war, Standard held the field in Mexico and in Central and South America.

This background to Deterding's American invasion is useful for what it tells us about the contrasting attitudes of the British and American governments.[126] Pearson could not have prevailed in his Mexican operations had not the British government supported them. Conversely, the Americans (i.e., Standard) were frequently at odds with Washington. The federal government was not interested in furthering Standard's cause and left it up to the oilmen to make their own way.

This indifference of official Washington was exploited by Deterding. He moved in, without fear of government interference. His only concern was how to proceed at least expense to himself and to his backers. He could import his own oil into the United States, but then he would have to reckon with the tariff. Or he could buy oil land in the United States and work out a distribution network. This latter plan, which he eventually followed, was expensive because prices of proven fields at this time were going for $100,000 an acre.[127]

With the considerable financial support on which he could draw from Europe this appears not to have been a great obstacle. Deterding went first to California, where he purchased potential oil lands in Coalinga. He developed and then sold that oil in Washington state, where he had formed a marketing system.[128] In this early phase of his endeavors, Deterding was at pains to conceal his foreignness. He may have feared provoking a challenge from Standard.[129] (It may also be, however, that he worried about inflated land prices, once it became known whom he represented.)

Eventually, Deterding came out into the open. The first corporation that he established in the United States in which no attempt at concealment was made was the American Shell Oil Co.[130] In setting it up, he used the prominent Wall Street banking house of Kuhn-Loeb.[131] Afterward, Deterding swore he had never seen the like of the New Yorkers for chicanery and double-dealing (which would seem to confirm Rockefeller's stance of keeping out of the New Yorkers' clutches).[132]

At the same time, one could speculate that Deterding's success in penetrating the United States was due to the Wall Streeters. They had no love for Rockefeller and therefore were willing to assist the European and collect their commissions at the same time. Of commissions there were plenty. In addition to his West Coast purchases Deterding bought oil properties in Oklahoma and in Kansas,[133] and he built refineries in Louisiana, Illinois, Missouri, and Delaware.[134]

At this point things may have looked bad for Standard. However, we will see the trust—or rather, the many companies formerly subsumed under it—revive eventually. It took the war in Europe to perform this feat. Indeed, the war was the American oilmen's salvation. It further revolutionized the oil industry, as it revolutionized the international state system.

OIL AS A WEAPON

According to Anthony Sampson, Samuel sparked the British navy's interest in oil. He and John Arbuthnot Fisher, first sea lord of the Admiralty, shared the view that, ultimately, the fleet must convert from coal; the advantages of oil were too many and too great. Indeed, Fisher was so set on this belief that his colleagues dubbed him the "oil maniac."[135]

When Samuel first was approached by the Rothschilds to take over selling their oil in the Far East, he traveled to Batum to study the oil business first-hand.[136] There he noted ships owned by the Nobels plying the Caspian powered by oil.[137] The ingenious Nobels had devised this application, which Samuel picked up on and adapted it to his own vessels.

Since that time, he had badgered the Admiralty, trying to get the navy to give oil a trial (Samuel's dream was that the navy would make him the exclusive supplier of oil for the fleet). The Sea Lords had not refused him outright; however, they moved slowly and with great care. As early as 1903 some tentative trials were run, and several submarines had actually been built that were oil-burning.[138]

The real impetus seems to have come when Fisher was made first sea lord; he got things moving. What had been holding things back was supply. Britain *had* coal, plenty of it; it had no oil. Thus, to abandon the former (a sure thing) for something for which no guaranteed supply existed seemed, to many, the height of folly.

The activity of the Germans apparently forced the issue. In the first decade of the twentieth century the Wilhelmian empire embarked on a course of becoming a world power, which, naturally, required the development of a strong military. Germany was laying down dreadnoughts, having proclaimed that it would surpass British naval strength.

As the Germans built bigger and bigger ships of war, Britain endeavored to stay ahead. There was a difficulty, however, because firepower could not be increased without invading space aboard ship given over to storing coal. Such space could be sacrificed, but only at a cost of reducing the speed of the vessel, and, as Fisher pointed out, in war speed is everything.[139] Britain's big ships were slowing down under the weight of the coal that they had to carry.

Fisher, the convert, could argue that oil showed the way out of the dilemma. Oil stored aboard ship took up far less room than coal; at the same time an oil-powered ship could be refueled at sea, whereas a coal-driven one was constantly having to put into port to refuel. Also, an oil ship required less personnel; the number of stokers could be cut almost in half.[140]

These were powerful arguments, which opened the way to other, equally powerful ones. For example, an oil-powered ship does not need a funnel; hence, the ship's guns can traverse a wider range, and there is less chance for detection, since coal smoke will appear over the horizon.[141]

By 1912 the British government was set to make the move to oil, and this naturally raised the question of which firm would be the navy's supplier. Standard was the obvious candidate—indeed, it was the only one; it alone had the resources to deliver a steady, sure supply of oil under any circumstances.

The choice of Standard would not have been to the liking of Samuel, who hoped that his firm, that is, the group to which his firm was affiliated, Royal Dutch/Shell, would be selected. However, Royal Dutch was not in Standard's class. It had lost its extensive holdings in Russia after riots gripped the Caucasus region in 1905. The firm retained other holdings in Sumatra, but, as noted earlier, one of its major fields there had failed relatively recently.

That left Romania, which Royal Dutch had been exploiting for some time, but there were problems there as well. Deterding was developing the Romanian fields along with the Deutsche Bank,[142] an association of which the admirals could hardly approve.[143] In the eyes of Britons, German banks were part of the state apparatus. Any move they might undertake could not be divorced from power politics. If Royal Dutch/Shell cooperated with them, it must be part of the German's machinations—or so the admirals believed.

Seen from this angle, the capitulation of Samuel to Deterding (whereby Samuel became part of Deterding's organization) was unfortunate. It meant that Samuel would never realize his dream of becoming the navy's oil supplier.

Despite misgivings, the British government did make a number of significant deals with Royal Dutch, and one in particular is of interest. It involved Germany and the Ottoman empire and was the catalyst for bringing both Great Britain and the United States into Iraq.

THE RACE TO THE MIDDLE EAST

The Middle East prior to World War I was an area of no special consequence. Indeed, the term had only just come into existence, coined by Admiral Alfred Thayer Mahon in an article in a London review.[144] Hence, the general public was not even aware of a specific locale called the Middle East. The Far East, yes; the Middle East, no.

For Europeans, the area had no commercial significance. Trade between Europe and the Middle East did not develop in the modern era until quite late, and it did not come about naturally. The British government promoted it for geopolitical reasons.[145]

In the period of the 1850s, Great Britain undertook to secure the integrity of the Ottoman empire against the rising power of Egypt's Muhammad Ali. Egypt, formerly a province of the Porte, had declared independence from it. The sultan's former viceroy not only broke from Ottoman control but essayed to take over the Levant, part of the sultan's domain. In repayment for a British naval blockade (which cut Muhammad Ali's supply line) the sultan granted Britain commercial concessions.[146]

Britain's free trade agreement with the sultan provided for, among other things, the elimination of internal tariffs and state monopolies, the reaffirmation of European capitulatory privileges, and the granting to Great Britain of most-favored nation status.[147] As an outgrowth of the agreement, the Ottoman empire and Great Britain began to exchange goods, and for a time a flourishing trade developed between them. Britain became the empire's leading foreign commercial partner.[148]

Ultimately, however, this trade slackened, and by 1909 exports had fallen to a low level, as had imports.[149] This was due to the condition of Turkish society—it was too backward to sustain an active trade. But, along with this, the empire had been driven to seek outside financial aid (a process begun with the Crimean War). The first Ottoman loan was subscribed in 1854 (floated by the Rothschilds, interestingly), and this was the prelude to an extensive loan business built up over the next 29 years.[150]

In 1875 the empire defaulted. It was estimated that over half the Ottoman budget was assigned to servicing external obligations, and new loans were having to be raised to pay the interest on earlier debts.[151] As the empire's creditworthiness dropped, interest rates rose, making it harder for the Turks to meet their obligations.

Moreover, once the empire had defaulted, London bankers shunned it. To be sure, the outstanding obligation had to be met, and for that a Debt Commission was formed, presided over by British and French banking interests. The Debt Commission functioned efficiently—the empire met all of its interest payments, although not without inflicting considerable hardship on the sultan's subjects.[152]

Nonetheless, as far as the The City was concerned, the empire was not an attractive place in which to invest; there was a general turning away from it—at least by Britain and, to a degree, France.

However, as interest on the part of these two slackened, Germany appeared on the scene, effectively offering itself as a suitor in their place.

REASONS FOR GERMAN INTEREST

This was the age of protectionism, when industry was harnessed to national objectives. As regards oil, France instituted a tariff on oil in 1893, and Germany essayed to make a similar move in 1913. Similarly, the United States moved to protectionism in the era of McKinley.[153] Only Great Britain, with its dominance of world sea-lanes and its virtual monopoly of the carrying trade, stood out against protection.

The development of the oil industry confounded the protectionist ideal. Both Germany and France were bereft of oil. The two states responded to the crisis, however, in quite different ways. France had colonies (e.g., in Algeria) where it was fairly certain that oil could be found in exploitable quantities.

However, France made no move to develop these resources, a neglect that was censurable, given the difficulties that this caused later on in the Great War. Behind France's high tariff wall sheltered a group of 10 refineries that monopolized the marketing of oil inside the country. The companies got their oil from Standard in a complex arrangement that allowed them to circumvent tariff restrictions and thereby set prices beneficial to themselves.[154]

The upshot was that France produced no oil, nor did it prospect for it in Algeria or anywhere else in the French overseas empire. Moreover, any attempt to develop a native supply was rigorously repressed.[155] All this was done so that the individuals controlling the Cartel Dix, as this combine was called, could make a good profit.

Germany was another matter. At the turn of the century, the Wilhelmian empire began a wide-ranging search for oil because, as stated earlier, Germany's military was not comfortable with having to depend on Standard for supplies. Initially, the Germans focused on Romania and Poland; later, they moved into Russia.

However, when the Russian fields were destroyed in 1905, this led the Germans to push their searches farther south, going all the way to the Ottoman empire. Berlin in 1902 had secured a contract to build the famous Berlin-to-Baghdad Railway, and under this arrangement the Germans were empowered to exploit minerals up to 20 kilometers either side of the right-of-way. At the time, Royal Dutch, too, was interested in developing oil lands in the Ottoman empire, and thus the parties agreed to cooperate.

The Berlin-to-Baghdad line was to run from the German capital through the Balkans to Constantinople and then across the Anatolian plateau to Mesopotamia (or, as it is known today, Iraq). From there it was to terminate at Baghdad.

For the sultan, the railway was a piece of essential infrastructure whereby he hoped to modernize his empire. Also, it would enable him to consolidate his hold over distant lands that, because of their remoteness, were practically autonomous. One such de facto autonomous region was Iraq. Although it sits next to Turkey's heartland, the country is cut off from it by high mountains peopled by wild tribes, mainly Arab and Kurdish. Once Iraq was breached by railway, troops could be dispatched to it fairly quickly, and that, the sultan believed, would bring the region under his control.

For Germany the railway served another function. Initially, it was a capital investment scheme for the German banks; by lending money for the project, the banks hoped to realize a significant return. However, as they began to see the potential for oil development, their thinking switched to that possibility, and at this point they brought Royal Dutch in on the deal.

The construction of the railway was one of the great dramas of the pre–World War I period, as it pitted Germany against Great Britain. Britain opposed the line for strategic reasons. The project, as laid out, would terminate in the Gulf, and this was not at all acceptable. The Gulf guarded a main approach to India and was therefore, in British eyes, part of their sphere. British ships patrolled the waterway, and there were British outposts spotted throughout it.[156]

The Berlin-to-Baghdad Railway scheme commenced its building phase in 1904, and before World War I the first sector (Baghdad–Samarra) was completed.[157] Thus, the line was set to advance north to Mosul, where (although it was not proved at the time) one of the world's richest fields of oil is located. At this point the Germans' hopes were dashed. The Ottoman empire experienced a revolt.

In 1908 the so-called Young Turk movement deposed the sultan, and that seemingly put an end to the railroad project and to German hopes of developing oil fields in connection with it. (The sultan, before he was deposed, had transferred ownership of the concession area to the privy purse.[158] This meant that, with him gone, the Germans' contract was invalid.)

The Germans, however, were able to resuscitate the deal with the sultan's successors. They did it by transferring the interest of the German banks to a specially created company, Turkish Petroleum. Participating in this new venture were Royal Dutch and another concern, the Turkish National Bank.[159]

The Turkish National Bank, despite its name, was a British company; at least, it was based in London. One of its principal shareholders was an Armenian, Calouste Gulbenkian. Gulbenkian devised the Turkish Petroleum Co. scheme and, in return, was to get a 15 percent interest in it.[160]

The British government did not want to see this project resurrected, for strategic reasons. London, therefore, took the tack of insisting that British interests be involved before it could go ahead.

The contract was overhauled, and now the Anglo-Persian Oil Co. took 50 percent of Turkish Petroleum shares; the German banks got 25, and Royal Dutch, 25, and, under a special provision, each of the latter gave up 2.5 percent to Gulbenkian, who thus ended up with 5 percent.

We have now introduced a new, important entity, the Anglo-Persian Oil Co. We need to talk about it.

THE DEVELOPMENT OF IRAN

In 1900 a British subject, William Knox D'Arcy—an entrepreneur who made his fortune prospecting for gold in Australia—determined to search for oil in the southeast of Persia.[161] D'Arcy, a biblical scholar, had been struck by allusions in the Bible to pools of naphtha that burned eternally in ancient fire temples; he shrewdly surmised that this might be oil.

For several years D'Arcy hunted for oil, expending his own capital. His search was unsuccessful until, on May 26, 1908, he struck oil using Col. Drake's drilling apparatus—not in the area that he had originally surmised but farther south in a place called Masjid-i-Suleiman, at the northernmost tip of the Gulf.[162]

Before he made his strike, however, he ran out of funds and, needing a resupply of capital, was on the point of appealing to Royal Dutch when the British Admiralty prevailed upon Earl Strathcona (who had developed the Trans-Canada Railway) to take up his concession.[163]

Strathcona formed a financial syndicate that included the Burmah Oil Co. of Glasgow, Scotland. The firm had some experience developing oil in the Far East, primarily in India. However, it was not a large operation, nothing on the scale of the two great trusts. At any rate, out of this combination (of Strathcona and Burmah Oil) the Anglo-Persian Oil Co. emerged.

The new syndicate, in its turn, got into difficulty and had to appeal—as D'Arcy had done—to the government. The D'Arcy claim was a difficult one to work. It was located in a remote region, to which supplies (including drilling rigs) had to be transported by mules. The temperature in the area routinely climbed above 100 degrees. There was continual harassment from the local tribes. On top of everything else, the Burmah Oil executives did not get on with D'Arcy's man on the spot.[164]

All of this probably could have been dealt with and eventually overcome, but the company's engineers seemed to have gone disastrously wrong in their attempt to construct a refinery, which they had located adjacent to the workings in Abadan. They were not sufficiently appreciative of the peculiarities of Persian Oil when they commenced to build, and thus the plant never really worked well.[165]

So complex and manifold were the problems of the malfunctioning unit that finally the company was forced to enter into a commercial arrangement with Royal Dutch whereby the latter agreed to market the company's kerosene. As a result of this early association, Deterding seems to have made up his mind to acquire Anglo-Persian, and Charles Greenway (Anglo-Persian's then-director) became as adamantly determined not to let him have it.

Greenway, a Scot, actively disliked Deterding.[166] One of the epithets that he fastened on him was "non-British." To be sure, this was the case; Deterding was a Netherlander. However, Greenway's characterization implied more than mere condition of national origin; he seemed to be hinting that there was something subversive about Royal Dutch.

Greenway, when it came time to appeal for funds, exploited this idea of the company's falling into the hands of foreigners. He lobbied the various departments of government on the basis that, if the government did not act, this non-British company (Royal Dutch) would take over the concession, which would cause incalculable damage.

This appears to have been a shrewd approach. Most of the men to whom Greenway was appealing were members of the Committee of Imperial Defense (described by Corley as "one of the most exalted official bodies of Edwardian England"[167]). These gentlemen took Greenway's warning seriously. At the same time, however, when Samuel got wind of it, he was furious.[168] Samuel was a parvenue, certainly; but no one could say that he was non-British.[169]

At any event, the ploy succeeded, as the admirals passed Greenway's appeal to the civilian arm of government, and that brought Winston Churchill—then first lord of the Admiralty—into the picture.[170] Churchill commissioned a study of the feasibility of the government's taking over the D'Arcy claim.

Here was a departure! Nothing of this scope had been suggested, certainly not by Strathcona or even Greenway. Indeed, no one ever had suggested that the British government get into the oil business.

Churchill's commission comprised a number of leading Britons and was headed by John (later Sir John) Cadman, a professor of mining at the University of Birmingham. Cadman and some of the commission members went out to Persia and returned to give the venture a glowing report.[171]

Based on this recommendation, Churchill gave the go-ahead to buy, the idea being that the Admiralty would assume control by purchasing 51 percent of the company's shares. Churchill did not publicize his decision but merely shared it with some interested individuals inside and outside government. Once their acquiescence had been obtained, the deal was done. Only when all details were settled did Churchill go before the Parliament, lay the matter out, and request approval, after the fact.[172]

This was an extraordinary decision that the government had made and clearly is something that one could speculate over endlessly. We have only one thing to say—the government was mainly motivated by price concerns. Churchill, in his speech to the Parliament, dilated on this. He spoke about the great trusts and, in particular, Royal Dutch/Shell, which, he said, was a money-making operation.[173] If the government were to become dependent on such an entity, he said, this could be a very costly proposition.[174]

On the other hand (said Churchill), were one to buy into Anglo-Persian, then price would be taken care of, as the Admiralty was assured a discount on future supplies, an arrangement that would obtain for some years.[175] This would guard against the most worrisome aspect of any contract arrangement—the likelihood that the oil price, constantly manipulated by the trusts, would fluctuate wildly.[176]

Also (according to Churchill) the contract contained guarantees about the overall operation of the company. Two government nominees would serve on Anglo-Persian's board who would vote only on matters involving national security. This was to reassure the public as to the propriety of the government's going into the oil business. (We will see that, despite Churchill's disclaimers, the government could not resist interfering on the commercial side.)[177]

We now can see what troubled the admirals. Because of the condition of the international market, the oil price could not be counted on to remain steady. Deterding, when pressed on this issue, refused to commit himself to more than a three-year contract. Samuel, when asked what he thought was a fair price for oil, said, whatever it would fetch.

These were excellent sentiments for one capitalist to confide to another, but nothing that would reassure the admirals. So, then, in labeling Deterding (and Samuel) as non-British, the admirals were saying that these men were not sufficiently dedicated to national interests.

True enough—capital knows no allegiance; it flows ceaselessly from one end of the world to another and is mistrustful of sentiment in any form; even sentiments of patriotism are inconsequential to it (if not downright counterproductive).

The question is, To what degree did the admirals protect themselves by arranging matters as they had? Was the government's proposal to buy Anglo-Persian a shrewd one? We will see that the arrangement made considerable difficulties later on, primarily with the oil producers Iran and, later, Iraq. The two countries let their concessions believing they would be operated as commercial ventures. But, in the case of Iran, the British government stepped in, and it was interested not in realizing revenue but in providing oil cheaply to the navy. Where did that leave the Iranian government, which was counting on making money off the sale of Anglo-Persian's oil in the form of royalties? (We go into the matter of how Iraq was similarly affected in the next chapter.)

OIL IN THE GREAT WAR

A big question about World War I is why the Allies devoted so much time and resources to waging the fight in the Middle East. This should have been a sideshow. Yet Britain was almost constantly active in this arena. Moreover, operations carried on by the British in the Middle East were not negligible. Churchill conceived the idea of storming the Dardanelles with a great flotilla.[178] That failed, as did Churchill's next big idea—to seize the heights overlooking the seaway by land. Some 40,000 Allied troops, mostly colonials, paid with their lives for this fiasco.[179] One wonders what Churchill and Lloyd George were hoping to accomplish.

A number of explanations have been advanced, but only one explanation carries weight, that the British were determined to take control of the area because of its oil.

After the Russian front collapsed, the oil fields of Baku were up for grabs, so to speak, as the Bolsheviks had begun to negotiate a handover to the Germans.[180] The Russians wanted out of the war, and the Germans wanted Russia's oil. So did the Turks, and the Turkish army was closer to it.

A race developed between the Germans and Turks as to who would first take over the fields. The Turks won, after which Turkish troops massacred the Armenian oil field workers and in the process set fire to derricks and other equipment.[181] This was a terrible waste.

All Germany had now in the way of oil came from Romania, and even here the Germans were strapped. The Romanians had tried to go over to the Allied side, and, when Germany descended on them, rather than give up the fields, they set them afire. It took Germany until almost the end of the war to restore the fields, and then only to 80 percent effectiveness.

By the year 1917 all of the combatants in the war—the Allies as well as the Entente forces—were running out of oil. The Allies, however, had a hope of replenishing their supplies, if the United States would come into the war on their side. For some time the Allies had gotten oil from America, but not in the quantities desired.[182] Then Standard stopped shipments entirely, once the U-boat war started. The company did not want to lose tankers, and so it shifted commercial operations to the Far East.[183]

Royal Dutch might have stepped in, but it did not have the enormous amounts of oil available that the Americans did, and, along with that, Royal Dutch, like Standard, was not anxious to lose tankers, and so it, too, shifted operations away from the war theater.[184]

In line with this, Deterding in 1915 did something that was to have far-reaching effects. He approached the British government with a proposal to make Royal Dutch (which was 60 percent Dutch, 40 percent British) into a British-controlled company.[185]

The question of making Royal Dutch British is obscure (one suspects it has been purposely kept so), but it does appear that Deterding had two things in mind when he made the proposal. One, the war had shown him that, after the armistice, he was going to need the protection of some strong flag, and the Netherlands was unlikely to serve him.[186]

Two, Deterding's determination to get his hands on Anglo-Persian had not abated. He would have liked to effect an amalgamation of all the major non-American oil companies, but, barring that, he at least wanted Royal Dutch to share in the Mosul concession.

By the 1920s two of Iran's most prolific wells were producing 586,000 and 880,000 tons a year (12,000 and 18,000 barrels a day), while in the United States wells were averaging less than 4,000 tons a year.[187] This was phenomenal, and, given the fact that the concession was so ideally located (midway between the Far East and Europe), it was bound to be a remunerative one. (To be sure, the Mosul concession was not part of Anglo-Persian's claim, but it was situated adjacent to it, and therefore the likelihood was that it, too, was sumptuously endowed.)

This idea (of having the British government assume control over Royal Dutch) never was implemented, but, while it was being debated, Deterding went out of his way to be of service to the Allied cause. He moved his headquarters to London from the Hague, and he personally took out British citizenship.

Deterding also agreed to sell oil at cost to the Indian government so the railroads there could go on operating. This freed the Burmah Oil Co. to ship its production to the Western front. However, this was only slight relief, as the Allied armies were consuming enormous amounts of oil, far more than they had ever anticipated.

The only satisfactory supplier was Standard. It was estimated that over the course of the war the Americans fulfilled 80 percent of Allied fuel requirements.[188] However, once the U-boat war started, and Standard pulled back, the Allies suffered.[189] In 1917 the Allied leaders went to the American president with a plea for tankers to move oil to the front. If they did not get the ships, they declared, they would lose the war. Wilson, galvanized by the request, prevailed on Standard to do what it could. The company agreed to divert tankers from the Far East, but in return it wanted compensation. The company expected that any ships sunk by the U-boats would be replaced. It wanted tankers that the Allies had sequestered at the start of the war returned to it. In short, Standard wanted to be paid for the help that it gave, and it was.[190]

The shift, once made, was effective. Oil started moving to the Allies just as the Germans were running out. The successful French campaign in the Balkans had cut the Germans' oil lines from Russia and Romania, which meant that Germany was practically cut off.[191] As the German general Ludendorff has written, after that it was a matter of time before Berlin would have to capitulate.[192]

What is interesting is how long it took the combatants to realize that oil was crucial. The awareness really did not come until late 1916.[193] Immediately after that we see a shift in Allied strategy. Particularly, the British changed course. They resumed operations in the Middle East, almost certainly because they were intending to seize the area's oil supplies.

BRITAIN IN IRAQ

Early in the war British and Indian troops had landed in Iraq.[194] They had tried to force their way up the Tigris River to Baghdad but were stopped by the Turks in one of the more embarrassing defeats of the war.[195] Now, at the very end of the war the British returned, and this time their campaign was more successful.

The attack of the British proceeded by fits and starts. However, by the time that the war ended, Britain did physically possess the oil region of Mosul, although the manner in which it took possession was controversial—it seized the area *after* the Turks had accepted a cease-fire.[196] At any rate, the takeover of Mosul set the stage for the one of the great, unexpected developments of the war—a grand fight over Middle East oil supplies between Britain and the United States.

At the end of World War I, two events occurred to disturb the tenor of U.S.–British relations. First, an outfit appeared that called itself the British Controlled Oilfields Group.[197] This entity went into Central and South America, where it began buying up available oil properties.

The group came to light only when U.S. oilmen encountered it by chance. The Americans had gone themselves into the Southern Hemisphere, meaning to acquire oil properties there, and found that the British had preempted them, having bought many of the parcels on which the Americans had their hearts set.

It rankled the Americans that they should have been beaten. It was especially vexing because, after the breakup of the Standard Trust, many of the former Standard subsidiaries needed new production sources, and Latin American countries were the likeliest and the most efficient sites for them to set up in.[198]

The British had outmaneuvered the Americans, and there was no use crying over that. Moreover, ways of recovering existed; the Americans were experienced in these. However, aspects of this business seemed odd. The Oilfields Group, it turned out, was not a private enterprise but rather a government-sponsored trust. It, like the Anglo-Persian Oil Co., was an arm of the British government. That did not sit well with the Americans.

It is difficult to get reliable information on the Oilfields Group, but it appears to have been an outgrowth of the Anglo-Persian Oil Co., chartered not in Britain but in Canada.[199] So here we have the Anglo-Persian Oil Co., in which the Admiralty held a controlling interest, and the Oilfields Group, operating under a similar setup. Then, of course, there was the Royal Dutch, which—if rumors were to be believed—had also come under British government direction.[200] All this smelled like a well-orchestrated plot to the Americans.

Also troubling was the settlement that Britain and France had devised for the Middle East, the so-called San Remo Agreement. In American eyes, this amounted to a carve-up of the region, using a device called the mandate. The mandate was a tutelage deal whereby Britain and France obligated themselves to introduce the Middle Easterners to self-government. On paper, the mandate had all the trappings of disinterested idealism.

In fact, as the Americans were led to conclude, the mandates were a facade, behind which the European powers were attempting to exploit the economies of Middle Eastern lands.[201] In particular, Britain and France were bent on taking over such oil fields as existed and, in the process, shutting the Americans out.

Under San Remo, practically every territory in the Middle East (and many outside it as well) was earmarked for exclusive development by French and British interests.[202] When American oilmen went out to the area (to test the agreement by trying to prospect in defiance of it), the British and French summarily expelled them.[203]

At that, the American government entered the picture. One would have expected Washington to resist helping the oilmen, who, in the eyes of many, were monopolists. In fact, no such antipathy obtained.

The government went to the aid of the industry with a great will. Indeed, the administration of Woodrow Wilson did this. Wilson informed the British that he expected American oil companies to be able to prospect in the Middle East—or anywhere else, for that matter.[204] There was a principle involved, Wilson averred, that of the "Open Door." As for Americans being shut out of the Southern Hemisphere, this was completely unacceptable; in America's eyes, this area constituted a sphere of interest.

The British government heard the objections of Washington; however, it would not do anything about them. Lord Curzon, the British foreign secretary, communicated several closely reasoned notes to the Americans in which he set forth London's case for behaving as it did.[205] The gist of the British argument was that Washington needlessly fussed. After all, America was presently producing seven-tenths of the world's oil; Britain was merely attempting to assure itself an independent source of supply.[206]

The U.S. Congress then threatened to pass legislation that would effectively punish British companies doing business in the United States. This would have made it impossible for foreigners to own property, and since Royal Dutch had extensive holdings in America, it, in particular, would have been hurt.[207] Another piece of legislation would have set aside oil lands for conservation. The lands would be designated by the secretary of the navy and could not then be sold to private interests.

Accompanying this activity in the Congress went a campaign in the press that claimed that the United States was running out of oil. Several respected bureaus of the federal government, including the Geological Survey, announced that, at the present rate of consumption, America could not hope to satisfy its energy needs past 18 years. In the rest of the world, however (it was claimed), oil reserves were good for 250 years.[208]

This was a confounding development. The Americans had expected that, after the war, world demand for oil would settle back.[209] Instead, consumption shot up enormously, and this was largely due to the popularity of the motorcar. In Great Britain alone the number of cars registered increased from 187,000 in 1920, to 1,925,000 in 1932.[210] In the United States between only 1919 and 1923, the registration of motor vehicles doubled to 15 million. From 1914 to 1928 registrations increased 14-fold from 2 million to 28 million, and the annual demand for gasoline rose proportionately.[211] Thus, Americans could not but be impressed that a great change had come about; projections showed world demand was unlikely to abate at least for the foreseeable future.

Another aspect of the "oil scare" is harder to fathom. A number of journals in the United States began to allege that Britain was plotting a war on America, an actual shooting war. Offered as proof was the fact that the Oilfields Group had bought property around the Isthmus of Panama. This, according to the press lords, meant that Britain was planning to seize the vital waterway.[212]

Britain protested vociferously against these allegations, but it could not hope to prevail. At the end of World War I, the United States was practically the only strong economy extant, and both Britain and France were hoping for infusions of capital from it. Once the Americans set their minds to extracting concessions from the Allies, they were bound to get them.

Britain eventually was made to back down. It did not surrender any of its property in Central and South America, but it did offer to open up the Middle East to the Americans—the oilmen would be allowed to share in the Mosul concession. Effectively, three companies were brought in on this—Standard Oil of New Jersey and of New York and the Gulf Oil Co.

THE CARRYING TRADE

What appears to have been driving American interests was the carrying trade. The United States had emerged from World War I with a huge armada of tankers, ships that it had commissioned to ferry supplies to the Allies. In 1920 it was estimated that America had some 1,465 of these vessels, representing a gross tonnage of 5,840,742.[213]

Since it had the ships, it wanted very much to use them. An obvious use would be for them to carry oil—getting it from one faraway place and taking it to another for sale. Out of this activity, it was expected, lucrative side benefits would accrue. The investment banking business and the insurance business might prosper. Railroads would gain as they transported goods to the great port cities of the United States.

Because of this combination (having a native oil industry and a great tanker fleet that enabled the oil companies to operate overseas), America now was poised to take a leap forward. Indeed, what America actually was essaying at this point was to displace Great Britain as the world's leading trader.[214]

More specifically, it was out to make New York the world's financial capital. This it could do if it could generate enough trade in dollars. Oil traditionally traded in dollars, and now, with the development of the motorcar industry, enormous amounts of oil were being sold, with more contemplated. Foreigners would be compelled to amass dollars, which they would then use to buy American products, and thus New York would become a great clearinghouse for an ever expanding lot of transactions. Ultimately, there was even the likelihood that the dollar would displace the pound as the unit of international exchange.

This was the bright prospect that appears to have been dazzling the American business community, a dream worth fulfilling. However, everyone had to get behind the effort. To do what? To push oil. Business, finance—all had to join in the campaign. With the country's elite falling in line behind the deal, the federal government could not possibly have stayed aloof.

This, it would seem, was why the government changed its stance from fighting the oil companies, to facilitating their affairs. However, it was not an unqualified backing that the companies got. The U.S. government was all for promoting the oil companies overseas—but not in the United States. For the government to have facilitated the *domestic* growth of the industry, it would have had, in effect, to repudiate the anti-trust actions of the previous administrations.

Since it was not prepared to do this, it had to parse matters carefully. Oil effectively divided into two spheres: at home things went on as always, that is, the federal government struck down combinations in restraint of trade wherever they appeared; conversely, the companies could count on full cooperation from the government as they expanded abroad. The oilmen were made aware that whenever they encountered difficulty anywhere in the world, they could expect U.S. government support.

Where does all this leave us? Obviously, the character of the oil industry had changed. It had now become truly internationalized, in the sense that the two great empires—British and American—were inextricably caught up with it. It is going to be difficult after this to state precisely where the line is drawn between the activities of the oil companies as businesses and their activities as agents of the twin imperialisms.

Moreover, this is a crucial distinction because, starting in the next chapter, we look into the relations between the companies and the oil producers, specifically in Iran and Iraq. These two had entered into contracts with businesses, entities that they presumed were interested solely in profit, not with empires bent on establishing geopolitical control.

NOTES

1. The name Seneca was meant to associate the product with the Indians, after the tribe of that name.

2. Hildegarde Dolson, *The Great Oildorado* (New York: Random House, 1959), 59.

3. Ibid., 82. It is important to note that, from the very first, American promoters of lamp oil were interested to get contracts overseas and that Europeans, along with Americans, were the first users of the product on a large scale.

4. Daniel Yergin, *The Prize* (New York: Simon & Schuster, 1991), 30. As to the large numbers of prospectors, it's interesting that the "oil rush" occurred right after the Civil War, when there were many discharged soldiers available for adventurous activity like oil exploration.

5. Mexico originally subscribed to this arrangement, but when the country became a big producer of oil, the government transferred the underground rights to the state.

6. The rule derived from English common law in respect to wild animals: *res ferae naturae* (he who captures a wild beast owns it). The idea is that if game crosses from one estate onto another, the owner of the estate on which the game is now found can take it. See Harvey O'Connor, *The Empire of Oil* (New York: Monthly Review Press, 1955), 45. The problem obviously does not arise with gold or iron or any other mineral that stays put underground—only with oil, which flows.

7. At the same time the oil fields are often ruined by unplanned, destructive drilling. One of the benefits of developing oil in the Middle East was that there the fields were state-owned, and hence the companies that undertook to develop them were able to do so on a planned basis.

8. Yergin, *The Prize*, 30.

9. Pierre l'Espagnol de la Tramerye, *The World Struggle for Oil* (New York: Alfred Knopf, 1924), 46, says that in 1870 there were 250 refineries in the United States.

10. For a good account of how the drawback worked, see Tramerye, *The World Struggle for Oil*, 45ff.; Dolson, *The Great Oildorado*; 260; Timothy Jacobs, *The History of the Pennsylvania Railroad* (Greenwich, CT: Brompton Books, 1988), 44. The definitive treatment, of course, is in Ida Tarbell's classic, *The History of the Standard Oil Co.* (New York: Peter Smith, 1950).

11. The question of whether the scheme originated with the railroads has never been settled. Ida Tarbell, who went most deeply into it, does not really set the matter to rights. At one point she says that certain refiners, whom she never names (Tarbell, *The History of the Standard Oil Co.*, Vol. I, 55), went to Rockefeller with the proposition. Elsewhere, she cites testimony by Flagler, Rockefeller's partner, in which he says that the scheme

was gotten up by two refiners, one from Philadelphia, one from Pittsburgh (ibid., Appendix 4, 280). Yet in another appendix to the volume (Appendix XXXII, "Producers' Appeal of 1878 to Governor John F. Hartranft of Pennsylvania," 383) she cites evidence naming the two railroad men who "initiated" the scheme. This last seems to be most likely. Because of the up-and-down nature of oil prices, the railroads were not making the money that they felt they should (Ibid., 81). They stood to gain if the price could be regularized. Also, it was a part of the original scheme that, after the drawback went into effect, all three of the participating railroads would share the revenue from oil shipments eastward. In other words, the three would agree not to undercut each other's rates. None of this could have been initiated by anonymous refiners, unless they were acting as agents for the roads.

12. Rockefeller's two original partners were Henry Flagler and Samuel Andrews. These men stayed with him throughout his career.

13. Dolson, *The Great Oildorado*, 260.

14. Tarbell in *The History of the Standard Oil Co.*, Vol. I, 61, shows how the system worked:

> The open rate from Cleveland to New York was two dollars, and fifty cents of this was turned over to the (Rockefeller group), which at the same time received a rebate enabling it to ship (before the drawback was tendered) for $1.50. At the same time, an independent refiner in Cleveland paid eighty cents a barrel to get his crude from the Oil Regions to his works, and the railroad sent forty cents of this to the Rockefeller group. A Cleveland refiner included in Rockefeller's group, however, could expect to get his crude oil shipped for just 40 cents.

Tramerye (*The World Struggle for Oil*, 54) quotes the following: "It was enough for the Standard or the South Improvement Association (the name of Rockefeller's group of protected refiners under the drawback system) to telegraph, 'Wilkinson and Co., have received a truck which only paid $41.50; screw them up to $57.50, and it was done.' "

15. The name South Improvement Association is meaningless. Rockefeller and his associates bought an existing charter of the state of Pennsylvania for a defunct organization called the South Improvement Association, and they kept the name.

16. Tramerye, *The World Struggle for Oil*, 54.

17. Tarbell, *The History of the Standard Oil Co.*, 62.

18. Those who did not wish the Standard stock could be paid off in cash, but Rockefeller conducted the appraisals, and many felt that he appraised under value.

19. Dolson gives an example of an affadavit that enrollees in the South Improvement Association had to swear to. Dolson, *The Great Oildorado*, 261.

20. For an insight into how Rockefeller went about this, see "The Affidavit of George O. Baslington" in Tarbell's *The History of the Standard Oil Co.*, 263.

21. Tarbell, 100.

22. Jacobs, *The History of the Pennsylvania Railroad*, 44.

23. Tarbell, *The History of the Standard Oil Co.*, Vol. II, 140. On page 81, Vol. I, of the same book Tarbell says: "The object (of Rockefeller's combination effort) is twofold: firstly, to do away, at least in a great measure, with the excessive and undue competition now existing between the refining interest, by reason of their being a far greater refining capacity than is called for or justified by the existing petroleum-consuming requirements of the world." Tarbell then goes on to say that a second requirement is to reduce competition between the railroads. Also Vol. I, 235.

24. Dolson, *The Great Oildorado*, 268.

25. Tarbell in her *History of the Standard Oil Co.*, Vol. II, 11, says:

Just how serious this situation was is shown by the difference in the cost of transporting a barrel of oil to seaboard by rail and transporting it by pipe. According to the calculation of . . . the president of the Reading Railroad, the cost by rail was at that time from thirty five to forty-five cents. The open rate was from $1.25 to $1.40, and the Standard Oil Company probably paid about 85 cents. . . . Now . . . oil could be carried in pipes from the Oil Regions to the seaboard for 16 2/3 cents a barrel . . . General Haupt (the engineer of the pipelines) calculated the difference in cost of the two systems to be 23 cents, enough to pay 28 per cent dividends on the cost of the line even if the railways put their freights down to cost.

26. The best account of this Potts-Rockefeller contest is in Tarbell, Ibid.

27. Jacobs, *The History of the Pennsylvania Railroad*, 45.

28. Ibid.

29. In addition to evidence cited in note 13, there is also material in Dolson's book that points to the conclusion that the railroad men got it up. This includes a letter, quoted in Dolson, in which Rockefeller shows apprehension about the scheme. Dolson, *The Great Oildorado*, 260–261.

30. At least one prominent economist believes that demand for oil is inelastic and that production costs, once it has been discovered, are low. Hence, the oil industry does not obey normal laws of supply and demand and tends toward cartelization. For a discussion of this theory see Peter Ellis Jones, *Oil: A Practical Guide to the Economics of World Petroleum* (Cambridge: Woodhead-Faulkner, 1988), xii.

31. O'Connor, *The Empire of Oil*, 50.

32. Tarbell, *The History of the Standard Oil Co.*, Vol. I, 20.

33. Samuel Andrews, testifying before an investigatory commission in Ohio in 1879. Ibid., 190. Another point worth bearing in mind is that the majority of stock was in the hands of only nine men, Rockefeller included. Therefore, the big beneficiaries of this scheme were able to become not just wealthy but extremely wealthy and, along with that, very powerful.

34. Ibid., Appendix XI. Also Vol. I, 79, 82, 190, 235.

35. Says Tarbell, ibid., Vol. II, 197, "Now it is generally conceded that the man or men who control over 70 percent of a commodity control its price—within limits, very strict limits, such is the force of economic laws."

36. Ibid., 131: "When the epidemic of trust investigation broke out in 1888, and the Standard Oil Trust was brought up for examination, there was a general public demand to have the matter cleared up. The first investigation of importance took place in February 1888, and by the direction of the Senate of New York State." Also see Anton Mohr, *The Oil War* (New York: Harcourt Brace, 1926), 40.

37. Another aspect of the trust activity that excited popular ire was the secrecy in which it shrouded its operations. Tarbell, *The History of the Standard Oil Co.*, Vol. II, 136, comments on this: "Consider the anomoly of the situation. Thirty-nine corporations, each of them having a legal existence, obliged by the laws of the state creating it to limit its operations to certain lines and make certain reports, had turned over their affairs to an organization having no legal existence, independent of all authority, able to do anything it wanted anywhere; and to this point working in absolute darkness."

38. The facts on this were actually brought out by Rockefeller himself. Testifying in a New York state commission of inquiry, he said that the trustees knew by reports and correspondence and by frequent consultation in New York with active promoters of each concern how the business went. Rockefeller's performance before these various investigatory commissions is puzzling. Before one, he would deny something, which

later on, before another, he would admit to. Nor does this seem to have come about because of confusion on his part. Under testimony, he always appeared the soul of self-possession. Ibid., 136.

39. Ohio Standard was both a holding company and an operating oil business. For details on how this worked, see George Sweet Gibb and Evelyn H. Knowlton, *The History of the Standard Oil Company, the Resurgent Years: 1911–1927* (New York: Harper & Brothers, 1956), 6f.

40. As a return for the transfer, the original Standard of Ohio owners were paid off in stock of the parent company.

41. In other words, the trust admitted the accuracy of the charge. Not only in the case of Standard of Ohio but with every one of the companies associated with the trust, this was the pattern that was set—the companies turned over their stocks to the trust to administer. Tarbell, *The History of the Standard Oil Co.*, Vol. II, 144.

42. Ibid., Chapter 18.

43. Yergin, *The Prize*, 97.

44. Much of this public hostility was generated by Tarbell's exposé, which appeared first as a series of articles in *McClure's* magazine.

45. In fact, the oil business from the very first was heavily involved overseas. Tarbell says that in 1897, the year before Rockefeller "first appeared as an important factor in the oil trade, refined oil was going into every civilized country on the globe." She goes on to say that "of the five and a half million barrels of crude oil produced that year, the world used five million, over three and half million of which went to foreign lands." Tarbell, *The History of the Standard Oil Co.*, Vol. II, p. 32; also Vol. I, 21. E. H. Davenport & Sidney Cooke, *The Oil Trusts and Anglo-American Relations* (New York: Macmillan, 1924), 86, argue that Standard was driven to go overseas by the demand to find markets for ever increasing production. (Tarbell notes this same dilemma when she writes, "A man with a thousand-barrel well on his hands in 1862 was in a plight. He had got to sell his oil at once for lack of storage room, or let it run on the ground" [28].) Alessandro Roncaglia, *The International Oil Market* (London: Macmillan, 1985) 53, says the anti-trust law drove Standard to concentrate overseas, because "U.S. anti-trust law forbade collusive agreements among producers within the U.S. territory, but had no application to events in foreign markets." Effectively, then, there are two interpretations as to why Standard went overseas so early and in such a big way—one, economic forces made it make the move, and, two, the government's hostility drove it to do so.

46. Harvey O'Connor, *World Crisis in Oil* (New York: Monthly Review Press, 1962), 37, 28. Also Tramerye, *The World Struggle for Oil*, 65.

47. O'Connor, *World Crisis in Oil*, 47.

48. The Deutsche-Amerikanische Petroleum Gesellschaft controlled 91 percent of Germany's oil imports as late as 1912. Mohr, *The Oil War*, 78.

49. O'Connor, *World Crisis in Oil*, 33. Also Tarbell, *The History of the Standard Oil Co.*, Vol. II, 210.

50. Tarbell, *The History of the Standard Oil Co.*, Vol. II, 192f.

51. For the effect on the Germans and others of upswings in the commercial price of oil, see ibid., 198ff. Tarbell tracks three separate phases in which Standard sought to drive prices up and was successful, and she shows the reaction in Europe. Writing of European response during the second phase, 1872 to 1879, she says that when the price went up,

[t]he exporters were angry. The buyers in Europe were angry. If the Americans are going to force up prices in this way, they said, we will not buy their refined oil. We will import their crude and refine it ourselves. We will go back to shale oil. A first result, then, of this attempt to hold prices up to a point conspicuously out of proportion to the raw product was that the export of illuminating oil fell off—they were less by a million gallons in 1878 than in 1877.

Elsewhere (205) she says,

In 1879 the exporters and buyers from all the great foreign markets had met in Bremen in an indignation meeting over the way Standard was handling the oil business. Remonstrances came from the consuls at Antwerp and Bremen to our State Department concerning even the quality of oil which had been sent to Europe by the Standard. [Said] a prominent Antwerp merchant: "I am of the opinion that if the petroleum business continues to be conducted as it has in the past in Europe, it will go smash."

Of course, at this time, as we shall see later, the Rothschilds started looking to develop the oil fields of Russia.

52. Tarbell, *The History of the Standard Oil Company*, Vol. II, 173.

53. R. W. Ferrier, *The History of the British Petroleum Company*, Vol. I (Cambridge: Cambridge University Press, 1982), 4.

54. O'Connor, *World Crisis in Oil*, 47; Robert Henriques, *Marcus Samuel* (London: Barrie & Rockcliff, 1960), 128; Tarbell, *The History of the Standard Oil Co.*, Vol. II, 210.

55. Tarbell, *The History of Standard Oil Co.*, Vol. II, 200.

56. Ibid., 206.

57. Allessandro, Roncaglia, *The International Oil Market* (London: Macmillan, 1985 p. 51; Jones, *Oil: A Practical Guide to the Economics of World Petroleum*, 7. Jones says that Rockefeller's companies were enjoined by the founder to become self-financing and not to attempt to raise capital through the banks.

58. Rockefeller's unwillingness to tolerate competition, even in Europe, was not irrational. The Europeans, once they developed the Russian fields, were closer to the European market than was Standard, and so there were unit cost economies that they could exploit. Also because oil from Russia was so cheap to produce (something we discuss later), it was coming onto the market at a great rate and depressing prices.

59. F. C. Gerretson, *History of the Royal Dutch*, Vol. I (Leiden: E. J. Brill, 1953), 210.

60. For a discussion of this, see ibid.

61. Yergin, *The Prize*, 58ff.

62. The area of Baku, where the richest fields are located, was previously an independent duchy, annexed to the Russian empire in the early nineteenth century. By 1829 there were 82 hand-dug oil pits, but output was tiny. The minuscule industry was run as a state monopoly. See ibid., 57–58; Henriques, *Marcus Samuel*, 70, which says that the czar did not allow independent prospecting until 1873.

63. Gerretson, *History of the Royal Dutch*, Vol. I, 213; Yergin, *The Prize*, 60.

64. Yergin says that "America's share of the world export trade in illuminating oil fell from 78 percent in 1888 to 71 percent in 1891, while the Russian share rose from 22 percent to 29 percent." *The Prize*, 62.

65. Ibid., 61, 62.

66. Ibid., 63f.

67. Robert Henriques, *Sir Robert Waley Cohen* (London: Seckjer & Warburg, 1966),

80, says that Samuel did not own the tankers but merely chartered them from Fred Lane, who comes up again.

68. This was known as "case oil." It was shipped in tins, crated two to the case, and could be an ordinary item of cargo, whereas "bulk oil" was shipped in tankers, loaded and discharged by pumps.

69. By 1911 Standard Oil (of New Jersey) had developed a tanker fleet of its own, but it did not directly control it. Under its direct control it had but five ships and six barges. It had another 26 steamers, two barges, and eight sailing vessels indirectly controlled through the Anglo-American Oil Co., its agent in Britain; and it had 23 additional tankers controlled through the German firm DAPG. Moreover, all these ships were European-made; Standard had no vessels built in the United States. Gibb and Knowlton, *The History of the Standard Oil Company, the Resurgent Years*, 154f.

70. Whether this was, in fact, a Rothschild-engendered scheme is not at all certain. Gerretson (*History of the Royal Dutch*, Vol. I, 210f.) makes a good case that the idea was originated by the Nobels. They confronted a problem moving their oil to the north of Russia. Because of the terrible winters, the oil had to be moved in spring and stored in tanks, to be distributed later on. Since the vessels that shipped the oil north along the Volga were tankers (on the order of those that Samuel and Rothschild later produced), it could be said that the whole "tank" scheme derived from the Nobel family.

71. For an excellent discussion of the significance of moving oil by tanker, see Gerretson, *History of the Royal Dutch*, Vol. I, 207f.

72. These contacts were not merely agents of Samuel's. They bought the oil from the Rothschilds, as did he, and their share of the profits from sales was prorated. Henriques, *Marcus Samuel*, 78.

73. Gerretson (*History of the Royal Dutch*, Vol. I, 214) says that Samuel did not originate the idea of moving oil through the canal; Standard did. It tried to get permission as early as 1895 and failed.

74. Yergin says oil from Batum to Singapore covered a distance of 11,500 miles, while oil from Philadelphia had to travel 15,000 miles. *The Prize*, 72.

75. Indeed, the British Rothschilds originally supplied the loan whereby Britain bought its controlling interest in the canal.

76. Yergin says that apprehension within the Rothschild family as to Standard's reaction very nearly killed the arrangement with Samuel, since one branch of the family did not want to take on the Americans, fearing the confrontation would be too bruising. Yergin, *The Prize*, 66.

77. Gerretson (*History of the Royal Dutch*, Vol. I, 214), says that for a time it appeared that the forces opposed to opening the canal would win out. Yergin further claims that the debate was charged with anti-Semitism, as the fight was portrayed as one of British versus Jewish interests (Samuel and the Rothschilds both were Jewish). *The Prize*, 66f. Henriques makes the same claim. Henriques, *Marcus Samuel*, 89.

78. Gerretson says that the Grand Duke Constantine Nicolaivich weighed in on this fight. Gerretson further claims that the intervention was crucial because the British government at this time was trying to develop an alliance with Russia and did not want to alienate ruling circles there. Gerretson, *History of the Royal Dutch*, Vol. I, 216.

79. Ibid., 217.

80. Henriques says that what the Americans feared was overproduction. They claimed that, in Russia, the oil flowed out of the ground unpumped, and the work was done with serf labor. Henriques, *Marcus Samuel*, 126.

81. Ibid., 143.

82. Yergin, *The Prize*, 72.

83. T.A.B. Corley, *A History of the Burmah Oil Company, 1886–1924* (London: Heinemann, 1983).

84. The secret of Rockefeller's early success in waging these price wars was that he could cut prices to harm a rival in one market and raise them in another so as to compensate for his losses. As long as the rival had only one available market, he could not win out against this strategy. Were the rival to secure an alternative market, however, he could then, in the same way as Rockefeller, raise prices in one part of the world to compensate for losses experienced elsewhere.

85. Ferrier makes a similar point in *The History of the British Petroleum Company*, Vol. I, 4.

86. Henriques says that the czar's action was triggered by the failure of a harvest (1891), followed by famine (1892), followed by pestilence (1893) and the death of a million peasants. Henriques, *Marcus Samuel*, 127.

87. Ferrier, *The History of the British Petroleum Company*, Vol. I, 8. The Russian fields peaked in 1901, and by 1914 Russia's share of world oil production had dropped to 16.4 percent from 51 percent.

88. Henriques, *Marcus Samuel*, 369.

89. The Rothschilds soon had an additional reason—in 1905, following news of Russia's debacle in the Russo-Japanese War, ethnic riots erupted in Baku, and the oil wells were set ablaze. Two-thirds of the producing fields were wiped out.

90. North Borneo was British-controlled, and therefore the Dutch government, which controlled most of the East Indies, could not shut him out of this particular area.

91. Yergin, *The Prize*, 114.

92. In the oil business at this time, to survive one had to have numerous sources of supply. This was because, as oil for motor fuel came more and more to be in demand, one could not keep pace with consumption. It was also the case that oil fields gave out (as subsequently happened in Russia), or the drills began sucking up water with the oil (as happened in Mexico).

93. For how the Dutch handled Standard's attempt to buy into the Djambi fields in Sumatra, see O'Connor, *World Crisis in Oil*, 53, also 38.

94. Kessler developed the fields; the man who initiated the operations was Aeilko Jans Zijlker. Zijlker effectively worked himself to death trying to exploit the claim, as did Kessler after him.

95. Ralph Hewins, *Mr. Five Percent* (New York: Rinehart, 1958), 63.

96. Gerretson, *History of the Royal Dutch*, Vol. I, 222f.

97. And also pay canal fees.

98. Henriques, *Marcus Samuel*, 264.

99. Ibid., 334. Henriques also says that 10 months before Samuel's contract with the Rothschilds came up for renewal, he wrote to his agent in Borneo reminding him that there had been negligible output coming from that concession. Ibid., 302.

100. Anthony Sampson, *The Seven Sisters* (New York: Viking Press, 1975), 57.

101. Yergin, *The Prize*, 117.

102. The full quote reads:

[O]il is the most extraordinary article in the commercial world, and the only thing that hampers its sale is its production. . . . There is no other article in the world where you can get the consumption as long as you make the production. . . . There is no need to look after the consumption, and as a seller you need not make forward contracts, as the oil sells itself. Only what you want is an enormous long, long purse to be able to snap your fingers at everybody, and if people do not want to buy it today to be able to say: "all right; I will spend a million in sterling in making reservoirs, and then in the future you will have to pay so much more." (O'Connor, *World Crisis in Oil*, 281)

103. Henriques, *Marcus Samuel*, 435f.; Yergin, *The Prize*, 124–125.

104. Mohr (*The Oil War*, 32) says that in 1899 there were about 1,672 motorcars in France, while about 600 were manufactured in the United States the same year. However, within 10 years the United States alone could boast 1 million cars, and the numbers in other countries, if not so great, were considerable. Also see Yergin, *The Prize*, 112.

105. Yergin, *The Prize*, 100.

106. Deterding concentrated initially on promoting concessions in the East Indies. Eventually, he came to control virtually all the fields in that part of the world. See Corley, *A History of the Burmah Oil Company*, 80f.

107. Yergin, *The Prize*, 122.

108. Ibid.

109. O'Connor, *World Crisis in Oil*, 43.

110. Ibid.

111. Henriques, *Marcus Samuel*, 490.

112. See Nubar Gulbenkian, *Portrait in Oil* (New York: Simon & Schuster, 1965), 120. For the breakdown of the board of directors of the new company, see Henriques, *Sir Robert Waley Cohen*, 130.

113. This was another innovation that Deterding supplied, that is, the notion of supplying oil from within markets instead of shipping it from a central location all over the world. This was a simple idea but ingenious nonetheless, since it obviously cut costs. Corley, *A History of the Burmah Oil Company*, 69.

114. For a description of how exactly Deterding handled this stock business, see Gulbenkian, *Portrait in Oil*, 86. This essentially was speculation. For the attitude of Standard toward speculation, we have the testimony of H. H. Rogers, quoted in Tarbell (*The History of the Standard Oil Co.*, Vol. I, 149–150). Speaking to a reporter, Rogers said, "Speculators have ruined the market. . . . To make an artificial increase, with immense profits, would be recognized as speculative instead of legitimate, and the oil interests would suffer accordingly. Temporary capital would compete with permanent investment and ruin everything."

115. Calouste Gulbenkian maintains that Deterding went to the United States on his concession-hunting foray at his insistence. Hewins, *Mr. Five Percent*, 61.

116. Yergin, *The Prize*, 100.

117. Ibid., 99. O'Connor (*World Crisis in Oil*, 60–61) says that between 1899 and 1911, Standard's average earnings of $79 million easily matched the capital stock of $98 million. Dividends averaged $40 million a year. The net worth in 1911 was $378 million.

118. The muckrakers were a group of independent journalists who penned numerous exposés of corruption at the turn of the century. In addition to Tarbell, Lincoln Steffens was perhaps the most famous of these. He wrote a work similar to Tarbell's—*The Shame of the Cities*. Tarbell's work appeared in 26 installments of *McClure's* magazine. It later became a book, *The History of the Standard Oil Co.*

119. Yergin, *The Prize*, 229ff.

120. Mexico, as mentioned earlier, was one area that, like the United States, conceded subsoil rights to property owners.

121. Tramerye, *The World Struggle for Oil*, 113.

122. Sampson, *The Seven Sisters*, 100.

123. Frank Hanighen, *The Secret War* (New York: The John Day Co., 1934), 53ff.

124. Ibid., 62.

125. Wilson regarded Huerta merely as a butcher.

126. Francis Delaisi, *Oil: Its Influence on Politics* (London: The Labor Publishing Co., Ltd., 1922), 25, 26.

127. Davenport and Cooke, *The Oil Trusts and Anglo-American Relations*, 70.

128. See O'Connor, *World Crisis in Oil*, 55.

129. Ibid.

130. Ibid., 57.

131. Hanighen, *The Secret War*, 101.

132. O'Connor, *World Crisis in Oil*, 57.

133. Ibid., 56, says Deterding paid $1.5 million for a half interest in three Indian reservations in Oklahoma.

134. Hanighen, *The Secret War*, 102.

135. For background on the Samuel–Fisher tie, see Yergin, *The Prize*, 155f.

136. Ibid., 154.

137. Ibid., 65, 116; also, Ferrier, *The History of the British Petroleum Company*, Vol. I, 4.

138. Corley, *A History of the Burmah Oil Company*, 80; also 3, where he says that as early as 1903, the navy had begun to negotiate long-term contracts for the provision of oil from the Burmah company.

139. Yergin, *The Prize*, 155; also, Davenport and Cooke, *The Oil Trusts and Anglo-American Relations*, 5.

140. Yergin, *The Prize*, 156.

141. Tramerye, *The World Struggle for Oil*, 18.

142. In 1912, 9 percent of Germany's oil imports fell to the Deutsche Petroleum Verkaufsgessellschaft, a company formed by the Deutsche Bank and Royal Dutch Shell (the remainder of imports came from Standard). This company's imports came from Galacia and Romania. See Mohr, *The Oil War*, 78–79.

143. Henriques, *Marcus Samuel*, 501.

144. Roger Adelson, *London and the Invention of the Middle East* (New Haven, CT: Yale University Press, 1995), 22.

145. P. T. Cain and A. G. Hopkins, *British Imperialism: Innovation and Expansion, 1688–1914* (London: Longman, 1993), 397ff.

146. Ibid.

147. Ibid., 400.

148. This was in the period between 1840 and the outbreak of the Crimean War in 1854. Ibid.

149. Ibid., 401.

150. Ibid.

151. Ibid., 402.

152. Ibid., 405.

153. Hewins, *Mr. Five Percent*, 26.

154. Delaisi, *Oil: Its Influence on Politics*, 47ff.

155. Ibid.

156. Britain secured its position in the Gulf by getting the petty sheikhs in the area to, in effect, put themselves under British protection. In return for their pledge not to alienate any of their land to foreign powers, Britain agreed to guarantee their sovereignty. The most significant of all these arrangements was the one made with Kuwait, which later came to be a principal upholder of British solvency. O'Connor, *World Crisis in Oil*, 49.

157. Stephen Longrigg, *Iraq* (London: Ernest Benn, 1958), 75.

158. Mohr, *The Oil War*, 86.

159. Davenport and Cooke, *The Oil Trusts and Anglo-American Relations*, 26.

160. Yergin, *The Prize*, 185.

161. Ibid., 134.

162. Ibid., 142.

163. Ibid., 141.

164. Ibid., 138–139.

165. Ferrier, *The History of the British Petroleum Company*, Vol. I, 8.

166. Ferrier in *The History of the British Petroleum Company*, Vol. I, 13, says Greenway acquired his intense dislike for the Royal Dutch people while serving with the trading company Shaw Wallace in India. He had dealings with both Royal Dutch and Shell, and this "left an indelible and unfavorable impression on him."

167. Corley, *A History of the Burmah Oil Company*, 90.

168. Royal Dutch was British by way of its ownership of Shell.

169. Henriques describes Samuel's protestations to the Admiralty that his firm was not "foreign," even though he got his oil from Russia by contract with a French company that had a long and unpronounceable Dutch title and was in Dutch territory and from contracts with other Dutch concerns in the East Indies and from Texas. Henriques, *Marcus Samuel*, 390. Also see Yergin, *The Prize*, 158.

170. Yergin, *The Prize*, 153.

171. Ibid.

172. Ibid., 160–161.

173. Davenport and Cooke, *The Oil Trusts and Anglo-American Relations*, 22. See also Henriques, *Marcus Samuel*, 541, where Henriques discusses a simultaneous rise in the price of gasoline by both the Americans and Royal Dutch, which angered the public in Britain. Ferrier in *The History of the British Petroleum Company*, Vol. I, 177, quotes a letter from Greenway written just before Churchill's speech in which he notes that "they [the government] must maintain a hold over the Anglo-Persian Oil Company (APOC) as this is the only part of the world under British control from which they can rely . . . on sufficient supplies to meet their requirements."

174. Ferrier in *The History of the British Petroleum Company*, Vol. I, 173, quotes a government official to the effect that "our [the British] political position in the Persian Gulf is largely the result of our commercial predominance, but that would be jeopardized if the Anglo-Persian were allowed to pass under foreign control by absorption in the Shell Company."

175. According to ibid., 179, Deterding refused to give the Admiralty anything more than a two-year contract for supplies.

176. Corley, quoting official British government sources, says in *A History of the Burmah Oil Company*, 90, that the problem of supply is not merely a commercial question; it is an imperial question of the first magnitude, particularly so for Britain a great power that lacked domestic supplies of oil.

177. Davenport and Cooke, *The Oil Trusts and Anglo-American Relations.*

178. C.R.M.F. Crutwell, *A History of the Great War: 1914–1918* (Oxford: Clarendon Press, 1934), 204f.

179. Ibid., 227.

180. Yergin, *The Prize*, 182–183.

181. Hewins, *Mr. Five Percent*, 119.

182. Tramerye, *The World Struggle for Oil*, 104–105.

183. Ibid., 106; Yergin, *The Prize*, 176.

184. Henriques, *Marcus Samuel*, 621.

185. There are quite a number of versions of how this came about. Corley gives what appears to be the most convincing, suggesting that Waley Cohen, Deterding's man, first raised the idea by suggesting that Burmah Oil and Royal Dutch/Shell could merge so that the latter would become a British-controlled company. Later, as negotiations over this progressed, Deterding suggested adding Anglo-Persian to the proposed merger scheme. Corley, *A History of the Burmah Oil Company*, 244f. See also Henriques, *Marcus Samuel*, 625f.

186. Henriques, *Marcus Samuel*, 414. Ferrier, in *The History of the British Petroleum Company*, Vol. I, 11, expresses this nicely this: "since oil is an internationally traded commodity with production and consumption centers often separated by vast distances, it is not surprising that the diplomatic dimension has been important."

187. Ferrier, *The History of the British Petroleum Company*, Vol. I, 398.

188. Yergin, *The Prize*, 178.

189. Ibid., 177.

190. O'Connor, *World Crisis in Oil*, 71.

191. Delaisi, *Oil: Its Influence on Politics*, 29.

192. Yergin, *The Prize*, 182.

193. Ferrier, *The History of the British Petroleum Company*, Vol. I, 235, says that, as a (British) Board of Trade memorandum revealed, the oil situation in 1915 excited little sense of urgency, for the full importance of petroleum products does not seem to have been fully appreciated until the latter half of 1916.

194. Cruttwell, *A History of the Great War: 1914–1918*, 339f.

195. The British were forced to surrender unconditionally; 10,000 combatants went into captivity.

196. For details, see Cruttwell, *A History of the Great War: 1914–1918*, 606f.

197. The best account of the British Controlled Oilfields Group is in Davenport and Cooke, *The Oil Trusts and Anglo-American Relations.*

198. Sampson says that after the breakup, the separate entities that formerly made up the Standard Trust were extremely vulnerable, with a dangerous imbalance between (their) big markets and (their) tiny supplies of (their) own crude oil. Sampson, *The Seven Sisters*, 75.

199. For background on this, see Tramerye, *The World Struggle for Oil*, 11, 143, 166; Hanighen, *The Secret War*, 152, 165; Mohr, *The Oil War*, 209, 213; L. Vernon Gibbs, *Oil and Peace* (Los Angeles: Parker, Stone, & Baird, 1929), 40, 58, 70.

200. Ferrier, *The History of the British Petroleum Company*, Vol. I, 376.

201. For the background to this, see Delaisi, *Oil: Its Influence on Politics.*

202. The San Remo Agreement is reprinted in ibid.

203. Davenport and Cooke, *The Oil Trusts and Anglo-American Relations*, 104; also Hanighen, *The Secret War*, 112.

204. In addition to carrying on a sharp correspondence with the British government, the administration oversaw some other developments. For example, the Congress called for a report from the State Department on Britain's alleged attempts to exclude Americans from the oil fields. This produced the Polk Report, which more or less averred that there was, in fact, such a policy adopted by the British. For the action of the Congress, see Delaisi, *Oil: Its Influence on Politics*, 34; for the State Department's report, see ibid., 39.

205. Davenport and Cooke, *The Oil Trusts and Anglo-American Relations.*

206. Mohr, *The Oil War*, 235.

207. Davenport and Cooke, *The Oil Trusts and Anglo-American Relations*, 181.

208. See Yergin, *The Prize*, 194.

209. Corley says that at the end of World War I, the United States was a net importer of oil. Corley, *A History of the Burmah Oil Company*, 285.

210. Ferrier, *The History of the British Petroleum Company*, Vol. I, 487.

211. Ibid., 542.

212. O'Connor, *World Crisis in Oil*, 132; Hanighen, *The Secret War*, 152; Tramerye, *The World Struggle for Oil*, 143–144.

213. Davenport and Cooke, *The Oil Trusts and Anglo-American Relations*, 73.

214. In line with this, Sampson gives an interesting aside. He says American oilmen were called to Washington at this time and told to "go out and get it," meaning they were to actively search for concessions in the Middle East and trust that the government would support them. Sampson, *The Seven Sisters*, 79–80. Davenport and Cooke throw a further interesting light on this by suggesting that Washington had to find a use for the ships, because it had added billions of dollars to the national debt to get them. Davenport and Cooke, *The Oil Trusts and Anglo-American Relations*, 70. Finally, Henriques, in *Sir Robert Waley Cohen*, 233, quotes an interesting exchange between Cohen and a Standard oil executive in which the latter boasts that, now that America has the ships, it will pretty soon displace Britain's leading role. This was in 1917.

CHAPTER 2

A Handful of Companies Gain Control of the Industry

What we have been trying to do up to now is show how a handful of companies were able to gain control of the international oil industry, and now we show how those same companies effectively operationalized a system for perpetuating the control that they had won. The reader will recall that systems are worked up in order to exclude others from benefits that the few system members enjoy.[1]

During the period of the 1930s the international oil system came to work in this way. The primary beneficiaries were the companies that we have been discussing, Jersey Standard, Royal Dutch/Shell, and Anglo-Persian, although, as we shall see, a number of others also were able to profit. This select group was known at the time (i.e., the 1930s) as the Combine. Throughout this chapter we refer sometimes to the Combine and sometimes to the cartel, because actually that is what this constituted.

The control setup did not just evolve. It was a response to circumstances that became manifest in the late 1920s and early 1930s. A set of conditions obtained that the companies were able to exploit to aggrandize themselves on a long-term basis. Indeed, the changes that the oilmen brought into effect were quite revolutionary, resulting in a restructuring of the oil industry.

Among the conditions was, first, a world surplus of oil, which developed in the 1920s. This was not a small-scale run-up in supplies. It was quite a large surplus, which disturbed many in the industry because it drove prices down to relatively low levels. It started accumulating in 1921, and by 1927 world production had risen to 1,260,000 barrels, an increase of about 17 percent over the output of the preceding year. Storage stocks reached unprecedented levels, totaling some 600,000 barrels in the United States at the end of 1927. The annual average price of a barrel of crude in the United States fell from $1.88 in 1926 to $1.30 in 1927. There was a further slippage in 1931 to 65 cents. Both the rise in production and fall in prices continued for some years thereafter.[2]

This price decline signaled the return of the bad old days of the 1870s, when Rockefeller and his associates (facing a similar dissolution of the market) implemented the South Improvement Association scheme, whereby they rationalized the refinery end of the business and eventually took control of the industry worldwide.

Another condition that facilitated the move by the oil giants did not actually come at this juncture; it had developed some time back. We refer to the appearance of a small number of so-called integrated companies.[3] Because these firms were integrated (i.e., had a much more complex organizational setup), they were more easily hurt by the run-up in oil supplies, and this compelled them to take extraordinary measures to protect themselves.

The final cause did not come until afterward, after the surplus had appeared and after the integrated companies had begun to close ranks. The very largest companies in the United States saw the need for tariff reform, which they got in 1932 from Herbert Hoover.[4] After this the system set, so to speak. The large, integrated firms then could ensure not only that they could make prices but that they could have ultimate say over which firms might enter the world oil market, an extraordinary control that they held onto until 1973.

The formula that enabled this great transformation to occur was surplus + integration + tariff = control. We discuss each separate element of the formula later in the chapter.

A caveat before we begin—the Combine (Jersey Standard, Royal Dutch/Shell, and Anglo-Persian) could not have transformed the industry on its own. The oil industry by the 1930s was such a sprawling, potentially chaotic affair that no set of discrete actors could have hoped to get a handle on it without help. Help came from the companies' governments. The 1930s marked the flowering of the era of cooperation among the companies themselves and also between the companies and their governments. What Great Britain and the United States did specifically to assist the cartelization process is gone into in this chapter.

We also will look into the development of the oil industry in Saudi Arabia. Saudi Arabia, Iraq, and Iran constitute the three main oil producers in the Persian Gulf. The rivalry between the three drives much of the action in the business. We are concerned with Saudi Arabia's rise because it ultimately comes to dominate OPEC, which control Iraq disputes, and this is what directly leads to the outbreak of the Gulf War.

Finally, just briefly, we touch on the question of exploitation. Two of the major oil producers in the Gulf, Iran and Iraq, believed that they were victimized by the oilmen; we want to assess that claim. In doing so, we give equal weight to what the companies did for the oil producers, as well as what they were able to reap for themselves.

THE ACHNACARRY AGREEMENT

We begin with the Achnacarry Agreement, the compact whereby industry leaders laid the basis for the international oil system.[5] This arrangement was conceived in 1928 in Achnacarry, Scotland, where the leaders of Jersey, Royal Dutch, and Anglo-Persian went to map strategy during a difficult time.[6] The three (Walter Teagle, Henri Deterding, and John Cadman) dissembled as to why they were meeting. To press inquiries, they replied they were enjoying a holiday, shooting grouse.[7] In fact, the meeting was not so inconsequential as that. Achnacarry was, in the author's view, one of the seminal events of the modern era.

Many explanations have been offered as to why the three got together and why they did so at this precise time. It is claimed that the meeting was in response to overproduction, cited earlier.[8] It is true that by 1925 the run-up had begun to affect prices.[9] The decline was not (as of 1928) alarming, but it was worrisome. It could have been a factor causing the meeting to take place.

Another suggested cause has to do with the reappearance on the world market of Russian oil, absent since before World War I. After the fall of the czarist empire, the Big Three oil producers expected the Soviets to fail and, in anticipation, bought oil concessions from Russian émigrés.[10] Obviously, the Soviet Union did not collapse, and once the Russians felt secure, they began producing oil, which they dumped on the European market.[11] This provoked the Big Three into mounting an embargo against them.[12] However, the embargo failed, as first one and then the other of the companies bought oil from the Russians, usually in secret.

Finally, Standard of New York bought a very large consignment, which it proceeded to market in the Far East.[13] This touched off a price war between Deterding and the New Yorkers that turned nasty, causing damage to both parties as it spread to the United States.[14]

This has been advanced as a reason for the Achnacarry meeting; that is, it was called to compose the bitter struggle among the giants themselves. All of these explanations have merit; each in its way may have been influential in bringing the meeting about. However, this was not all there was to it; something else motivated the men to assemble.

Overproduction had gone on long enough that a class of speculators had arisen who regularly were purchasing surplus oil and selling it at prices that undercut the prices of the largest oil dealers.[15] Indeed, the speculators had become so entrenched that they had their own spot market in which to trade. Allowed to continue, the situation world have deprived the cartel of its control. It is likely that this is what galvanized the Big Three to meet at Achnacarry.

In Scotland the three drafted a program of seven points, to which they pledged adherence.[16] A close reading of the program shows that, indeed, the oilmen were concerned about speculators; each point seems to have been formulated with speculative activity in mind. For example, the three promised to keep production down to 1928 levels. They also agreed to sell any surplus that might develop to each other at a price agreed on at Achnacarry. They pledged not to buy oil from anyone other than themselves, no matter at what temptingly low price it might be offered.

Further, they agreed to share facilities. All of the companies were, during this period, oversupplied not only with oil but with tankers and refineries.[17] Thus, if any one of the Big Three needed a facility in a certain part of the world, rather than build anew, it would use an existing plant, the property of an erstwhile rival.

Another point had to do with pricing—the so-called Gulf-plus agreement. This one needs to be dealt with at length, and we save that discussion for later.

Had the Combine been able to carry through on these points, it might have reversed the deteriorating trend; the speculators might have been overcome, and the Combine would have regained market control. However, nothing could be done along these lines until a further step was taken—the Combine needed to draw other large firms into the agreement; in particular, it had to involve several American concerns.

Most of the difficulty plaguing the oil industry at this time derived from the behavior of Americans—not so much Jersey Standard and Standard of New York (which had undergone a name change; it was now Socony-Vacuum) but other large, integrated firms that had grown up in the United States since the 1911 Supreme Court dissolution decree. There were about 16 of these, and their combined production was too significant to ignore. Unless these others could be induced to cooperate with the cartel, the bad situation would only get worse.

Teagle, therefore, after the Achnacarry Agreement was concluded, returned to the United States to try to sell his compatriots on accepting the plan worked out in Scotland.[18] In this he was largely successful. Early in 1929 the American firms formed the Export Petroleum Association, Inc., to limit oil production to the 1928 level, which, in turn, would reduce the amount of American oil going overseas.[19]

Why did Americans agree to support Achnacarry? They seem to have been worried about the British.[20] Anglo-Persian had made a significant find in 1908, when it brought in the Masjid i Suleiman field; it then followed that up with another big strike in Iraq on October 15, 1927. The latter flowed at a rate of between 50,000 to 100,000 barrels a day for several days.[21] Royal Dutch brought in the Los Barossos well of the La Rosa field in the Maracaibo Basin of Venezuela in 1922; it blew out at a depth of 1,500 feet, with uncontrolled production estimated at 100,000 barrels daily.[22] All three finds were so-called flush fields, meaning that the oil did not have to be pumped (as was the case with most American wells); it rose to the surface under its own pressure.

This much new oil coming onto the market was worrisome—it meant that the British were now able to withstand a price war. If the Americans undercut them, they could fight back.[23] Were a struggle to develop (the outcome of which could not be predicted), this would hurt all parties. Under the circumstances, it would have been wise for the Americans to fall in line with the Achnacarry Agreement.

In any event, the Export Petroleum Association was formed, and immediately a problem arose, namely, how to win the approval of the U.S. government for the plan that the oilmen were proposing to embark upon. Such a course of action ran counter to the U.S. government's position on combinations in restraint of trade. American companies, as far as the U.S. government was concerned, could not band together for purposes of reducing production. That ultimately would affect prices, which were supposed to be set by market forces.

Teagle sought to win over the government by going directly to the president (then Herbert Hoover) and making the oil industry's case for cutbacks.[24] At the same time, he moved on another front. Working through the American Petroleum Institute (API), the trade association of the American oil industry, he organized a nationwide public relations campaign.[25]

The campaign was built around the idea of "conservation." It promoted the concept that present oil extraction techniques in the United States were wasteful and that, by adopting other methods, considerable savings of oil could be achieved.[26] There were a number of resource-saving techniques that the API promoted.[27] However, the institute's main push was for quotas.

The large oil companies wanted to stabilize oil prices, which could be done by calculating the amount of oil coming onto the market and adjusting flow to demand.[28] This sounds reasonable; at the same time, however, it was controversial. After all, what was it that the government was being asked to do? Allow the industry to set quotas, which the large companies would predetermine.[29]

Ultimately, the oilmen's approach was doomed. The government might sympathize with their plight, but individual politicians would not risk their careers doing anything to contravene the Sherman Anti-Trust Act. Americans supported that law because they mistrusted Big Oil, and, in particular, they did not like Standard Oil.[30]

Teagle found this out when he approached Hoover to lay out the program of the Oil Export Association. Government lawyers called in by the president to evaluate the scheme pronounced it unacceptable.[31] Hoover indicated willingness to cooperate; however, assistance must be based on respect for the Sherman Act (which was to say, respect for popular opinion).[32]

While Teagle and the rest of the oilmen thought that one over, catastrophe struck—not once but twice. In 1929 the New York Stock Market collapsed, issuing in the Great Depression, and, along with that, in 1931 the famous East Texas field was discovered. This was a flush field on the order of those that the British recently had been discovering. Its size dwarfed anything that had been found in the United States to date. By the end of 1931 the area was producing 340,000 barrels per day and a new field was being opened up every hour.[33] Moreover (as the name suggests), the field was huge—it encompassed the whole eastern part of the largest state in the Union.

Someone said that, if the Lord Almighty deliberately wanted to destroy the American oil business, he could not have done better than to open up East Texas.

East Texas all but delivered the coup de grâce to the oilmen. Until it appeared, the industry's problems with overproduction, while serious, were manageable. East Texas threw so much oil on the market that it seemed that the flow could never be stanched.[34] Immediately, thousands of Americans descended on the East Texas fields to stake claims, hoping to make their fortunes.

COPING WITH EAST TEXAS

Once East Texas came in (and the Depression hit), it became clear that getting production down would not be easy. The result of the twin crises was to destroy solidarity among the oilmen. Each big company now began fighting for market share, and in the process more and more oil was put on the market, and that, of course, only drove prices down further.

However, Teagle and the Standard leaders did not give up. They went to Hoover and proposed that the U.S. government *impose* national oil quotas, in other words, devise a scheme to arbitrarily limit production. Hoover was not about to do that. He was not going to promote a rise in gasoline prices in the midst of the Depression, when Americans were cash-strapped.[35]

Hoover suggested that Teagle take his case to the governors of the major oil-producing states. They might be willing to prorate (the technical term for quota applications).[36] The principal oil states in those days were California, Oklahoma, and Texas, and Teagle went to the governors of each with his proposal.

Specifically, he asked the governors to regard oil produced in excess of the agreed upon quotas as contraband and to set up a process whereby it could be confiscated.[37] This, Teagle said, would reduce the glut, and the market would return to normalcy.

The governors of Oklahoma and California were willing to cooperate, but not Texas; Texas was the holdout.[38] Texas had a long history of populism.[39] Indeed, this one state, prior to 1911, had specifically prohibited the old Standard Oil Trust from operating inside its borders.[40] (Standard of New Jersey had gotten around that by acquiring a half interest in Humble Oil, which then functioned as its affiliate.[41]) This widespread anti-trust sentiment, so pervasive in Texas, checked Teagle's scheme.

The American oil industry now underwent a significant realignment of forces, brought about by Teagle's attempt to promote prorationing. Practically all the large oil companies had swung over to Teagle's side, agreeing with him that prorationing was the course to follow. This did not mean that they ceased battling for market share. They publicly came out in support of conservation (which meant that they supported the quotas).

This obvious preference of the big companies for quotas soon had a countervailing effect—it caused the small producers in the United States to mobilize. The small producers came out in opposition to the prorationing.[42]

Under normal conditions, the independents (as the small producers called themselves) would have had no chance against the large, integrated firms. However, in this instance the "little guy" had a number of things going for him. The principal activity (in the prorationing fight) went on in Texas, which, as we said, was well populated with freethinkers. Moreover, once East Texas came in, the state was deluged with wildcatters, who also tended to be radicals.

The independent oil producers ran what amounted to mom-and-pop operations. On average, they did not own more than a few acres, from which they made barely enough to live on. But, as there were so many, once mobilized, they constituted a sizable constituency. It did not take the independents long to form an organization of their own, the Independent Petroleum Association of America (IPAA), which they used to combat Teagle and the API.[43]

For a time the battle of the associations swung back and forth, with now the lobbyists of Big Oil appearing to win, now the IPAA. Initially, the independents were compromised by the positive appeal of Big Oil's conservation message. Eventually, however, the small operators found a counterargument to it.

The independents declared that the integrated companies' claim of being conservation-minded was disingenuous. What the big companies really sought was to hold onto markets—markets that by right belonged to the independent producers (this was the independents' claim). A handful of big companies controlled the market for oil in the eastern part of the United States, which they supplied from South American holdings.[44] Monopoly control was perpetuated because South American oil, being cheaper to produce, undercut the price of North American production.[45] However, the recent fall in prices in the United States was changing that, as independents were able to compete with the big companies.

Unexpectedly, the independents proposed a deal—if the API would support a tariff on foreign oil, the independents would support prorationing. This was a surprising stance for the IPAA to have adopted because not all of their members could accommodate such a position. Indeed, the very smallest producers and small refiners might expect to be ruined if this was agreed. At the same time, however, the proposal split the API forces. The major international oil companies (like Jersey Standard) initially rejected the offer, while some integrated firms, especially those not operating in a big way overseas, approved.[46]

As a counterproposal, the large, integrated firms suggested voluntary cutbacks on imports—Standard of New Jersey announced that it would limit production in Venezuela, and Royal Dutch said that it would shut down substantial quantities of production in Romania, the Dutch East Indies, Mexico, and Venezuela.[47] However, the big companies subsequently reneged on this, after government lawyers warned anew that such action would violate the anti-trust laws.

After this, Jersey Standard and a number of the other big firms agreed to support a tariff. An act of Congress that went into effect in June 1932 set import taxes ranging from half a cent per gallon on crude oil to four cents a gallon on lubricants.[48] With that, the international oil market was compartmentalized.

This was a highly significant development. It meant that there was now an overseas market for oil and a domestic (U.S.) one. Between the two was a tariff wall, which created the compartmentalization by keeping foreign oil from coming into the United States. This is where the Gulf-plus pricing arrangement mentioned earlier comes in.

Under Gulf-plus the large overseas firms had agreed to abide by prices set in the United States at the Gulf of Mexico. By doing so, they effectively kept the price of American oil up, because, obviously, by setting overseas prices at the American level they could not undercut the domestic market.

With that concession, the independents lost all incentive to oppose the Combine. Safe and secure behind their tariff wall, they were reasonably sure of surviving, and most of these mom-and-pop operations asked for nothing more. (Interestingly, the agreement between the Combine and the independents was paradoxical, because all along the Big Oil producers had been promoting conservation, and here they had agreed to a deal that kept the most inefficient producers in business.)

This historic compromise well served the interests of the Combine. It allowed its members to follow through on their scheme of creating a great world-girdling cartel, something that they had been aiming for since Achnacarry.

How did the tariff affect this? Well, it reduced the area that the cartel had to control. The United States having been, as it were, abstracted out of the picture, what was left? The Soviet Union. But by this time (1935) the Soviet Union, which had been dumping oil in Europe since 1920, was doing less of that. The Russians, once they got their economy going, needed all their oil for themselves; they virtually ceased to compete with the Western companies.[49]

There were also South America, Dutch Sumatra, and the Middle East, all significant oil producers.[50] Sumatra was taken care of—Royal Dutch reigned supreme in that part of the world. The Middle East was, by and large, dominated by APOC; and South America was shared between Jersey and Royal Dutch, with some participation by Gulf (which at this stage was a member of the cartel, along with Socony-Vacuum).

One could say that the tariff was a gift. The oil giants would never, on their own, have suggested that the U.S. government make such a move. Standard of New Jersey, Royal Dutch, and the other big, integrated companies were too fearful of a government takeover; Washington could at any time (it was feared) have declared oil a public utility.[51]

Under Hoover, the companies might not have had to fear anything so drastic. But Franklin Delano Roosevelt (FDR) was in the White House now, and FDR staffed his administration with individuals whom the oilmen looked on as anti-business—men like Harold Ickes, about whom we have more to say later.[52]

At the same time, though, during this period Roosevelt was cultivating business, and the API profited from that.[53] For example, under prodding by the API, Texas did finally enforce prorationing (the Texas Railroad Commission called for martial law in the East Texas fields, which brought the Texas Rangers in to police the quotas)[54]; and later the so-called Connally Hot Oil Act was passed.[55] This specified that any attempt to move oil in excess of the quota across state lines would result in seizure of the "contraband" material and its subsequent confiscation.

All this had the effect of regulating the American oil industry, something that, a short time ago, had been despaired of. The majors were not slow in taking advantage of this new setup. In the United States they cashed in on higher prices, while, internationally, they reaped benefits from their cartel relationship.[56] They actually divided the overseas market into regions.[57] In each, they set quotas for selling their oil, and in this way they eliminated competition among themselves.

To ensure that the new rules held, the Combine created an office in London, where top executives of the companies met monthly to review events and plan ahead. (Of course, all of this was going on in secret.)

The Combine members also signed long-term contracts to supply each other with oil at discounted prices.[58] We talk more about this later on, but essentially the effect of this was to further bind the members; with the contracts in place, they had no interest in price-cutting.[59]

All this activity, so obviously collusive, was justified by the big American concerns on the grounds that it went on overseas. The companies claimed that they were covered by the Webb-Pomerene Act, which permitted American companies to coordinate their activities overseas, so as to compete against foreign corporations. However, Webb-Pomerene specified that American companies could do this only if their activity did not affect the American market.

How could Jersey and the rest make such a claim when their adherence to Gulf-plus pricing kept oil prices up in the U.S. market? Obviously, the companies' argument was a weak one. We will see how trouble developed over this.[60]

One other point to note. At about this period the Combine began expanding overseas by buying up additional oil properties.[61] These were not properties for which the members had prospected; rather, they *took* properties away from competitors. The institution of the U.S. tariff forced some companies to rethink their global strategies, it now being no longer in their interests to expand overseas. Standard Oil of Indiana was one such case. Jersey bought Indiana's South American holdings in 1932 for $140 million.[62]

Indiana had been spending millions to build up its foreign marketing organizations. To firmly establish a place for itself in overseas markets would have required an additional outlay of money. However, if a tariff or embargo were levied on oil imports to the United States, Indiana's huge investment in Venezuela and Aruba would be jeopardized by reason of its inability to market most of its products in the United States.[63]

Thus, Standard of New Jersey found that it could profit from Standard of Indiana's inability to accommodate a changed situation. Jersey got a lucrative property out of Indiana's predicament. One could almost say that a natural selection process was at work—a few companies (like Standard of Indiana) that seemed on the point of becoming multinationals had to pull back, while others (like Jersey Standard) consolidated already strong positions.

At the same time, however, two companies were actually co-opted into the Combine. Joining Standard of New Jersey, Royal Dutch/Shell, Anglo-Persian, Socony-Vacuum, and Gulf were Standard Oil of California (SOCAL) and the Texas Co. (Texaco). These two, along with the original cartel members, made up what later came known as the Seven Sisters, the elite that for many years dominated the international oil business.

To understand how SOCAL and Texaco became cartel members, we need to revisit a subject discussed in the last chapter, the movement of the cartel into the Middle East, specifically, the Persian Gulf region. A connection exists between this and the eventual shape of the international oil system.[64]

THE RED LINE AGREEMENT

A feature of the old Turkish Petroleum Co. (TPC) concession was that all of the parties agreed not to seek concessions in what was then the Ottoman empire.[65] This was a demand of the British, who were mistrustful of Germany's activities in the Persian Gulf; Britain did not want Germany to establish a strategic position in the Gulf on the pretext of developing commercial relations there.[66]

When the deal was renegotiated (as it was in 1914 to permit the Anglo-Persian Co. to come in), the restraining clause was kept.[67] Britain remained suspicious of Germany's long-term strategic ambitions. Additionally, Anglo-Persian's director, Greenway, wanted to keep Royal Dutch from going off on its own, acquiring fields in the Gulf that Anglo-Persian might want to acquire for itself.[68]

After the war, when the Germans were defeated, and when the TPC reformed (and the name changed to the Iraq Petroleum Co. [IPC]), the restraining clause was still kept.[69] Now it was the two junior partners—Calouste Gulbenkian and the French—who insisted on this. They feared being left out in any carve-up of territory by the senior partners, Royal Dutch, Anglo-Persian, and by the several American firms that were then participants.[70]

Gulbenkian is supposed to have drawn a red line on the map of the Middle East that took in all the territory of the old Ottoman empire, except Kuwait and Egypt.[71] That was the area, he maintained, that could not be developed except by the consortium as a whole. Gulbenkian's action came to be styled the Red Line Agreement. This is what gave final shape to the international oil system; it determined who ultimately got to be a member.

ENTER SOCAL

Although the great oil companies bound themselves to observe the Red Line Agreement, companies outside the agreement were not so constrained. In the 1930s, after the major shakeout in the American oil industry, there were not a lot of American firms trying to poach on the IPC's holdings. There was one, however, Standard Oil of California (SOCAL).

Based on the West Coast of the United States, SOCAL had grown up in isolation. Of all the Standard entities, it was probably the least under the control of Rockefeller and the original directors. Consequently, it was something of a loner, doing what it wanted, not mindful of anyone.[72]

Another thing about SOCAL—at the time of the dissolution it practically was an integrated company, unusual for a Standard affiliate. Most Standard companies found themselves at the breakup lacking components that would have enabled them to function as integrated firms. SOCAL had everything, even down to a rudimentary marketing setup.[73] This freed the company to develop independently, and by the mid-1920s it was actively engaged in looking for oil properties overseas.

In 1928 SOCAL acquired a concession to develop areas of Bahrain (see map) originally held by Gulf, which got the concession in 1927 from one Frank Holmes, who got it from the skeikh of Bahrain.[74] Holmes was an adventurer who cadged concessions from the skeikhs and then offered them to interested oil companies.

Gulf knew when it bought the concession that it might not be able to work it (because it was a member of the IPC and thus bound by the Red Line Agreement).[75] In fact, when Gulf appealed to its partners for an exemption, it was turned down.

The British were not eager to facilitate further American penetration of the Gulf. The other partners were also mistrusting. It was now well into the 1930s; the Depression was under way, and the oil glut was intensifying. Whatever oil there might be in Bahrain seemed best left underground.

Indeed, Standard of New Jersey earlier had been offered the Bahrain concession by Holmes and had refused it, partly because it was worried about glut.[76] (Standard's geologists had advised that there was no oil there; they also had looked at Saudi Arabia and pronounced it unpromising.)[77]

So all members of the IPC voted against Gulf's being allowed to exploit the Bahrain concession, and it dutifully went along, selling out to SOCAL. As a nonparticipant in the IPC, SOCAL did not need to be concerned about the Red Line. However, it did have to take into account the opposition of the British government, which, at the time, held Bahrain as a protectorate. The company agreed to form a brand-new outfit that would be incorporated in Canada.[78] With that, SOCAL was given the go-ahead to begin operations.

In 1932 SOCAL brought in a gusher; the very first well that it sank in Bahrain came in under its own pressure. The new well was determined to have a potential of several thousand barrels of oil a day, which caused consternation among the

IPC members.[79] In the meantime complications had developed on two other fronts.

KUWAIT

In 1927 Gulf got a concession from Holmes to explore for oil in Kuwait.[80] Kuwait was not part of the Red Line Agreement. However, because Britain had Kuwait, too, under its protection, the company sought to accommodate London, as SOCAL had done. It agreed to take Anglo-Persian into partnership. At first the British firm held back, but, when Gulf agreed to a special marketing formula, it agreed.[81] This turned out to be a lucrative deal for APOC. In 1938 the Burgan field came in, the richest discovery in the Middle East down to this day.[82]

Shortly after this, in 1933, SOCAL jumped from Bahrain to the mainland of Saudi Arabia, having obtained a concession from the Saudi ruler Abdul Aziz Ibn Saud to explore the eastern (Hasa) province.[83] SOCAL again proved successful, bringing in another rich well (this did not come, however, until 1938).

At that SOCAL found itself with quite a lot of oil on its hands, which it had to find a market for. The natural market was Asia, but SOCAL had no outlets there. In 1936 SOCAL had agreed to share its concessions in Bahrain with the Texas Co., on a 50:50 basis; Texas, in return, had granted SOCAL a 50 percent interest in its Far Eastern market facilities. Now, in 1938, the deal was extended to include Saudi Arabia, and a new company was formed, the California Arabian Standard Oil Co. (CASOC).

This outfit formed the basis for the creation later (in 1947) of the richest and ultimately the most powerful oil group ever formed, the Arabian American Oil Co. (ARAMCO), a lash-up between SOCAL and the Texas Co., on one side, and Jersey and Socony, on the other. The deal merits extensive treatment, but we will postpone that until later in the chapter.

ARAMCO typified the pattern of control worked out by the Combine. Essentially, it was the same setup as the IPC, an arrangement of interlocking partnerships within which companies share information with each other, so as to do long-term planning. We see this kind of setup develop in Venezuela.[84] Ultimately, everywhere that significant oil finds are made, the companies resort to this mechanism in order to keep rivals out.

The sharing-out-of-the-industry proved extraordinarily lucrative. According to the Senate report on *The International Petroleum Cartel*, by 1952 (when the report was written), the companies making up the cartel collectively controlled 98 percent of the crude oil production of the Middle East, 94 percent of the production of the Eastern Hemisphere, and almost 45 percent of the Western Hemisphere (and they also were the controllers of refining, transportation, and marketing all over the world).[85]

It is important, too, to note what the companies were controlling—*oil*, the lifeblood of the capitalist system. So it was not just commercially that they were involved; the cartel members were becoming political actors.

THE GRAVITY SHIFT

In the late 1930s the center of gravity of the oil industry lay in the Western Hemisphere, particularly Venezuela, Mexico, and the United States. But, then, as discussed earlier, the Americans enacted a tariff, and oil from Venezuela became less attractive. Moreover, in 1935 the strongman leader of Venezuela, Vincente Gomez, died. Gomez had pretty much let the oil companies operate as they wished (as long as he got his reward).

But when he died, his successors started preaching nationalization. This naturally upset the oilmen; at the same time, they were successful in forestalling such action. Then, the war erupted, and suddenly the offtake from Venezuela skyrocketed, and the Venezuelans, with plenty of money coming in, forgot about nationalizing the fields.

The wheel took another turn, as it were, when the U-boat war commenced. Now Venezuela's take from oil sales plummeted, and this revived the sentiment for nationalization.

Apparently, this determined the oilmen to begin transferring their operations. With the U.S. tariff in place Venezuela was no longer that desirable, whereas the Gulf, being located midway between Europe and Asia, was becoming more so. Also appealing was the ease with which oil could be produced in this part of the world. In some areas it practically leaped out of the ground.

One other factor might have influenced the cartel's decision to shift the center of gravity away from the Western Hemisphere to the Persian Gulf. In 1938, Mexico nationalized its oil industry, and after that began exploiting the bulk of its resource for itself in order to modernize the country.

It is also likely that the oilmen anticipated nonconfrontational relations with the host governments in the Persian Gulf. The states of the lower Gulf were all monarchies or emirates. Iraq was a kingdom; Iran, an empire. In other words, these were all anachronistic entities, hence inherently weak and presumably tractable.

The companies' view of what they would find in the Gulf was accurate up to a point. They encountered a warm reception among the sheikhdoms of the lower Gulf, but in the two larger states in the north, Iraq and Iran, the reality proved different. Both countries, from the 1930s on, continually pitted themselves against the foreign presence in their midst, a presence that, at the time, was fundamentally tied to oil.

That the natives should quarrel over the terms of their contracts with the companies is only natural, but the Iraqis and Iranians were disturbed far beyond this. They felt themselves victims of imperialism, and that was a political judgment.

So, at this point in the narrative, a shift of focus occurs. We have been dealing almost exclusively with commercial matters, and disputes were between companies—Jersey, Royal Dutch, APOC. Now, we switch to governments—not just the Western powers (which have already become involved) but lesser lights such as the governments of Iraq and Iran.

We are going to look first at British dealing with Iran, and then at how four of the companies (Anglo-Persian, Royal Dutch, Jersey, and Socony), through the IPC, behaved toward Iraq.

We will see that the dealings of the companies with both parties (Iran and Iraq) were pretty ruthless; that is, the oilmen got their way, no matter what; and, although the native governments might protest, and even in some cases resort to violence, in the end they were firmly squelched.

After we have treated affairs in the northern Gulf in some detail, we will shift to the southern portion of the waterway and specifically to events in Saudi Arabia. There, the cartel, as a whole, ran into an unexpected lot of trouble having to do with the aforementioned independents SOCAL and Texaco.

THE CASE OF IRAN

The oil dealings of Iran with the British were disturbed almost from the time that the original concession was signed. Animosity crystallized, however, over an incident that APOC seems to have provoked. In 1917 the company's president, Charles Greenway, arbitrarily withheld royalties from Tehran after the APOC pipeline was cut by Bahktiari tribesmen, an event that produced some loss of revenue for the company.[86]

Greenway wanted compensation and, until he got it, made up his mind that he would not pay royalties. Greenway's stand is hard to justify. From the start of APOC's operations, he had the Bahktiaris on retainer, precisely to safeguard the line.[87] The company recognized—correctly—that the Persian government could not provide protection, not in so remote a region.

But the Bahktiaris soon fell in with German agents who induced them to sabotage the APOC's property. If anyone could have been said to be at fault, it would seem to have been the APOC, which could not make the Bahktiaris deliver on the deal that they made.

In fact, there was more going on here than meets the eye. Greenway had ambitions to make APOC a rival of both New Jersey Standard and Royal Dutch. With this in mind, he continually sought to expand company operations.[88] In 1915, for example, APOC formed a subsidiary, the British Tanker Co., and built that into a major shipping line by the end of the war. Greenway also, in 1917, acquired the British Petroleum Co. (BP), formerly the Europaische Petroleum Union, a German firm established in 1906 in Britain. The British government sequestered it during the war.

At some point it seems to have occurred to Greenway that, as the APOC expanded, the Iranians stood to gain. The original contract stipulated that Tehran was entitled to 16 percent of company profits, *irrespective of where those profits came from.* To Greenway, it was unacceptable that the Iranians participate in downstream ventures like BP.[89]

So, at the same time that he withheld royalty payments, Greenway offered to settle his dispute with Tehran, *if the Iranians agreed to renegotiate the concession.* He offered a quid pro quo—if Tehran agreed to a payment of two shillings a ton for the liftings of Iranian crude (and gave up its 16 percent cut of the profits), he would forget about compensation and resume paying royalties.[90]

This, it would seem, was a crude attempt at coercion, which the Iranians most certainly would have seen through. Once they perceived that Greenway wanted something from them, they would then have subjected the deal to scrutiny.

Ultimately, the APOC was hoist on its own petard over this. Some background is necessary, however, to appreciate how it came about.

After World War I, Lord Curzon wanted to make Iran into a British protectorate and, with that in mind, had Percy Sykes draw up the 1919 Anglo-Persian Treaty, which provided for British assistance to Persia through the setting up of military and financial missions and by a loan of £2 million (pounds).[91]

The treaty was signed by the Iranian government but proved so unpopular that the Iranian *majlis* (parliament) refused to ratify it. In the interval between when the government approved and the *majlis* rejected the treaty, Greenway went ahead and drew up a revised contract that effectively dealt Iran out of any share of downstream profits. Further, Greenway called on his government for support in getting Iranian government approval of the new agreement.[92] (The British had a number of high Iranian officials on retainer in those days, and the British ambassador approached these men, requesting aid.[93])

At the same time, however, the Iranians made a corresponding move. Despite the unpopularity of the 1919 treaty, they asked the British government to fulfill one of its provisions. They wanted the British adviser promised them. London dispatched Sidney Armitage-Smith, a former assistant secretary to the British Treasury. The Iranians asked him to look into the matter of withholding royalties, pending fulfillment of APOC's claims.[94]

Armitage-Smith enlisted the services of a Scottish accounting firm, William McLintock, and that firm, after looking over the company's books, decided that APOC was not dealing fairly with Tehran. For example, the damage to the pipeline, which the APOC had assessed at £402,887, amounted to no more than £20,000. Moreover, the firm contended that Iran was not responsible for the pipe-cutting incident since Tehran had declared neutrality in the war and since Britain had invaded its territory. McLintock also discovered that APOC, while claiming damages from Iran (for the severed line), had at the same time charged £10,000 a year for the damages as operating expenses. thus lowering its nominal profits and also lowering the royalties payable to the Tehran government.[95]

Confronted with what must have been embarrassing revelations, Greenway withdrew his claim for compensation and made restitution, paying up the arrears in royalties. However, he did not include profits of subsidiary firms (i.e., downstream operations), and when the Iranians pressed him on this, Greenway threatened to detach those firms from APOC, which would have been a great hardship for the company but would effectively have taken them out of the reach of the Iranians.[96]

At this point Armitage-Smith intervened and, in effect, rewrote the original

D'Arcy agreement. The new version specified that Tehran was entitled to 16 percent of profits of the APOC, but only from that portion "defined and calculated" to be derived from Persian oil.[97]

All of this haggling over profit calculation became somewhat academic when, in 1921, the Tehran government was overthrown in an army-led coup. The officer who engineered the takeover, Reza Khan, had himself appointed, successively, war minister, prime minister, and ultimately emperor of Iran (the founder of the Pahlavi dynasty).

This man was an enigma. Considered by some to have been a great nationalist and by others a pirate, it is difficult to characterize him in any satisfactory way. There probably was a lot of the pirate in him, in common with all of his immediate predecessors on the throne of Iran. At the same time, however, Reza was different in one major regard. He seems to have appreciated that, to hold onto power, he had to acquire modern weapons, which only the West could supply. He therefore cultivated the British and kept open his lines to the APOC, while at the same time driving the hardest bargains with the company that he could.

The shah constantly was in need of cash, and so in 1929 he reopened the issue of renegotiating the D'Arcy contract. The shah wanted Iran to have an equity holding in the APOC. The new president of the APOC, John Cadman, saw nothing wrong in this. He would approve giving Iran *nonvoting, inalienable* shares. However, in return, he wanted Iran to accept a fixed royalty of 2s (shillings) a ton based on the amount of oil produced (in other words, the APOC was back to demanding that Tehran surrender its profit-sharing agreement). In addition, the area of the concession would be reduced to 100,000 square miles, and (in compensation for that) the concession would be extended 30 years.[98]

The Iranians then made counterproposals, thinking to improve their position. At this, Cadman broke off discussions, and in the meantime, the stock market collapsed in New York, which put paid to the whole business.

The Iranians brought the matter up again in 1931, and this time they had shelved the idea of equity. However, they wanted a new basis for providing royalties and taxes. The negotiations led to the drafting of an agreement that raised APOC's royalty payments from 16 percent to 20 percent of the net profits on all operations connected with Iranian oil. The additional 4 percent was in lieu of taxes.[99]

The Iranian and British negotiators were on the point of signing this deal when, figuratively speaking, a bomb burst. This was 1932, and the company, without warning, informed the shah that royalties for 1931 would be only £306,870—less than a quarter of the royalties of the year before.[100] When the shah demanded to know the reason for this, Cadman pointed out that they had just passed through what was later determined to be the trough of the Depression, in which the company had had a particularly bad time of it.[101]

So furious was the shah that he ordered the company's file brought to him, and before witnesses he consigned it to the fire.[102] Effectively, he had unilaterally canceled the concession.

This drove the British government to intervene. Over objections of Cadman, who wanted to resolve the matter by personal diplomacy, London put the matter before the Permanent Court of International Justice at the Hague (which, technically, had no jurisdiction, the court not being empowered to arbitrate commercial disputes).[103] At the same time, Anthony Eden, then undersecretary of state for foreign affairs, threatened that his government "was prepared to take all such measures as the situation may demand."[104]

This veiled threat may have intimidated the shah.[105] He reopened negotiations and virtually gave in to all the company's demands. The renegotiated deal was quite complex, but the major points dealt with royalty payments (to be based on oil liftings, not profit sharing); taxes (the Iranians would not levy taxes); and representation (the shah could appoint a representative who would be empowered to receive all information to which company shareholders were entitled and to attend meetings of the company's board of directors). Other points involved the scope of the concession (it was reduced to 100,000 square miles) and the duration (it was extended until the year 1993).[106]

Two points to focus on here. Once the issue was fairly joined (between the shah and the company) the *matter was taken out of the hands of the APOC.* The British Foreign Office managed the confrontation from then on.[107] Thus, for all of Churchill's insistence (before World War I) that the APOC was a business and that the British government had no intention of interfering in its affairs, when matters turned crucial, London elbowed the oilmen aside and took charge.

The other point to note is the vulnerability of the oil producer, in this case Iran. The Iranians could not stand up to the company when the latter could rely on support from its home government, particularly when there was an implicit threat of military action. The shah appears to have been caught off-guard by the decisiveness with which London intervened, an indication that he believed Churchill's disclaimer about the British government's not getting involved in commercial matters.

THE CASE OF IRAQ

Parallels exist between the experience of Iran with the oil companies and that of Iraq. The Iraqis, too, developed grievances against the British. However, in their case the hostility boiled up from below from the people who took arms against the IPC and against the British officials who served the mandate authority. In this, the people acted against their leaders, who were strong supporters of the British.

The first Hashemite king of Iraq, Feisal, was not an Iraqi. He was a Saudi, the son of the so-called *sherrif* of Mecca, a religious dignitary who early in World War I declared for the Allies and subsequently led an Arab revolt against the Ottoman caliph.

Feisal, as the *sherrif*'s eldest son, took a prominent part in the revolt, and, as a reward, the British installed him as king of Syria. However, the French, who claimed the mandate for Syria, deposed Feisal, and, as a kind of consolation prize, he accepted the throne of Iraq.

The British had gotten the mandate for Iraq; fine for them, since they were intending to exploit the oil there. But, as stated in Chapter 1, Iraq was a primitive place, the most remote and in many ways most forbidding region of the old Ottoman empire. The people were fractious to an inordinate degree; they barely would submit to authority. In the south were fierce Shia tribes, and, in the north, rough Kurdish hillsmen.

The British looked on Feisal as someone who could command the loyalty of the disparate groups, for the reason that, whatever else, the Iraqis (Arabs and Kurds) were Muslims. Feisal was of the family of the Prophet (i.e., he could trace his lineage back in a clear line of descent). That, the British felt, should command respect.

Feisal also had great personal charm, which enabled him, over time, to make a place for himself in the esteem of his subjects.[108] It would seem, then, that, overall, the British chose well; Feisal was not half bad as a ruler.

Along with that, Feisal did not trouble the British greatly. He gave them most of what they wanted, except in one area—he originally stipulated that, before he would consent to assume the throne, Iraq must become independent; he would not rule a mere mandated territory.[109] The British gave in on that, a significant concession, as we shall see.

Having set Feisal on the throne, the British then had to maintain him in power, which was not easy, for the reason that it cost them quite a bit of money, which they did not have.[110]

The British decided to rule on the cheap, as it were. To police the territory, they called in the Royal Air Force (RAF).[111] This was the first known use of airpower as a constabulary. The British twigged to the concept in 1921, during a revolt of Shia tribesmen in the south.[112] The RAF daunted the tribesmen, who could not find a proper response to aerial targeting.[113]

In time, the British expanded the use of the RAF, sending it on all sorts of assignments. For example, it would bomb the tribes to soften them up for visits from the tax collector. It bombed preemptively—at the first rumor of revolt, the planes would be dispatched to incinerate croplands.[114]

This sort of thing eventually provoked bitter opposition outside Iraq. The American consul in Iraq, for example, called aerial targeting "hunnish and barbaric."[115] Such a personage as Lord Curzon evidently agreed, and the issue of bombing came up over and over in the British Parliament.[116] Still, the British did not cease using the RAF—they could not, as long as they were strapped for cash.

The British innovated in another area, their tribes policy. They reconstituted tribal society in Iraq, making the headmen or chiefs into landed property owners.[117] Land that formerly had been held in common was assigned to the chiefs, who became, as a result, very wealthy men.

Of course, the chiefs then had to defend themselves against their newly dispossessed tribesmen, which they did by supplying themselves with thuggish bodyguards—in the north, among the Kurds, these were the *pesh merga*; in the south, they were styled *hushiyyah*.

These newly propertied tribal chiefs formed the backbone of British control over Iraq; they also became the bane of Feisal's existence—he could do almost nothing against them.[118] Tribal chiefs packed the Parliament, where they worked hand in glove with the British.

Joining Feisal in antagonism to the tribes were Iraq's army officers. British-instituted policies rendered the army inferior to the tribes, and the officers resented this.[119] Also against the British (and the chiefs) were the Shia devines of Najaf and Karbala and the Iraqi middle class, such as it was.[120]

Thus, we see that Iraq, from the first, was a country divided against itself. Feisal tried during the early years of his reign to rectify this bad situation. An Arab nationalist, he wanted to make Iraq into a real nation. He scored some successes, but then (unfortunately for Iraq) he died, prematurely. After his death, his party (that is, the clique that had surrounded him) went over to the British, lock, stock, and barrel, as it were.

This party was led at the time by one Nuri Said, a so-called *sherrifeen* politician.[121] A strong figure, Nuri was also extremely pragmatic. He perceived that the fate of Iraq lay with the British, a condition that he was not disposed to resist.

The other strong personality of the time was Abdul Ilah, the cousin of Feisal, who became the prince regent. When Feisal died in 1933, he was succeeded by his son Ghazi, who himself died early (in 1939), leaving his son, Feisal II, as heir presumptive.[122] However, Feisal II was a minor when his father passed away, and so he was put in charge of Abdul Ilah.

These two, Nuri and Abdul Ilah, were Great Britain's men. London had all confidence in them, and they repaid that confidence well.

Had Iraq been better managed and had the revenues from oil been sufficient to bestow prosperity on the land, Iraqis might have tolerated Nuri and Abdul Ilah (and the British). Instead, Iraq, although sitting on one of the greatest pools (perhaps the greatest pool) of oil in the world, was, during all the time that the British controlled it, a poor, poor country. This brings us to our main area of concern—oil policy in Iraq under the British.

TOUGH NEGOTIATIONS

Under the original concession, Iraq was tipped to get 10 percent equity in whatever private company was formed to exploit the oil.[123] France was to get 20 percent, and the British interests (Anglo-Persian and Royal Dutch) the remaining 70 percent.[124]

When later the Americans were brought in, and the deal was renegotiated, complications arose, as the Americans had their own ideas about how it should be structured. They proposed that the member companies buy their oil from IPC at cost, plus a little over to cover IPC expenses.[125] This meant, in effect, that IPC was to become a nonprofit enterprise.

Why would the members want to be associated with a company that was nonprofit? The answer is that, although IPC was nominally nonprofit, this did not mean that there were not profits to be made, albeit in a roundabout manner. All of the major participants in IPC were integrated companies, which meant that they did not sell crude oil on the open market. They used it themselves, passing it through their own refineries and selling it through their marketing setups in Europe, the Far East, or wherever. By taking profits downstream, on product (not crude), the companies could enhance their tax picture, which is discussed later.

To be sure, not all the members of IPC could benefit in this way. Gulbenkian certainly could not. Gulbenkian was Gulbenkian; a lone individual, he had no company, much less refineries and marketing arrangements. Similarly, the French were somewhat disadvantaged by the American proposal. To be sure, the French wanted crude at cheap prices. But, along with their nonprofit idea, the Americans also were pushing for IPC to adhere to the principle of the Open Door, and that made problems for the French.[126]

Recall that the U.S. State Department had insisted that, when the oil lands of Iraq were opened to exploitation, it must be on a nonrestrictive basis; the Americans were insistent on there being free competition.[127] Thus, they had worked out an intricate scheme whereby 192 square miles of the IPC concession would be set aside and divided into 12 parcels of 16 square miles each, which the original IPC members would bid for at auction.[128] After that, according to the Americans, the rest of the concession territory (some 159,000 square miles) would be made available through yearly auctions at which not less than 24 plots of 8 square miles each would be offered and to which outsiders would be invited to bid, along with the original concession holders.[129]

The French had assumed that they would have access to all of the potential oil lands subsumed by the old Turkish Petroleum concession. They did not like having to bid on a restricted portion. As may be imagined, Gulbenkian was not anymore pleased by what the Americans were proposing, nor, we may assume, were the British.[130]

The Iraqis, if anything, were most distressed of all. As stated earlier, they had assumed that they would get at least a 10 percent equity in IPC.[131] However, once the Americans proposed (and the other members agreed) to make the company nonprofit, Iraq's hopes for equity were dashed. What was the point of having equity in a nonprofit concern?[132]

Moreover, the Iraqis did not learn that they would lose their equity until late.[133] The nonprofit arrangement was struck by the IPC members without informing them.[134] When the Iraqis did learn about it, they fought hard to upset the deal. However, they had not much hope of prevailing. In the end, they fastened their hopes on the auction scheme.

Iraq could only benefit from opening up a vast portion of the IPC territory to outsiders; the more outsiders who were involved in developing Iraqi oil, the less the Iraqis would be at the mercy of the original concession holders.[135] Again, however, the Iraqis' hopes were dashed, because the non-American members of IPC eventually talked the Americans (at this stage, Jersey, Socony, and Gulf) into scrapping the Open Door principle and abandoning the plot-auction idea.[136]

As a compensation to Iraq, the members offered to divide the concession. The members would take all of the original TPC concession, comprising the 192-square-mile portion discussed before, plus almost 32,000 more square miles that embraced the *vilayets* (provinces) of Baghdad and Mosul to the east of the Tigris River. A new concession was then created, the so-called Mosul Petroleum Co., which effectively took up all the lands west of the Tigris; this was turned over to Iraq for outside bids.[137]

Pleased at this new arrangement, the Iraqis advertised the parcel, and a competent bidder soon was secured—the British Oil Development Co. (BODC), a syndicate comprising British and Italian entrepreneurs.[138] However, after sealing the deal, the new combination failed to find any oil, and after a relatively short time it abandoned the concession.

At that point, the original IPC members took over the abandoned portion, which meant that they now had in their hands practically all of northern Iraq in which to explore for oil. What about Iraq? What happened to it?

Essentially, it got the same deal that Iran got—that is, it settled for 4s per ton on liftings.[139] No share of the profits, just royalties based on volume. Iraq did benefit, however, in one respect. It held out for, and got, payment in gold; Iran had settled for sterling.[140] Hence, when Britain went off the gold standard, and sterling was depreciated, Iran suffered; Iraq did not.

Even on liftings, however, Iraq was at a disadvantage, because for a long period these did not amount to much. We go into this in the next chapter. Here it's enough to say that (before World War I) IPC virtually closed down the Mosul concession, and later on, when it got control of vast oil lands in the south of the country (around Basrah), it refused to develop those as well. Effectively then, Iraq's gains from the protracted negotiations were quite clearly limited.[141]

EXPLOITATION

We want now to discuss the question posed at the start of the chapter, whether the countries were exploited or not and, if so, to what degree. The answer would appear to be that, on one level, they certainly were. Take the request of both Iran and Iraq for equity. They saw it as a way to increase revenue. The companies would not go along, because (in the companies' eyes) with equity went control. Control was something that the companies meant to preserve at all costs.

The countries could reply that control at this stage of the relationship was farthest from their minds. But the companies could only suspect such disclaimers. Why, if there was no intention of seeking control, did the countries insist on having a seat on the company board?

Sitting in on meetings and looking over the companies' statements of account could only enhance the countries' understanding of how the companies operated, and, there (in the oilmen's view) was where the trouble lay. *The companies operated as a cartel.* Cartels were *illegal* organizations. Perhaps not in Britain or France, but this certainly was the case in the United States.

Many techniques of operation that the companies adopted out of necessity (because otherwise they could not manage the unwieldy apparatus of their organization) would be perceived, in the public's eyes, as shady, if not downright criminal. To safeguard against being exposed, the companies put a tight clamp on the dissemination of information.

No one, unless he or she had a demonstrable right to know, was permitted to learn the secrets of the inner circle. In the eyes of the individuals who ran the cartel, the rulers of Iran and Iraq did not have that right and therefore were excluded.

This argument was not likely to impress the countries. They could counter that the information that they sought was not privileged, or at least it ought not to have been. It was information that was vital for the countries to know; namely, on what basis were the companies figuring their profit? The countries' royalties were based on that estimate; the countries simply wanted to know if the estimate was fair.

Here, it would seem, is where the exploitation comes in. This was not a short-term relationship between companies and countries. The latter could see the enormous amount of infrastructure that was being amassed. They knew of the wealth that was accruing to the companies through the development of the producers' oil resources. What the countries did not know were precise details of the operation. Nor could they work it out for themselves, for the reason that this was a cartel with which they were dealing. The cartel did not conduct its business by arm's-length bargaining. Everything—even down to the price at which the oil would be sold—was arbitrarily set by the companies.

The companies treated the countries as dependents (in the countries' view). They expected the countries to accept what was being offered them on trust. This, as far as the countries were concerned, was demeaning, particularly as these were sovereign states. *Britain did not conquer Iran in the war.* Iran had remained neutral in that conflict. In the case of Iraq, it was true that Britain practically had created it, but Feisal, as a condition of assuming the throne, had stipulated that Iraq must be independent, and Britain had gone along with that. Thus, the two countries felt that they had rights that Britain was bound to respect.

Over the years, this resentment at being so treated festered until it exploded into violence. The violence, as might have been expected (given the sociological makeup of the place) developed first in Iraq. In Iran relations were much more pacific; this may have been a function of the Iranians' having maintained their independence, after a fashion.

Iraq was colonized by the British; there can be no doubt about this. At the same time, the colonization policy was not at all easy to effect. Batatu has estimated that between 1919 and 1958 (when the British finally were ejected from Iraq) there were no fewer than 30 significant violent outbreaks of one sort or another.[142]

The worst of these involved urban violence, and a lot of this can be blamed on the British. When the latter instituted their policy of using the RAF, they drove thousands of peasants off the land. It was not merely the aerial harassment that agitated them; they also were exasperated by their rough treatment at the hands of the landowners.

These so-called *shurugis* (easterners) converged on Baghdad, where they took up residence in shanty towns outside the city. Generally, they lived in hovels, built on refuse dumps. British medical inspectors who encountered them there claimed that they were "pathological specimens."[143]

Batatu says that over time the numbers of *shurugis* swelled to 100,000.[144] The slum dwellers would erupt on the slightest provocation. The Baghdad government, to contain the disturbances, bolstered the police, and when, after World War II, more money became available (from the sale of oil), Nuri turned Iraq into a veritable police state. (We have more to say about this when we discuss the coming of the Ba'th and Saddam Hussein.)

Macaulay, writing of the Englishman's attitude toward the Irish at the time of James II, says the following:

> The Englishman compared with pride his own fields to the desolate bogs whence the Rapparees issued forth to rob and murder, and his own dwelling with the hovels where the peasants and the hogs of the Shannon wallowed in the filth together. He was a member of a society far inferior, indeed, in wealth and civilization, to the society in which we live (Macaulay's England), but still one of the wealthiest and most highly civilized societies that the world had then seen: the Irish were almost as rude as the savages of Labrador.[145]

All in all, this seems a pretty good description of the British attitude toward the Iraqis under the mandate.

THE ARAMCO DEAL

The shift of the oil industry's center of gravity away from Venezuela toward the Middle East ought to have pleased the CASOC officials. In fact, it was otherwise, because essentially what this did was force a confrontation with the cartel that CASOC would rather have avoided.[146]

After making test borings on their Saudi concession, SOCAL and the Texas Co. were surprised to find it much bigger than they had expected.[147] Texas and SOCAL were prepared to put small to medium amounts of oil on the market, but large amounts would only destabilize the international oil system.[148]

The Big Three—Jersey, Royal Dutch, and Anglo-Iranian (the name was changed in 1934)—had gone to great lengths to rationalize the industry in order to make it profitable. All of the agreements into which they had entered (Achnacarry, the Red Line) were directed to this result. The agreements were in the nature of inhibitors; that is, they were meant to *reduce* production.

SOCAL and Texas could hardly expect to throw tons of new oil onto the market and escape censure from the cartel. Indeed, censure was the least of it—the cartel had ways of preventing outfits like CASOC from acting against its wishes. Thus, CASOC was in a bind—how to market its oil against the opposition of the cartel?

CASOC emulated Greenway of Anglo-Persian, who, in pre–World War I days, had faced a similar test. Greenway had oil that he had to market from flush fields of southern Iran.[149] His rivals, Royal Dutch and Jersey, conspired to prevent him, and so he struck a deal with the Admiralty whereby it bought his production on a long-term contract basis at a relatively low price.

CASOC now did pretty much the same thing. Two of its executives, W. S. Rodgers (president of Texaco) and H. C. Collier (president of SOCAL), went to Washington, where they interviewed a number of top bureaucrats, putting virtually the same proposition to each—CASOC wanted the United States to advance the Saudi king Abdul Aziz $6 million annually for the next five years against the security of CASOC oil products, which the company would deliver to the U.S. government for the king's account.[150] CASOC would make the oil available on a long-term contract basis at a low discount price.

This was a neat, three-way deal. CASOC could dispose of its oil without having to engage the cartel in a price war.[151] The U.S. government would get a guaranteed supply of oil in wartime. The king would be subsidized. One might well ask, however, Why have the government pay the money to Abdul Aziz? Why not pay directly to CASOC?

It would appear that CASOC executives anticipated trouble on this score; that is, if the government bought oil directly from them. Nonparticipating oil companies would surely object to such an arrangement; they would create a fuss, which would alert the American public; in the end, CASOC could be hurt. So, it seems, the executives contrived this means of getting around the awkwardness.

Even at that, the deal was not an easy one to effect. To take it completely out of the realm of the commercial, CASOC further suggested that the purchases be portrayed as a security measure. The U.S. government could declare Saudi Arabia vital to U.S. interests and then steer lend-lease Abdul Aziz's way. It might even be possible, according to the CASOC plan, to have Britain subsidize the king, using part of their lend-lease from the United States.[152]

Among the top bureaucrats whom the executives approached, the most influential was Harold Ickes. Roosevelt's energy czar heard the executives out and then discussed their proposition with the president. Interestingly, Roosevelt did not reject the matter out of hand, probably because, after two years of fighting, the U.S. government had come to realize that it had overestimated its oil reserves; they were being used up at a furious rate.[153]

Roosevelt agreed to propose Abdul Aziz for lend-lease, although he is supposed to have remarked, "How we are to make a democracy out of this outfit, I don't know."[154]

In the end, lend-lease did not go through. Whether it was because Roosevelt, the consummate politician, perceived the dangers (i.e., of exposing this matter to the American public) is not known. At any rate, the deal died.

However, Ickes was not content to leave it there. He came up with a plan whereby the government should buy CASOC—*buy it outright, 100 percent.* Ickes was that kind of politician. He would size up a situation according to his lights, and once he had found a way through—or thought that he had—he would bull ahead on it.

We leave Ickes for a moment and look at something happening on another front. It appears that the State Department, too, was developing a plan for U.S. control of Saudi oil.[155]

INTERNATIONALISM AT STATE

In 1941 the State Department appointed Max Thornburgh a petroleum adviser and tasked him to develop a coherent policy for foreign oil.[156] By 1942 Thornburgh had drafted a report in which he suggested that the United States develop an international cartel to manage oil resources for peace and war. Subsequently, others at State suggested bringing the British in on the effort.[157]

It's hard to figure what Thornburgh and the others at State had in mind with this proposal. It has been suggested that they wanted the United States to enter the existing cartel of Jersey, Royal Dutch, and Anglo-Iranian.[158] Anderson says the plan was consistent with the long-range interest of those companies already established in the Middle East.[159]

Thornburgh never spelled out precisely what he was after; he rather suggested that the government *think* about taking such action, and he further speculated that, because of the war, the public could *probably* be expected to go along.[160] In other words, the public, which ordinarily would look with disfavor on any such activity, might approve if it was portrayed as serving the war effort. Thornburgh clearly was tiptoeing around the issue, and for good reason. Getting the U.S. government involved in a cartel was no mean proposition.

It is the author's belief that the plan could not have envisaged regulating oil worldwide, not if, as indicated, the British and American governments were expected to cooperate. The only company over which Britain had control was the Anglo-Iranian Oil Company (AIOC)—it owned the majority of its stocks. However, that one company, because it was known to be a British *national* concern, was shut out of practically all producing areas around the globe, except the Gulf.[161]

In any case, we now have three schemes in play involving Saudi Arabian oil. SOCAL and Texaco are scheming to sell it to Washington; Ickes (at this point unbeknownst to the CASOC executives) is set to put Washington into the oil business by buying CASOC; and the State Department is doing whatever it is doing (as we said, it's difficult to fathom exactly what the State Department was after).

We deal first with Ickes' plan to buy CASOC. It met with an immediate, firm rebuff. When Rodgers and Collier revisited Washington, and Ickes sounded them out about it, they were (in the words of Anderson) "surprised and shocked."[162] That was not what they had had in mind.

At the same time, the two were not so put off that they broke off discussions. In fact, after giving the matter thought, they returned to tell Ickes that they might be willing to let the government have a third share in CASOC (and there also seems to have been some discussion of Washington's building a refinery for them).

Ickes, after consultations with the Navy and War Departments, decided that he could go along with that, and he so informed the companies. After considerable haggling, a deal was crafted. In return for a one-third interest in CASOC, for which the government would pay $40 million, Washington would have a preemptive right to purchase up to 51 percent of CASOC's production in peacetime and 100 percent in war, and (along with that) it could block sales to third parties if it were deemed in the national interest. Except for those restrictions, CASOC would continue to operate as a normal commercial enterprise.[163]

That was the deal, but it never got very far. Oilmen are not known for keeping projects of this magnitude secret; word got around, and when Jersey and Socony-Vacuum heard that the government was thinking of buying into CASOC, they became upset.[164] In response, they mobilized the Foreign Operations Committee of the Petroleum Administration for War, a group comprising heads of all the major oil companies whose job was to monitor the use of petroleum overseas in wartime. In a public statement, the committee came out strongly in favor of private—not public—development of foreign oil supplies.[165]

Moreover, the Texas independents, too, got involved, the same independents that, in the 1930s, had scuttled the prorationing scheme of the majors. They also opposed Ickes' plan of buying into CASOC. They feared that the government would be co-opted by the overseas producers and that this would open the way to importation of cheap oil to undercut the price of the domestic product.[166]

It does appear that some in the government were thinking along these lines. James C. Sappington, assistant petroleum adviser under Thornburgh, had drawn up a memo in which he noted that the importation of cheap foreign oil would cut sales of U.S. oil and thus would conserve American production for wartime emergencies.[167] Sappington was asking that oil be seen primarily as a strategic, not a commercial, product. It was this sort of thinking that the independents deplored, and so now they began to mobilize.

A formidable array of forces was shaping up against the deal, and one would have supposed that Ickes would have appreciated this and not gone on with it. Not Ickes. In the end he had to be reined in severely by forces that had the power to make him comply.[168]

Jersey and Socony inserted themselves directly into the picture. According to Anderson, on October 15, 1943, Ralph Davies, former vice president of Standard Oil of California (and at this time Ickes' deputy), escorted John Brown, president of Socony-Vacuum, into Ickes' office. There, Brown informed Ickes that his company and others in the foreign field did not like the idea of government competition. That same afternoon the government's oil czar announced that he was taking himself out of the CASOC negotiations.[169]

Rodgers of the Texas Co., who was scheduled to see Ickes after his meeting with Brown, said, "I have done a lot of trading in my day, but I never saw anything happen like this before. . . . At 11 o'clock in the morning, I thought we were together on the thing (the plan for Washington to buy into CASOC). At 2 o'clock in the afternoon, without any preliminaries at all, we were told the deal was off."[170]

What Ickes seemed incapable of appreciating (or did not want to understand) was that, by building up CASOC, he was promoting a rival center of power to the cartel. CASOC, with U.S. government backing, would inevitably engage in competition with the cartel, with all the destructiveness that would ensue from such a contest.

In any event, as of October 15, as far as developing Saudi oil was concerned, only one scheme remained in play—the State Department's proposal for the United States and Britain to join forces in some sort of condominium.

That one, too, foundered, but not before it had been carried quite a ways along. For a time there was regular communication between officials at the highest levels of the British and American governments, and some intense exploratory sessions were held in London and Washington. In the end, however, the deal broke down over problems with the exchange.[171]

British officials, looking to the end of the war, anticipated trouble on the exchange front, particularly involving oil. Oil traded in dollars. If American companies (and also British-based companies like Royal Dutch, which traded in dollars) sold oil in the commonwealth, Britain would have to exchange the dollars for sterling.

Since the British economy had been pretty thoroughly blasted by the war, the value of sterling could be expected to be low when the war was over; it would then become a real hardship to have to keep up the exchange. Britain wanted to shut dollar oil out of the commonwealth, giving preference to oil from the AIOC, a company that traded in sterling.

The United States would not go along with any such arrangement. Washington was looking to consolidate the free trade regime as soon as the war was ended through agreements like Bretton Woods; it consequently looked on the British proposal as a move toward protectionism. So the condominium discussions went nowhere. (We look at this exchange problem anew in the next chapter.)

Eventually, the Texas independents, working through their powerful senator Tom Connally, killed the condominium proposal outright,[172] which meant that, as of 1944, things were back to where they had started—there was all of this new oil set to come out of the Gulf, and unless something was done, the market was going to be swamped by it.

The problem was solved, but in a most unorthodox—and, one could say, devious—manner.

In October 1946, Jersey and Socony appealed to the British government to break the Red Line Agreement. London refused.[173] The Americans then brought suit to breach it, their lawyers arguing that the agreement had already been broken, since Gulbenkian and the French government both had "collaborated" with the Axis during the war.[174]

The lawyers claimed that since Vichy France was allied with Germany in the war and because Gulbenkian had resided in Vichy for some time while the war was going on, this constituted collaboration.

Finally, after extensive negotiations with the British, the latter went along with the Americans' contention. To be sure, the British were well compensated. Jersey agreed to purchase 800,000,000 barrels of crude from Anglo-Persia over 20 years; Socony made a similar pledge for some 500,000,000 barrels.[175] Jersey also pledged to build a pipeline for AIOC from Iran to the Mediterranean (interestingly, a promise on which it later reneged).

As soon as the Red Line was declared invalid, Jersey and Socony bought into CASOC. Contracts were signed on March 12, 1947, and, as a result, the two became part of the Arab American Oil Co. (ARAMCO), CASOC's Saudi Arabian affiliate.[176] As finalized, Jersey took 30 percent of ARAMCO, Socony-Vacuum 10 percent.

Immediately after that the new partners demanded that ARAMCO *raise* the price at which it was selling its oil, to match the Gulf-plus price. SOCAL and Texas refused, but Jersey and Socony held fast, and, after considerable haggling, the former were made to give in.[177]

As a result, CASOC's scheme, which had been to undercut the cartel—and thus capture a larger share of the market—was sabotaged. The high price of American oil was maintained, and this had the salutary result (from the standpoint of the cartel members) of preserving stability in the system.

It would appear, then, that Jersey and Socony contrived to break the Red Line Agreement in order to preserve the cartel. Of course, in the process, they did well for themselves—ARAMCO became one of the most successful business endeavors of all time.

The neatness of the deal was it not only got the cartel off the hook, it compensated Britain. Britain *was* the AIOC, inasmuch as it owned 56 percent of the company's stock. AIOC never had the outlets of its chief rivals in the cartel (Jersey and Royal Dutch), and, as a consequence, it always had difficulty moving its oil. During the war it had increased production from Iran and now, with the war ending, it was going to have to move that extra production on the world market.[178]

The deal Britain made with Jersey and Socony—to buy AIOC production for up to 20 years—solved that problem (of how to move the excess), or at least it seemed to. There was still a problem of whether Jersey and Socony could sell their oil inside the commonwealth (because of exchange restrictions). We look at that complication in the next chapter.

To sum up, then. . . . During the war, it would appear, the U.S. government became impressed with the value of oil, and also with the relatively limited nature of U.S. resources in that department. Since the South Americans were becoming restive (i.e., getting themselves caught up in various nationalistic agitations) it made sense to look farther afield for new areas to exploit, and the Persian Gulf seemed to recommend itself.

However, because of the Red Line Agreement, and because the whole area was a British sphere, the Americans were not going to be allowed in—not as long as the cartel companies were willing to stand by the Red Line Agreement.

It may be then that the State Department's negotiations with the British—in the Anglo-American Agreement talks—were attempts to work out a modus operandi whereby the Americans could come into the Gulf; that is, to find a way whereby Britain would be induced to allow them to enter.

But, if that was the case the issue was complicated by the presence already in the Gulf of the American cartel members (Jersey, Socony and Gulf). The three were not going to assist in opening up the southern Gulf to the likes of SOCAL and Texaco.

Therefore, it was not until Jersey and Socony had worked out their separate modus with the independents (SOCAL and Texaco) that a way was finally found, irrespective of any State Department involvement.

That would appear to be what all of the State Department intriguing was over. The author *thinks* this was it; the whole thing is so obscure it's hard to tell for certain.

NOTES

1. See Introduction, note 3.

2. Henrietta Larson et al., *New Horizons, History of the Standard Oil Company (New Jersey), 1927–1950* (New York: Harper & Row, 1971), 60. J. H. Bamberg in *The History of the British Petroleum Co.*, Vol. II (Cambridge: Cambridge University Press, 1994), 111, gives similar figures but says that the price did not fall to $1.27 until 1929.

3. Technically, the first integrated oil company was Standard Oil, which in 1897 entered the field of production in a small way after previously having been involved in all other areas of the business. However, the first truly integrated firm—that is, one that sought out production properties—was Royal Dutch. U.S. Senate, *The International Petroleum Cartel, Staff Report to the Federal Trade Commission, Submitted to the Subcommittee on Monopoly of the Select Committee on Small Business* (Washington, DC: Government Printing Office, 1952), 37–38. Harold Williamson et al., *The American Petroleum Industry* (Evanston, IL: Northwestern University Press, 1963), 7, says Standard oil "innovated" the concept of the integrated firm.

4. Norman Nordhauser, *The Quest for Stability, Domestic Oil Regulation: 1917–1935* (New York: Garland, 1979), 47.

5. For the most detailed discussion of Achnacarry, including the precise language of some of its more important provisions, see U.S. Senate, *The International Petroleum Cartel*, 197f.

6. Bamberg in *The History of the British Petroleum Co.*, Vol. II, 109–110, says, in fact, that officials of the Anglo-Persian Co. and the Burmah Oil Co. drew up the agenda (including the program to be acted upon) prior to Achnacarry and that the heads of the three companies merely ratified the program presented to them. It also appears that two other companies attended the meeting—Standard Oil of New York and Gulf—and that these two later became members of the original cartel, but junior members.

7. Ibid., 110.

8. The glut first developed in 1920 with the discovery of the Huntington Beach field in the Los Angeles Basin. This was followed by an even greater strike at Signal Hill in Long Beach, and then another important field was discovered at Santa Fe Springs in Southern California. Then in 1926 several big fields were discovered in Oklahoma. Norman Nordhauser, *The Quest for Stability: Domestic Oil Regulation, 1917–1935,* 8. According to Nordhauser (28), by November 1926 more than 100,000 barrels per day of high-grade crude oil flowed from the wells in Oklahoma, and by July 1927 the field reached its peak daily output of half a million barrels.

9. George Sweet Gibb and Evelyn Knowlton, *The History of the Standard Oil Company, the Resurgent Years, 1911–1927* (New York: Harper & Brothers, 1956), 420.

10. U.S. Senate, *The International Petroleum Cartel*, 197f.

11. Bamberg in *The History of the British Petroleum Co.*, Vol. II, 112, says that already in 1924 an importing and distributing organization, Russian Oil Products Ltd. (ROP), was competing in the British market with subsidiaries of the three market leaders. By aggressive price-cutting ROP increased the value of its sales, mostly benzine, from £500,000 in 1924 to nearly £4 million in 1929.

12. Gibb and Knowlton, *The History of the Standard Oil Company, the Resurgent Years*, 356.

13. According to Larson et al., writing in *New Horizons*, 305, Standard of New York was one of the few American companies at this time that did not have to worry about outlets abroad. A successful marketer overseas, it was purchasing supplies from Romania, Russia, Persia, Burma, and the Dutch East Indies.

14. Ibid., 305f. Standard of New York was not cowed by Deterding's action of taking the fight to the United States. Indeed, it moved into the British market, promoting its recently introduced ethyl gasoline, in competition to both Royal Dutch and Anglo-Persian. Williamson et al., *The American Petroleum Industry*, 529; also U.S. Senate, *The International Petroleum Cartel*, 197f.

15. Williamson et al., *The American Petroleum Industry*, 526, say

> By the mid-1920s, other groups were beginning to challenge the market position of the major companies. . . . Included among the challengers were the marketing subsidiaries of such American companies as Cities Service and the Texas Co., several small but well established British marketing firms, and a number of other British companies, commonly referred to in the trade as "pirates" and which, according to one authoritative source, "were brought into the market through three factors, the profitability of the business, the richness of the concentrated municipal markets, and the availability of supplies of gasoline, particularly at the public wharves near these markets. The pirates

purchased their supplies from private brokers who had picked up spot cargoes of American, Roumanian, Mexican or Russian oil at bargain prices, and resold them at cut prices to those dealers willing to retail unbranded products."

16. U.S. Senate, *The International Petroleum Cartel*, 200f.
17. Ibid.
18. Bamberg in *The History of the British Petroleum Co.*, Vol. II, 111, says that Teagle took the initiative of trying to line up support for the Achnacarry Agreement among his fellow American producers.
19. U.S. Senate, *The International Petroleum Cartel*, 202.
20. For a discussion of the impact of new discoveries on the American oil industry, see ibid., 40. For the impact of these developments specifically on Jersey Standard, see Larson et al., *New Horizons*, 5, 61. Larson writes, "The basic weakness of the foreign marketing affiliates (of the American companies) was their dependence upon American products while their leading competitors sold products made from lower-cost crude oils produced on large concessions in Venezuela, Persia, and other countries." Further, the foreign fields that the Britishers mainly were exploiting had geographical advantages. For years, Deterding had been arguing the good sense of supplying markets from within their geographical region. See Corley, *A History of the Burmah Oil Company, 1886–1924*, 69.
21. U.S. Senate, *The International Petroleum Cartel*, 59, footnote 55.
22. Gibb and Knowlton, *The History of the Standard Oil Company, the Resurgent Years*, 389.
23. U.S. Senate, *The International Petroleum Cartel*, 206, points out that as long as America was the world's principal resource of oil, it was to nobody's advantage to undercut the American price in any foreign market, unless the undercutter was willing to risk a price war—a war that the dominant American companies, because of their size and location, would surely win. Also see ibid., 40.
24. Nordhauser, *The Quest for Stability*, 64; also Bamberg, *The History of the British Petroleum Co.*, vol. II, 111.
25. Larson et al., *New Horizons*, 66. The U.S. Senate report of the Temporary National Economic Committee, 1941, 6, says the API was dominated by the majors, and the strongest voice among the majors was that of the former Standard companies. See the monograph on *Control of the Petroleum Industry by Major Oil Companies* (U.S. government report, n.d.).
26. As the big oil companies saw the issue, unregulated, rapid, close drilling disturbed conditions underground, so that, inevitably, oil could no longer be brought to the surface except by economically unprofitable means. Nordhauser, *The Quest for Stability*, 33. Elsewhere, on 34, Nordhauser says, "Interior Department publications implied . . . that the country was on the verge of an oil shortage, while, it was hinted, an enormous amount of oil and gas was being poured into rivers or blown into the air by wasteful wells." On p. 67, Nordhauser says the big oil companies also opposed "low production, or so-called stripper wells, wells which had to be put on the pump to continue functioning and which often pumped oil for years at a rate of less than a barrel a day."
27. As, for example, unitization, as had been carried out by Anglo-Persian in the Gulf. See U.S. Senate, *The International Petroleum Cartel*, 208; for details of Jersey Standard support for unitization, see Larson et al., *New Horizons*, 88.
28. The Senate committee investigating control of the petroleum industry found that oil companies talked about "conservation," but they were really interested in "stabilization" (i.e., of prices). Conservation, according to the report, means saving limited re-

sources so that they may be used by later generations. Stabilization, on the other hand, applies to efforts to obtain improvement in the economy, regardless of the effects on efficiency. Stabilization, based on market demand, the report concludes, is basically a form of monopolistic control. See *Control of the Petroleum Industry by Major Oil Companies*, 12.

29. Some businessmen saw stabilization as a good thing, since it eliminated price wars. But this was predominantly the sentiment of Big Business. According to Ellis Hawley, in *The New Deal and the Problem of Monopoly* (Princeton, NJ: Princeton University Press, 1966), 83, "Small firms often existed only because they offered lower prices to offset consumer preference for advertised brands." Nordhauser in *The Quest for Stability*, 33, says "The word 'conservation,' as used by industry leaders, became synonymous with the call for a suspension of the anti-trust laws."

30. Hawley, in *The New Deal and the Problem of Monopoly*, 426, writes, "The Sherman Act . . . was one that was deeply rooted in American traditions, one that over the years had acquired the strength of moral precept, and therefore enjoyed 'unquestioned public acceptance.' Any revision of the law, to be sure, was extremely difficult. Even the slightest change was usually treated something like 'an amendment to the prayer book.' " Also operating here was distaste for the industry generated by revelations of the Teapot Dome scandal. Nordhauser, *The Quest for Stability*, 17.

31. According to Larson, et al., *New Horizons*, 306, Teagle thought that the export association would be allowed under the Webb-Pomerene Export Trade Act of 1918. This measure had been enacted to permit competing American companies to form associations for the sole purpose of engaging in export trade, provided they did not thereby restrain that trade of any domestic competitor or commit any act that enhanced or depressed prices or substantially lessened competition within the United States.

32. On the government's unwillingness to sanction the scheme and the reasons given, see Larson et al., *New Horizons*, 66.

33. Yergin, *The Prize*, 247.

34. Nordhauser, *The Quest for Stability*, 69.

35. Nordhauser in *The Quest for Stability*, 38, says that Hoover was reluctant because members of his administration feared that the federally imposed stabilization might mean higher prices and that the public would blame the Hoover administration for this.

36. *Control of the Petroleum Industry by Major Oil Companies*, 15; Nordhauser, *The Quest for Stability*, 34.

37. Ibid.

38. Williamson et al., *The American Petroleum Industry*, 542; also Nordhauser, *The Quest for Stability*, 63f., 74f.

39. For history of populism in Texas, see Nordhauser, *The Quest for Stability*.

40. Ibid.

41. Ibid.

42. Nordhauser, *The Quest for Stability*, 50.

43. According to the U.S. government report, *Control of the Petroleum Industry by Major Oil Companies*, 14, "[P]rorationing works a hardship on the nonintegrated operator and works to the advantage of the majors who have many sources of crude oil. When the output of wells is restricted, the cost per barrel is increased and a longer time is required for the nonintegrated operator to amortize his investment. Usually, the small operator has a very limited amount of capital and is often forced into bankruptcy, since he can operate his wells only in a very limited way."

44. See Nordhauser, *The Quest for Stability*, 47f.

45. Ibid.

46. Nordhauser, *The Quest for Stability*, 51. As for those smaller companies that found the deal attractive, Nordhauser lists Barnsdall, Phillips, and Skelly.

47. U.S. Senate, *The International Petroleum Cartel*, 229; also, Nordhauser, *The Quest for Stability*, 77.

48. Larson et al., *New Horizons*, 66; also, Nordhauser, *The Quest for Stability*, 79.

49. U.S. Senate, *The International Petroleum Cartel*, 249.

50. To be sure, there was also Mexico. But Mexican fields were despaired of at the time; they had begun to show significant water traces. As for Sumatra, it was not in the league of Persia and Venezuela.

51. Nordhauser, *The Quest for Stability*, 15.

52. Ickes, for example, felt that the National Industrial Recovery Act (NIRA) codes (discussed later) were deliberately promoting monopoly and were responsible for an increased number of identical bids on public works contracts. See Hawley, *The New Deal and the Problem of Monopoly*, 73.

53. Roosevelt was inaugurated early in 1933. In June approval was given to the NIRA, and in August a code of fair competition in U.S. oil was approved under the act. U.S. crude oil prices rose sharply, the East Texas field price for Grade A crude advancing from 50 cents a barrel in July, to one dollar in October. Bamberg, *The History of the British Petroleum Co.*, 114.

54. Williamson et al., *The American Petroleum Industry*, 541; also Nordhauser, *The Quest for Stability*, 83.

55. Nordhauser, *The Quest for Stability*, 160.

56. Royal Dutch during this period had a sizable American operation under the American Shell logo.

57. U.S. Senate, *The International Petroleum Cartel*, 236.

58. Ibid., 45.

59. Ibid., 208: "[In the 1930s] the United States was producing at increasing costs by tapping deeper reserves and by use of stripping operations in its older shallower fields. United States domestic production in these areas tended to be high-cost as compared with the flush production of Venezuela and the areas of the Middle East then being opened."

60. Peter Ellis Jones, in *Oil: A Practical Guide to the Economics of World Petroleum* (Cambridge: Woodhead-Faulkner, 1988), 19, says, "The effect of the system was to maintain U.S. prices and at the same time provide a very attractive profit to the major companies on their low cost international production, particularly in the Middle East." This was the case because, no matter where the oil was shipped to (e.g., Italy from the Persian Gulf), the buyer would have to pay as if it had been shipped from the Gulf of Mexico.

61. U.S. Senate, *The International Petroleum Cartel*, 197.

62. George Philip, *Oil and Politics in South America* (Cambridge: Cambridge University Press, 1982), 45.

63. P. H. Giddens, *Standard Oil Company (Indiana): Oil Pioneer of the Middle West* (New York: Appleton-Century-Crofts, 1955), 489.

64. U.S. Senate, *The International Petroleum Cartel*, 67, 72.

65. For the exact language of the original agreement, see ibid., 66.

66. Ibid., 47.

67. Ibid.

68. Ibid.

69. Ibid.

70. U.S. Senate, *The International Petroleum Cartel*, 58.

71. Ibid., 66, footnote.

72. The *Petroleum Times of London*, writing about SOCAL on May 2, 1936, said, "Fight for markets has been under reasonable control . . . 'gentlemen's agreements' are the order of the day, and what each large oil company fears more than all else is the entry of a powerful newcomer in the established order of the world markets. . . . [t]he vast strides of international scope the Standard Oil Company of California has made in a relatively few years at least proves that romance is not yet dead, but it may lead to disturbing factors." Quoted in George Stocking, *Middle East Oil, a Study in Political and Economic Controversy* (Kingsport, TN: Vanderbilt University Press, 1970), 87.

73. Anthony Sampson, *The Seven Sisters* (New York: Viking, 1975), 45.

74. U.S. Senate, *The International Petroleum Cartel*, 24.

75. Ibid.

76. Ibid.

77. Ibid.

78. John A. DeNovo, *American Interests and Policies in the Middle East* (Minneapolis: University of Minnesota Press, 1963), 203, writes that "Britain insisted that the concessionary company (to be formed by SOCAL) be British registered, that the managing director and a majority of the other directors be British subjects, and that no rights granted by the [sheikh] be under direct non-British control. Effectively that would have precluded SOCAL from running its own company. After the compromise whereby the company was registered in Canada was worked out, the Americans still were handicapped, to the extent that all dealings between them and the government of Bahrain had to be conducted through the British political agent."

79. U.S. Senate, *The International Petroleum Cartel*, 73.

80. According to DeNovo, *American Interests and Policies in the Middle East*, 204, Gulf got the concession after Anglo-Persian had first turned it down.

81. Irvine Anderson, *ARAMCO, the United States and Saudi Arabia* (Princeton, NJ: Princeton University Press, 1981), 40.

82. According to DeNovo, *American Interests and Policies in the Middle East*, 206, as had been the case with Bahrain, the jointly owned British–American company had to be registered in Britain. According to Stocking, *Middle East Oil, a Study in Political and Economic Controversy*, 115, as a guarantee that Gulf's participation in the development of Kuwait would not unduly disturb international oil markets, Anglo-Persia made an agreement with Gulf that provided, among other things, that Kuwait oil would not be used to "upset" the marketing position of either company at any time or place.

83. DeNovo, *American Interests and Policies in the Middle East*, 207.

84. Stocking, *Middle East Oil, a Study in Political and Economic Controversy*, 127, says,

> The common interest of the four corporate entities that accounted for virtually the whole of Middle East production not only depended on their relations as joint owners of producing enterprises but was strengthened by various contractual or partnership arrangements between and among two or more of the four. Royal Dutch-Shell and Anglo-Iranian were closely associated not only as joint owners of IPC but as joint marketers throughout much of the Eastern hemisphere, including the United Kingdom and Ireland, much of Africa, the Near East, Ceylon, India and Pakistan. . . . Jersey and Socony conducted their production and refining operations in the Dutch East Indies and their

marketing activities over a considerable extent of the Eastern hemisphere through the Standard-Vacuum Oil Company in which they had a 50 percent ownership.

85. These estimates of control of crude oil supplies are based on data from the U.S. Senate report, *The International Petroleum Cartel*, 24.

86. R. W. Ferrier, *The History of the British Petroleum Company*, Vol. I (Cambridge: Cambridge University Press, 1982), 358f.

87. Zuhayr Mikdashi, *A Financial Analysis of Middle Eastern Oil Concessions: 1901–65* (New York: Frederick A. Praeger, 1966), 35.

88. Bamberg, *The History of the British Petroleum Company*, Vol. II, 6.

89. Ibid., 360f.

90. Ibid.

91. George Lenczowski, *The Middle East in World Affairs* (Ithaca, NY: Cornell University Press, 1962), 167.

92. Bamberg, *The History of the British Petroleum Co.*, Vol. II, 362.

93. Mikdashi, *A Financial Analysis of Middle Eastern Oil Concessions*, 16.

94. Mostafa Elm, *Oil, Power and Principle* (Syracuse, NY: Syracuse University Press, 1992), 19.

95. Ibid., 20.

96. Ibid., 21.

97. Ibid.

98. Ibid., 29–30.

99. Ibid., 30.

100. Ibid., 31.

101. Elm says that the Depression had reduced the company's profits by 37 percent, but the royalties had dropped 76.2 percent. Ibid., 31.

102. Ibid.

103. Ibid., 32.

104. Bamberg, *The History of the British Petroleum Co.*, Vol. II, 37.

105. Elm suggests that there was outright intimidation, saying, "[W]hat brought about this unfortunate outcome was the Shah's desperate need for money and great concern for British warships in the Persian Gulf." He then quotes Cadmen, saying that " '[the Shah] was intensely suspicious of the Company's activities in southern Persia . . . and in Persian Kurdistan.' " What he is implying is that the shah feared the British would raise the tribes. Elm, *Oil, Power and Principle*, 38.

106. Bamberg, *The History of the British Petroleum Co.*, Vol. II, 50.

107. Ibid., 37.

108. Edith Penrose and E. F. Penrose, *Iraq: International Relations and National Development* (London: Ernest Benn, 1978), 82.

109. Ibid., 47.

110. As the Penrosees say in ibid., 43, the British at the end of World War I were determined that their overseas colonies should pay their own way.

111. Peter Sluglett, *Britain in Iraq, 1914–1932* (London: Ithaca Press, 1976), 203.

112. Ibid.

113. The head of Britain's air forces in Iraq said, "[I]f the Arabs have nothing to fight against on the ground, and no loot to be obtained, and nobody to kill, but have to deal with airplanes which are out of their reach, they are certain to come in and there will be no risk of disaster or heavy casualties such as are always suffered by small infantry patrols in uncivilized countries." Ibid., 265f.

114. Ibid.

115. Ibid.

116. Ibid.

117. For a discussion of British tribal policy, see ibid.

118. Ibid.

119. Penrose and Penrose, *Iraq: International Relations and National Development*, 82f.

120. Ibid.

121. Originally known as the *sherrifeen* officers. These were individuals, mostly Arabs who had been trained in Ottoman military schools, who allied with the British, particularly with Lawrence of Arabia in his famous Arab Revolt. After the war, they scattered throughout the Middle East and formed nationalist cores in various capitals.

122. Ghazi is a controversial figure, considered by some to have been a proto-Arab nationalist leader, by others a mental case. See Penrose and Penrose, *Iraq: International Relations and National Development*, 94.

123. This was under the terms of the Long–Berenger agreement. Ibid., 58f.

124. Long–Berenger left open the possibility of another 10 percent for native interests if certain conditions were met. This extra 10 percent would have been made good from the foreigners' shares.

125. According to Penrose and Penrose, the Americans insisted on this point, because otherwise they would have had to pay double taxation to the British (since IPC was a British company) and to their own government. See Penrose and Penrose, *Iraq: International Relations and National Development*, 61.

126. Ibid., 59–60.

127. See the discussion of the San Remo Agreement in Chapter 1.

128. According to Penrose and Penrose, the Americans' original proposal was subsequently amended. It was worked out that, instead of 12 parcels of 16 square miles each, it would be 24 of 8. See Penrose and Penrose, *Iraq: International Relations and National Development*, 64.

129. U.S. Senate, *The International Petroleum Cartel*, 55–56.

130. Why, then, would all these disgruntled partners have agreed to the Americans' proposal in the first place? Evidently, because the American State Department had set its heart on this, and America, as described in Chapter 1, was in a position to make problems for both the British and the French.

131. Ferrier, *The History of the British Petroleum Company*, Vol. I, 584.

132. To be sure, Iraq would have gotten a share of the crude to dispose of, but, as was the case with Gulbenkian, Iraq did not want crude as much as it wanted money.

133. Ferrier, *The History of the British Petroleum Company*, Vol. I, 583.

134. Just as the original negotiations over San Remo had been concealed. It was only belatedly that the Americans learned the full purport of what the British and French had agreed.

135. Penrose and Penrose, *Iraq: International Relations and National Development*, 64.

136. Indeed, the proposal had been successively watered down. For example, the scheme was amended so that, after the initial auction, the IPC members could participate in the follow-up one as well. Moreover, they were to open the bids, which were to be sealed. This gave them a huge advantage, since they could always underbid any outsider.

137. U.S. Senate, *The International Petroleum Cartel*, 70, 85.

138. Penrose and Penrose, *Iraq: International Relations and National Development*, 68.

139. Ibid., 65. Iraq got another concession from the IPC, namely, an arrangement that would link royalties to profits, defined to include the estimated profit on refined products made from Iraqi oil—but the arrangement was not to come into effect for 20 years. Subsequently, however, the IPC repudiated this concession.

140. Ibid.

141. Ibid., 73.

142. Hanna Batatu, *The Old Social Classes and the Revolutionary Movements of Iraq* (Princeton, NJ: Princeton University Press, 1978), 468.

143. Ibid., 134.

144. Ibid.

145. Lord Macaulay, *The History of England* (London: Penguin Books, 1968), 244.

146. Bamberg, *The History of the British Petroleum Co.*, Vol. II, 330.

147. Davin Painter, *Private Power and Public Policy* (London: I. B. Tauris, 1986) 35, says that Saudi Arabia's production went from 500,000 barrels per day in 1939 to over 5 million bpd in 1940. See also Anderson, *Aramco, the United States and Saudi Arabia*, ix.

148. Anderson, *Aramco, the United States and Saudi Arabia*, 28: "By 1941 the three structures that had been tapped were estimated to have reserves of 750 million barrels, and the existence of numerous similar untapped structures clearly indicated that potential reserves were much greater."

149. The effect of this, of course, was to avoid having to invade the marketing territory of either of the two giants (Jersey or Royal Dutch). The British government was a kind of floating resource for Anglo-Persian, a market that had not existed previously but that could absorb as much oil as Anglo-Persian could send its way.

150. Painter, *Private Power and Public Policy*, 33.

151. Anderson, *Aramco, the United States and Saudi Arabia*, 56.

152. Ibid., 8, says that, prior to World War II, the British provided Abdul Aziz with a subsidy, which was ended in 1927. British–Saudi relations were not good due to British support for the Hashemites, whom Abdul Aziz drove out of the Arabian peninsula during World War I. The subsidy was reinstituted, however, in 1940. Ibid., 30.

153. According to Painter, by this point in the war, Allied planners had grown concerned about America's ability to keep drawing on its oil resources. The feeling was that the United States could drain itself to supply the Allied war effort. Painter, *Private Power and Public Policy*, 35.

154. Anderson, *Aramco, the United States and Saudi Arabia*, 32.

155. Painter says that Undersecretary of the Navy William Bullitt suggested to Ickes that he try for a majority control of CASOC. Painter, *Private Power and Public Policy*, 36.

156. Thornburgh was a former executive of Bahrain Petroleum. He left there in 1941 to go to State. Anderson, *Aramco, the United States and Saudi Arabia*, 32, 69.

157. Ibid.

158. This was the idea of more than one prominent American when, later on, the proposal or a version of it was publicized. On Senator Owen Brewster's reaction, see Painter, *Private Power and Public Policy*, 62.

159. Anderson, *Aramco, the United States and Saudi Arabia*, 68.

160. Painter says that "the transformation of the domestic oil economy raised ques-

tions about [America's] traditional self-sufficiency in oil." He then cites statistics showing that, on the one hand, U.S. proved reserves of oil increased from 6.7 billion barrels in 1919 to over 19.5 billion in 1941. On the other hand, the tremendous increase in reserves and production was paralleled by increases in consumption. Between 1919 and 1941 oil increased its share of total U.S. energy supply from 12.1 percent, to 31.4 percent. Painter, *Private Power and Public Policy*, 9.

161. Governments did not want to deal with it; for example, Peru and Colombia in South America shut it out.

162. Anderson, *Aramaco, the United States and Saudi Arabia*, 58.

163. Ibid., 61.

164. Ibid.

165. Ibid., 96–100.

166. Ibid.

167. Ibid., 75.

168. Ibid., 98.

169. Ibid., 63.

170. Ibid., 65.

171. Ibid. 96.

172. Ibid., 106.

173. Ibid., 94.

174. U.S. Senate, *The International Petroleum Cartel*, 97, 145.

175. Bamberg, *The History of the British Petroleum Co.*, Vol. II, 303.

176. Anderson, *Aramco, the United States and Saudi Arabia*, 158.

177. The cartel companies exploited an obscure clause in the partnership agreement. Even then, elements in SOCAL resisted until, according to Blair, Jersey prevailed upon members of the Rockefeller family, who were influential in SOCAL to influence the company executives to give way. Blair, *Control of Oil*, 39.

178. Keith Hutchison, "Crude Oil Politics," *America's Energy*, ed. Robert Engler (New York: Pantheon, 1980), 218.

CHAPTER 3

The Fall of Mosadeq and the Triumph of the Oil Cartel in the United States

By the period we are about to cover (roughly the late 1940s through mid-1950s), a fundamental change had affected relations between the cartel and the political order. Effectively, the cartel was released from controls that formerly the order had been able to exert over it. This came about in the following way.

The original intent of Rockefeller and Deterding had been to rationalize the oil industry. The product of that effort was the international oil system, which we have been discussing.[1]

Once the system was in place, it then became necessary to perpetuate it. For that, support was enlisted from politicians in various countries, but most notably the United States and Britain.

Effectively, this gave the politicians a stake in the system by making them complicit in its operations. This, in turn, effected a change in the relation between the governments and the oil companies, in effect, upending the customary relationship.

To a degree, the companies became more powerful than the governments. This is not to say that the separate companies became so; rather, the companies acting together as units of the cartel did this.

The upshot was that, whereas previously the international oil system comprised seven companies and Britain (by virtue of the British government's owning 56 percent of AIOC), now the United States, too, became, if not a system member, then an entity that was becoming enmeshed in its affairs.

In this chapter we look at instances that show the strength of the cartel and its ability to treat the Great Powers on a more or less equal basis.

The first involves Britain and that country's problems with the currency exchange, a matter touched on briefly in the last chapter.

THE CURRENCY CRISIS

Britain emerged from World War II in a difficult position. Its infrastructure was badly damaged and needed to be rebuilt. For this, matériel was required that could be supplied only by the United States.

U.S. businessmen were eager to cater to Britain's needs but wanted to be paid in dollars. As Britain's supply of hard currency was low, the U.S. government extended it a line of credit for $3.2 billion. The money was advanced with the understanding that sterling would continue to be convertible.[2]

By 1947 Britain had run through its credit line and still was experiencing economic hardship.[3] As Britain essayed possible strategies for alleviating its problem, one area of difficulty stood out—an inordinate amount of Britain's dollar reserve was going to pay for oil.

Right after the war, oil for Europe originated mainly from U.S. companies operating abroad.[4] Until Britain's oil industry recovered, taking oil from the Americans made sense.[5] However, by 1947 British oil companies were back online. Hence, Britain had to reconsider its position—why go on paying out scarce dollars to Americans when British firms could supply all of Britain's oil needs?

A partial answer to this question was that Britain could not, under agreements that it had with the United States, discriminate against American companies. For example; it was a partner to the so-called Bretton Woods Agreement and several other compacts, the aim of which was to open up world trade and put an end to protection. Any attempt by Britain to favor its own companies and put obstacles in the way of American firms' doing business overseas would be resisted by the United States.

Also significant in this regard is the Marshall Plan, which America got up, in large part, to help Britain. Through the plan, Europeans were provided with food and fuel. Some $16 billion was committed in this way over the four-year life of the program.

Administering the relief effort was a large bureaucracy, the so-called Economic Cooperation Authority (ECA). The ECA laid down all sorts of restrictions that had to be complied with to get aid. Some were not too onerous; some were quite intrusive.

The ECA did not merely dispense cash; it monitored how the money was spent. It did this because many in the United States looked on the plan as a boondoggle. For example, one of the aims of the plan was to get Europeans to switch from coal to oil. Europe's coal industry had been virtually destroyed in the war, and, with a shortage of miners (many of whom had been casualties of the war), it seemed efficient to utilize oil, a nonlabor-intensive industry.[6]

This, of course, suited the U.S. oilmen, up to a point. The Europeans, looking to optimize their situation, did not want to take product; they wanted crude.

Thus, they intended to use Marshall Plan funds to build refineries. By refining their own oil, they believed that they could save themselves money.

From the standpoint of American independent oil producers this was unacceptable—the independents exported product and saw European attempts to build up a refinery capacity as an effort to do them out of a market. The independents complained to the ECA, and the ECA denied the Europeans funds for refinery construction.

With this kind of surveillance it was almost impossible for the British to do anything involving American aid that the Americans were set against. At the same time, however, Britain's financial problems were so pressing that the newly elected Labour government in Britain was forced to act.

Labour moved toward protectionism gradually. In the spring of 1949, on instructions of the Bank of England, British banks refused to convert sterling for oil purchased outside the sterling bloc.[7] The Scandinavian countries, by and large, fell into this category, as did some other non-Commonwealth countries.[8]

Britain's decision particularly hurt ARAMCO. The richest partner in ARAMCO, Jersey, had a large network of overseas affiliates, some of which were affected by London's embargo. Socony, too, was well endowed with affiliates in countries overseas. Indeed, because these two had such affiliates, the two original ARAMCO partners—SOCAL and Texaco—invited them into the Saudi concession.

Just as ARAMCO was set to move large quantities of Saudi oil, the British, as it were, had thrown a spanner in the works.[9] Also at this time, Britain worked out another arrangement that hurt the Americans. It promoted a number of barter deals with foreign countries. For example, in South America the British arranged to supply the Argentines with British oil in return for Argentine beef.[10]

All of these special deals ran counter to specific international agreements that the British had entered into with Washington. Of course, the Americans were upset—not only the oil companies but the American government, as well.

Washington's ability to check the protectionist tide was, however, undercut by developments at home. Beginning in 1948 and stretching into 1949, the U.S. economy had gone into a recession. British imports to the United States had dropped precipitously, and this made Britain's exchange situation intolerable. In September 1949 Britain devalued its currency.[11]

Once Britain devalued, it then became imperative to cut down on its dollar exchanges. In December 1949 Britain initiated a substitution policy. Affiliates of American oil companies *inside* the sterling area were forbidden to sell dollar oil if sterling was available. Only when British companies had expended their stocks could the affiliates take on dollar oil.[12]

This action upset the British members of the cartel. Hearing of this decision, the AIOC executives insisted that the government explain the necessity of its action to the Americans. The executives wanted it made clear that AIOC had no part in this; otherwise, said the executives, the Americans will think that they were trying to undercut them.[13]

Responding to Britain's action, the Americans came up with a number of counterarguments. They claimed, for example, that Britain could not determine "dollar oil" on nationality factors alone. Many subsidiaries with which Britain dealt were, in fact, multinational firms in which British and Americans held an interest.[14]

Britain replied that it had taken care of this objection by figuring percentages. For example, if Americans owned 25 percent of a given subsidiary, 75 percent of the company's production was reckoned sterling oil, only 25 percent dollar.[15]

A point well taken. However, the Americans went on to claim that many subsidiaries *perforce* did business in dollars. All oil equipment, for example, had to be paid for in dollars (because practically the only manufacturers of such equipment were American); also local taxes and expenses usually were paid in dollars (because most foreign states preferred it this way).[16]

To be fair, the Americans argued, Britain should take into account these obligatory dollar costs when figuring its percentages. If Britain would do this, the Americans would work to get the "dollar content" of their oil down. There would then be only a small percentage of sterling that would have to be converted.

Britain showed interest in the plan, and the two sides discussed it. Nothing came of it, however, as the two could not agree on the precise dollar cost of the oil in question.

This disagreement might not have been so bad had it not been for the Saudi connection. The Americans had made specific commitments to the Saudi king Abdul Aziz. If now they could not move oil from the kingdom in what effectively amounted to half the oil-consuming world, how were they going to retain the concession?

The Americans asked the State Department for help. State had been following the crisis with great misgiving. It understood the effect of this on the cartel, and it tended to side with the companies. However, other departments of the U.S. government were not so partial. Indeed, some were quite hostile.

For example, ECA was not overly friendly. The ECA had discovered, as it worked to alleviate energy shortages in Europe, that the cartel companies overcharged on their deliveries. This came about through the Gulf-plus pricing arrangement, discussed in the last chapter. The companies charged *as if* shipping from the Gulf of Mexico, when in fact their oil could come from anywhere. The ECA demanded that this practice (known as phantom freight) cease, and it was discontinued, but not before it had engendered considerable bitterness.

Along with ECA, the Treasury Department was hostile. Some officials high up in the Treasury could not see why the companies did not let the matter go—let the British exclude American oil (for however long it took them to get back on their feet); the Americans (the Treasury officials claimed) could stand it. The officials pointed to the depletion allowance, which entitled the companies to large write-offs on their income taxes and which ensured them a huge return on their operations. One Treasury official accused the oilmen of behaving like "monopolists." He rebuked the oilmen for expecting the U.S. government "to pull their chestnuts out of the fire."[17]

Despite all this, State did intervene, couching its argument along security lines. State made the case that Britain's policies were harmful to America's defense effort. According to State, Saudi Arabia would be most hurt by the British policy; it would cost the kingdom (by State's calculations) $45 million a year.[18] Britain must realize (said State) that America intended Saudi Arabia to be its "back-up supplier of oil."

According to the State Department, America had imposed heavy demands on its energy resources in the last war. Were there to be another great conflict, the United States must have an alternative source of energy outside the United States. America's policymakers decided that Saudi Arabia was to be that outside resource.[19]

This argument, as several British commentators were quick to point out, did not make sense. If security were America's primary concern, why did it choose an alternative supplier located under the nose of the Soviet Union? How did the Americans propose to defend their client?

Effectively, State had no answer to that. However, as the U.S. military seemed disposed to support State's argument, there was no gainsaying it. Still, it is not at all likely that the British would have relented and opened their markets to American oil had not the Korean War intervened.[20]

Once that developed, there was no problem finding new outlets for Saudi oil (and, indeed, for oil from anywhere). In addition, the effect of Marshall Plan aid was beginning to be felt. More and more European countries were switching to oil from coal, and, as a consequence, oil from the Middle East—due to its proximity to Europe—was becoming more in demand.

Britain and the American companies came to terms. Britain agreed to discontinue oil rationing, and the Americans were allowed to supply the increased demand. On their side, the Americans agreed to get their dollar costs down to a level that Britain could accept. In the end, the Americans were treated equally with British and British-Dutch companies.[21]

In this example we see how the companies were able to exploit their State Department tie in a contest of wills with an American ally, Britain. In the next case we look at how the American companies were able to enlist two powerful departments—State and Treasury—to get their ways.

THE SAUDI 50:50 SPLIT

One feature that stands out about the preceding instance is the solicitude of the ARAMCO companies for the Saudis. Ordinarily, a powerhouse like ARAMCO would not be so solicitous of a native producer, which usually could be made to rewrite concession terms (as we saw the Iraqis do in the case of the IPC). In the case of the Saudis, a complicating factor intervened.

Sometime back, the State Department had urged ARAMCO to allow American independents into the peninsula. This was an attempt by the department to behave evenhandedly toward the independents and the big international oil companies. Against their better judgment, the majors went along, agreeing to surrender rights to the so-called neutral zone (see map) if the Saudis would extend them rights in offshore territories.[22]

The swap had turned out badly for ARAMCO. One of the American independents, J. Paul Getty, offered Abdul Aziz a truly lucrative deal compared to what the king was getting from ARAMCO. Getty (the owner of Pacific-Western Oil Co.) paid the Saudis $.55 a barrel royalty (ARAMCO was paying only $.33). He also gave an initial payment of $9.5 million, an annual payment of $1 million, and Saudi rights to purchase shares in Pacific-Western. Finally, Saudi Arabia was promised one-eighth of production profits and one-quarter of refinery profits.[23]

The fact that Getty could make such an attractive offer led Abdul Aziz to conclude that ARAMCO could do better. Consequently, he signified his desire to renegotiate the concession, unless ARAMCO "rectified" matters on its own. Under the original contract, ARAMCO was obliged to return within 90 days areas that it did not intend to exploit. This clause had never been enforced, only because the Americans had been able to talk the king out of making good on it.[24]

If now the king were to insist on fulfillment, this could break the cartel's monopoly hold on the Gulf, and that, in turn, could threaten the cartel's grip worldwide. Cartels have to check independents whenever the latter attempt to free ride. An independent that latches onto a substantial oil supply (and one that is likely to be available over time) can always, by setting its price just under the cartel price, find buyers. Such unfair practices (as the cartel viewed them) act as a solvent on the system.

A way had to be found to close off the peninsula to independents like Getty. By way of accomplishing this, ARAMCO once again had recourse to the U.S. government. ARAMCO executives lay Abdul Aziz's demands before their friends at State. State's immediate response was, in effect, to suggest a reworking of the Getty arrangement. Why, said State Department officials, did ARAMCO not surrender more of the unexploited Saudi lands? This would satisfy the king, and it would be in line with America's stated policy of the Open Door.

The companies had come to grief already over the Open Door; they would not get into this fix again. Instead, ARAMCO officials proposed to offer Abdul Aziz a 50:50 profit-sharing arrangement (the king had been demanding this ever since Venezuela had gotten it in 1949). The company could afford it. At the same time, however, it would not do to hand the king this concession; that could lead to "leapfrogging" (in other words, where other countries make similar demands and in some cases seek to top the original offer).[25]

ARAMCO officials had something novel in mind. Under the scheme that they had worked out, Abdul Aziz would be asked to tax the company, something that was not part of the original concession agreement. This seems an odd scheme for businessmen to propose. Ah, but wait a bit; there was a catch. Once the king agreed, the way would then be open for ARAMCO to forgo paying taxes to the United States. Jersey was looking to transfer U.S. tax payments to the king, thereby granting him a 50:50 split without cutting into the company's profit margin.[26]

Under U.S. law, American firms doing business overseas (and subject to foreign taxes) could be exempted from paying taxes at home. This is done so the companies will not be dunned twice. At the same time, however, American law excepts royalties. Relief is accorded only if the Americans pay taxes *that the natives, too, are required to pay*. Royalties are considered exceptional exactions and do not count.[27]

ARAMCO wanted Abdul Aziz to tax his people—a practically unheard of notion, since the bedouin would hardly submit to this; in their view, the king was obligated to buy their loyalty. Along with that, ARAMCO expected the U.S. government to approve the royalties-for-taxes swap *in advance*. In other words, the oilmen wanted State's assurance that, if the king complied (by taxing his subjects), Washington would approve the transfer of American taxes to him.[28]

Despite friends at State, this was not an easy deal to arrange. Nor was it a propitious time to propose it. Right after the war, allegations had been leveled against the oil companies, accusing several of collaboration with the Axis. This prompted calls for congressional investigations.[29] There were now no fewer than 20 such investigations in progress (not all against the oilmen; Congress was looking into all sorts of anti-trust matters).

Despite the unfavorable climate, State did obtain conditional approval for the deal from the secretary of the Treasury.[30] In a somewhat convoluted arrangement State got the Treasury to let ARAMCO deduct taxes over a 10-year trial period, at the end of which Treasury would review the arrangement and then decide whether to okay it.[31]

Confident that the deal was approved, ARAMCO advised Abdul Aziz to go ahead and pass his income tax law. The king did, but he exempted from payment anyone in the royal family, armed forces, and religious figures, and anyone who had an income less than 20,000 riyals or who paid the *ẕakat* (religious tax). This worked out to just about everyone in the kingdom except ARAMCO.[32]

In respect to the U.S. government, the implications of the reform were immense. According to Painter, in 1950 ARAMCO paid the U.S. government $50 million in income tax, while the Saudis received $66 million in royalties. In 1951, claiming a credit for taxes paid in the kingdom, ARAMCO paid only $6 million in U.S. income taxes. Saudi Arabia, in contrast, received almost $110 million from the company.[33]

Here, then, we have a classic example of oilmen's getting the government to assist them. As to any benefits that the government may have derived from the deal, that's problematical. If one accepts that Gulf oil was a security asset, the 50:50 split may have been worth the loss of U.S. tax revenue.[34] We have more to say about this later on.

At the same time, there can be no doubt that the oil companies gained commercially by consolidating their hold on the Gulf. This was (and is) the richest oil repository in the world and also the one from which oil could be most cheaply extracted. Along with that, its location is ideal. In 1950 ARAMCO opened a pipeline from near the Persian Gulf to a terminal in Lebanon. This enabled Saudi oil to flow both ways—to the Eastern and Western Hemispheres. With that, the kingdom became the oil industry's true center of gravity.[35]

We are now set to look at yet another instance. In this one, the companies actually top the deal that they have just gotten, and this time they do it by manipulating one department of the U.S. government against another.

RETURN OF ANTI-TRUST

We have been talking about State and its ties to Big Oil. The obverse of this relation was that of the Justice Department to the American people. Justice considered itself a popular advocate, an attitude that became manifest at the end of the war, when it took up the cudgels against Big Oil, initiating several anti-trust investigations.

The investigations were launched in a climate of widespread popular antagonism—not just toward oil; bigness per se was anathematized.[36] According to Sobel, America has gone through several phases of corporate growth-through-merger.[37] The last large-scale instance of this phenomenon was in the 1920s, when, says Sobel, 1,100 firms disappeared in 1929.[38]

Then in the 1930s mergers declined, for a good reason. The earlier merger activity had been effected through exchange of securities, and in Depression times securities were not all that attractive.[39]

Also, those corporations that survived the Depression had no need to restructure, as they, usually, were strong and vigorous. They went into the war in good shape and grew only stronger while the conflict raged.[40]

After the war, merger activity started up again, but this was different from what had gone on before. Now it was conglomerates that formed as companies expanded horizontally.[41] This was a type of activity that the American public could ill comprehend. Americans could not see why a vacuum cleaning business would want to buy up an insecticide company. At the same time, it was impossible to overlook the fact that companies were dying off. Whether they were being taken over by natural competitors or by firms that simply had excess capital that they wanted to invest was not important—the important thing was net effect.

Opportunities for small business were disappearing. The class that, for decades, had seen itself as crucial to America's growth was becoming marginalized. Dismay among members of this class was soon transformed into anger.

It should not be surprising that a lot of the anger targeted oil. At the turn of the century, little businessmen had applauded Ida Tarbell's attack on Rockefeller and the Standard Oil Trust. They were incensed by what they saw as pandering to the monopolists (when the courts reinterpreted the anti-trust laws to accommodate the Wilsonian liberal view of business–government relations). Now they reacted to revelations of alleged oil industry collaboration with the Axis. (Jersey supposedly conspired with I. G. Farben to sabotage Allied efforts to develop synthetic rubber.[42])

Such accusations rekindled the ire of the anti-oil forces. Joining the small business community in fighting the cartel were the Progressives, who were the original trustbusters. They saw the oilmen as innovators and principal promoters of the trust concept. They wanted the anti-trust cases revived and felt that the accusations of collaboration justified this.[43] In addition to charges of collaborating, accusations were made of overcharging the military for oil deliveries and of sales to the Axis (through foreign subsidiaries) while the war was going on.

Arrayed alongside the small proprietors and Progressives were elements of the labor movement. Not all the movement, to be sure—many in labor's ranks mistrusted the Sherman Act, used against them by past administrations.[44] The United Mine Workers (UMW) union, however, saw its relation to oil in zero-sum terms—a gain for the cartel was a loss for it.[45]

Finally, the oil industry itself was divided—the independents harbored great mistrust of the international companies like Jersey, despite the fact of the independents and cartel having just struck a deal.[46] It would appear that the two groups were naturally enemies—no matter how many deals that they might conclude, they did not trust each other.

All of these separate constituencies now aligned against Big Oil, and this produced a rash of federal investigations. The most notable were those of the Anti-Trust Division of the Justice Department, the Federal Trade Commission (FTC), and the Senate's Small Business Committee. The real start of this investigatory surge, however, was the report of the FTC.[47] *The Report to the Federal Trade Commission on the International Petroleum Cartel* drew the greatest attention and formed the underpinning for several investigations of the industry in the postwar years.

The international oil companies viewed the FTC report as quite dangerous, a deadly serious attempt to curtail their power and influence. Government staffers who put together the report amassed volumes of data, going to the heart of the cartel's operations. The report is a monument of investigative reporting.[48]

DETAILS

During Franklin Roosevelt's second term as president, the Anti-Trust Division of the Justice Department was taken over by Thurmond Arnold, a professor at Yale's Law School.[49] Arnold announced his intent of reactivating an arm of government that, after National Recovery Administration (NRA) days, had grown moribund.[50]

Arnold instituted a number of investigations and did for a time succeed in rejuvenating the anti-trust movement; then World War II intervened. To Arnold, the outbreak of the war made the cause of anti-trust only more crucial. In his view, the cartelization of industries impeded America's ability to mobilize for the conflict.[51]

Nonetheless, battle lines formed as the Navy and War Departments argued for discontinuance of trustbusting on grounds that the big firms supplied the "sinews of the war effort."[52] In 1943 Roosevelt created the War Production Board (WPB), with the power to absolve firms from anti-trust action if their services were deemed essential to the national defense.[53]

The appearance of the board sounded the death knell of anti-trust in the United States, and soon afterward Arnold resigned. However, once the war ended, a number of government departments renewed the fight, impelled by a number of factors.

For one, the Swedish government (while the war was going on) instituted a widely publicized investigation in which it determined that the Achnacarry Agreement, presumed to have lapsed, was, in fact, still operative.[54] Also there was the matter, mentioned earlier, of the companies' alleged collaboration with the Axis. Strong anti-trust senators, like Owen Brewster of Maine, insisted that the charges be ventilated.[55]

However, according to Kaufman, the real impetus to reopening the investigation was the appearance of the report on the international oil cartel.[56] The FTC, on its own, had undertaken to investigate cartels in several industries during the war years. Then, in 1949, it decided to turn its attention to oil.[57]

It was out of this that the report came. The FTC investigators used the subpoena powers of the government, which enabled them to acquire never-before-revealed information on cartel activity. It is no exaggeration to say that, had the FTC report never been written, we would have no clear idea of how the cartel operated. Prior to the report's appearance, Tarbell's revelations (in the last century) provided the only insight into the arcane world of oil.

Nor had the FTC drawn the line at investigating U.S. cartel members only. It initially had tried to go after the British and British–Dutch components as well. However, the latter successfully blocked the attempt, and so the commission limited its probe to the American firms.[58]

What is so impressive about this investigation is its breadth—it is a system-wide view of the cartel, commencing with the 1928 Achnacarry Agreement and stretching up to 1952. Indeed, so exhaustive was the fact-finding effort that much information subsequently had to be excised on grounds of national security.[59]

Despite all this, the investigation might never have become public had not the Senate's Small Business Committee chairman, John Sparkman, gotten hold of a copy of the report and, against the wishes of high-ranking officials of the

Truman administration, leaked it to the press and then, on his own, promoted an investigation.[60]

All this transpired immediately after the war, when, as stated, Americans were sympathetic to an attack on Big Business. This shaped up as the greatest essay at trustbusting since the last century. At least that was the feeling when the investigation was launched. In fact, it turned out quite differently. The cartel was able to deflect the attacks. However, to understand how it did, the reader must know something about Iran's attempt to nationalize its oil industry in 1953, because that was the issue that the oilmen exploited to wriggle off the hook, as it were.

IRAN

Near the end of World War II, the Iranians offered Jersey an oil concession that, as soon as Royal Dutch heard about it, led it to request similar treatment. Up to this time, only AIOC had been involved in Iran. The negotiations between the Western oil companies and Iran were sensitive because the concessions proffered were in the north, Russia's sphere.[61]

The Soviets, on learning of the offers, sent a representative to Tehran to demand an oil concession for themselves. It would appear that the Iranians had overreached. Thinking to involve the United States in their affairs, they had offended their powerful northern neighbor.[62]

With Russian troops stationed on Iranian territory, Tehran could not simply brush aside the Soviets' demand. Therefore, it sought to temporize. The then-prime minister Ahmad Qavam-ul-Saltaneh journeyed to Moscow to discuss matters.[63]

The war was fast winding down, and, under the arrangement that the Allies had worked out, all foreign troops were to be out of Iran within six months of its conclusion. As soon as Germany surrendered, Britain pulled out. The United States also withdrew. The Russians, however, stayed on. Thus, the Iranian position was compromised—they had hoped to reject the Russians' request, once the latter withdrew. But, now, since the Russians were not leaving, the Iranians were in a bind.

Then in the far northwestern corner of the country a breakaway movement appeared. Elements in Azerbaijan and, just to the south of that, in Iranian Kurdistan declared independence. The Iranians, in attempting to put down these separatist movements, encountered Soviet troops that refused permission to enter the affected areas.[64]

It appeared that the rebellions (at least the one in Azerbaijan) had been fomented by the Soviets as a way of pressuring the Iranians into granting the oil concession.[65] The Iranians had to succumb; they agreed to a concession but conditioned their acceptance on approval of the *majlis* (parliament), which body would not meet until all foreign forces had left the country.

The reader needs to be aware that the Allies invaded Iran during World War II and deposed the old shah and put his young son, Mohammad Reza, on the throne, after which they opened a corridor to Russia from the Gulf, and over this corridor they ferried supplies to the Soviet army.

The invasion was a blatant violation of Iran's neutrality, and the *majlis*, to protest against it, had dissolved itself, vowing not to reassemble until all foreign troops had left the country. In addition, it voted penalties for any Iranian official who discussed concessions with foreigners without the *majlis*' approval. (The stipulation was set, incidentally, by Mohammad Mosadeq, about whom we have a great deal to say shortly.[66])

The Russians accepted the terms of disengagement by withdrawing, which allowed the *majlis* to reconvene. But, then, the *majlis*, instead of agreeing to the Russians' concession, turned it down.[67]

In the West, this development was greeted with great elation. In the process of fending off the Russians, the Iranians had exploited American fears of a Russian takeover of the country. At the urging of Truman, Tehran had sent a delegation to the United Nations to protest alleged Soviet sponsorship of the movements.[68]

Once Moscow was rebuffed by the *majlis*, Washington and London took this as a clear win for the West. What the two overlooked was that the *majlis*, in rejecting Moscow's bid, passed the so-called Single Article Law, in which it promised to review *all* foreign oil concessions, a shaft aimed at the AIOC.[69]

It is interesting that the Russians accepted the result. They had clearly been outmaneuvered by the Iranians in a way that was somewhat humiliating. However, although they blustered, they did nothing. Elwell-Sutton implies that, in fact, once the Russians saw that they were going to lose, they exacted a promise from the Iranians that they would review the AIOC contract.[70]

What is also interesting about this whole affair is how it played into the Americans' campaign against the Russians. Truman had promulgated his famous Truman Doctrine, the purpose of which was to save Greece and Turkey from communist pressures. The Marshall Plan component of the doctrine had encountered opposition in Congress from representatives who wanted to steer clear of European affairs.

To overcome this resistance, Truman preached a crusade—America (he averred) was taking arms against an alien belief system that threatened the United States, even though it was located far away. Supposedly, the Soviets were aiming to subvert Third World countries on which the United States counted as future trading partners.

Iran fit into the president's strategy. He portrayed the Iranian Communist Party, the so-called Tudeh, as a fifth column set up by the Soviets to bring Iran into the Russian sphere.[71] As a consequence of Truman's maneuver, Iran, which until then had been of no significance to the United States, now came to be seen as the eastern flank of the European–American defense system.

In any event, the British and Americans were wrong to dismiss the review of the AIOC concession. The Iranians were serious about this and looked for only an opportunity to start the process. This came in 1949 with news that the Venezuelans had gotten their 50:50 split. Once this was publicized, agitation for renegotiating began in earnest.[72]

THE 1951 OIL CRISIS

At this point, Britain was ruled by a Labour government, which lacked the confidence of its predecessor, the Conservatives, a situation that arose, in part, from Labour's having been so long out of power. Along with this, the Labourites were attempting to nationalize the commanding heights of Britain's economy. An extraordinarily radical proposal, this earned them numerous enemies, and, of course, this only added to the party's vulnerability.

All in all, Labour, as of 1949 (when the nationalization business got going), was beleaguered and, perhaps for this reason, overly aggressive. It would not give way even on minor points that probably would have been conceded by a more self-assured government.

One point that Labour was absolutely determined to defend was the status of AIOC as Britain's biggest overseas earner. Labour intended that the AIOC should be as profitable as possible, to bring money into the country. In line with this, it taxed the company heavily.

During the war, Britain had enacted an excess profits tax, which it discontinued once the war was over. However, almost immediately afterward the Labour government reinstituted the tax, which substantially increased the government's share of company earnings. In 1948 Iranian royalties from the AIOC came to £9.17 million; tax revenues to the British government were £18.03 million.[73]

When the Iranians learned of this spread, they (as Bamberg says) were strongly aggrieved at the apparent inequity of the figures.[74] The revelation proved doubly noxious, as Iran's share of company profits was deducted *after* British taxes had been paid. Thus, the more that the company gave to Britain, the less Iran had for itself.[75]

There was another inequity, as Iran viewed it. After the war, Britain forbade the payout of dividends to shareholders. It did this to win trade union backing for voluntary wage restraints. Initially, this was merely a suggested policy; however, by 1951 Britain had enacted it into law, when the voluntaristic approach appeared not to be working.

As a condition of Iran's 1933 contract, Tehran received annual dividends on company profits. Iran did not actually pocket the dividends; rather, they were deposited in an escrow account to be paid when the concession had expired. Here, now, Iran was losing out, as immediately after the war the dividend payments were discontinued.[76]

While all this was going on in England, in Iran the economy was in a deplorable state. During the war the country had gone through a terrible inflation and then immediately afterward it experienced a brief, sharp deflation when successive wheat harvests failed.[77] The elements of the population hardest hit by this were the civil servants and peasants.

Thus, starting in 1947, the Iranian leadership, which throughout the war had been docile, began importuning the West (i.e., the United States and Britain) for a new deal. Mohammed Reza Shah, successor to the deposed Reza, found himself in an anomalous position; that is, he was driven to seek succor from the parties responsible for undermining his dynasty.

MOHAMMED REZA SHAH

Prior to the move by Britain, the Soviet Union, and the United States into Iran, the political situation of the country had been stable. The deposed Reza was a tyrant, but an effective one. He had a clear idea of what he wished to accomplish and throughout his career firmly adhered to it. Effectively, the Pahlavi House, under Reza, could look out for itself.

Mohammed Reza did not have the tyrannical disposition of his father. Indeed, his father—whatever ambitions he may have had for his son—handicapped the boy. Mohammed Reza was a stammerer, a condition brought on, according to confidants of the shah, by abject fear of Reza. Evidently, the father was as fierce and demanding of his son as he was of his courtiers.

Then came the war, and without warning the Allies whisked the old shah into exile, leaving Mohammed Reza bereft, having to fend for himself in a hostile environment. Counted among his enemies were the so-called oligarchs, a clique of 1,000 families. Owners of vast estates, the families looked on the Pahlavis as usurpers.[78]

Before the war old Reza had curbed the power of the families, but then, during the war, under the encouragement of the British, the class revived. As they had done in Iraq, the British encouraged the families in order to be able to wield them as a club against the Pahlavis. London wanted security in the southern oil fields and friends in the capital. In the south, the extensive and powerful Qashqai and Bahktiari tribes gave physical protection; in Tehran, the landowning class formed a pro-British bloc.

To be sure, the Shah had an army, but this institution was in need of weapons, for which money had to be found. For the young shah, everything came down to acquiring funds, and, since the British were not helpful in this regard, it was to the Americans that he made his appeal.

The shah put out feelers immediately after the war, exploiting somewhat tenuous ties to the United States.[79] He asked for a loan from the International Bank for Reconstruction and Development (IBRD), and the bank responded by asking for a plan of how the money would be spent. The Iranians brought in an American consulting firm, headed by Max Thornburgh (the same whom we met in the last chapter). Thornburgh produced the so-called Seven-Year Plan, which would have cost $650 million.[80]

The plan envisioned the modernization of the country, as expected. However, important segments of Iranian society did not want to see the country modernize; in particular, this was the case with the Shia clergy and the *bazaaris* (Tehran merchant class).

Among Middle Eastern religious groups, the Shia clergy are probably the most impatient of temporal authority.[81] Their relations with the Pahlavi House were always strained, and, as traditionalists, they viewed with misgiving any attempt to modernize. Once the Seven-Year Plan became known, the clerics doubled their opposition to the palace.

The *bazaaris* also disapproved of the plan, inasmuch as it bolstered industry and encouraged exports, measures that the *bazaaris* felt would harm their interests. The *bazaaris* were then, and remain today, a powerful force in Tehran and hence in Iranian politics. In addition, they were longtime allies of the clerics, and so it was natural for these two forces to team up.

Thus, the shah's money-raising attempts, while certainly justifiable—given the deplorable economic condition of Iran—put the palace on a collision course not only with nationalist elements (suspicious of any opening to the West) but with the traditionalists as well.

Immediately, however, the nationalists gave trouble. Prime Minister Qavam told the British ambassador that national sentiment was enflamed against the AIOC and, therefore, that Tehran would have to move ahead with the Single Article law; that is, it would have to review the AIOC concession.[82]

The prime minister claimed that this would be a perfunctory business, about which the company need not be alarmed. Iran knew, said Qavam, how much it owed to the company and would do nothing to harm it. That seemed reassuring.[83]

The British were thus prepared when, on December 1, 1947, Qavam—in an intensely nationalistic address delivered nationwide over the radio—claimed that the AIOC's concession would have to be reexamined.[84] Almost immediately, however, they were shocked to learn that Qavam had fallen from power, to be replaced by a virtual nonentity. Coincidentally, Tudeh Party cadres took to the streets of Tehran to agitate for the review.

Britain canvassed a number of politicians friendly to it, and all cautioned against underestimating the depth of feeling on this issue. Iranians know, said the sources, that Venezuela was getting a much better deal than Iran; the concession would have to be modified.[85]

THE NEGOTIATIONS BEGIN

In August 1948 the AIOC sent a delegation to Tehran to discuss Iranian concerns. This produced a revised contract, the so-called Supplemental Agreement. The agreement was handed to the Iranian government in April 1949 in Tehran by the AIOC president, Sir William Fraser. It stipulated that, instead of accumulating dividend payments in a lump sum to be released to Iran at the contract's expiration, the funds could now be turned over annually. This, Fraser explained to the Iranian officials, should satisfy the shah's need for cash.[86]

The revision to the contract was made possible because the British government gave way on certain contested points, such as its refusal to sanction the payout of dividends. Even so, the company's offer was hardly munificent. The Iranians had been expecting a 50:50 split, and the company had not budged an inch on that.

However disappointed the Iranians may have been, they agreed to go along. However, they wanted the company to guarantee that the yearly handover would not fall below a specified amount. Iran remembered its 1933 embarrassment, when a sharp, unexpected fall in royalty payments sank the government's Five-Year Plan.[87]

Fraser complained that the market, not the company, would determine the dividend; still he agreed to the Iranians' appeal. The Supplemental Agreement was signed. In addition to the terms discussed, it raised the royalty from 4s to 6s per ton, retroactive to 1948. The Iranians assured the British that, with these revisions, early ratification of the agreement by the *majlis* could be expected. That, as it turned out, was too optimistic an assessment.

RISE OF NATIONALISM

A lot of forces converged in 1949, the year the Supplemental Agreement was sent to the *majlis*. We first look at the fate of the IBRD loan. The shah embarked on his visit to the United States in October 1949 and did not attempt to disguise that he was going to Washington to solicit alms. He failed. After spending several months in America and interviewing Truman and other leaders, the shah returned home empty-handed.

He appears to have been operating on misinformation. He went to America believing that Washington, caught up in the Cold War, would support Iran, a country that the Americans called a bastion of the free world under siege by the communists.

This was true. The Americans did look on Iran as embattled, but they also felt that the shah was corrupt. After having "lost" China, the Americans were sensitive about whom it backed. Quite a number of Americans attributed China's "fall" to the moral dereliction of Chiang Kai-shek and felt that Washington ought never to get involved with "grafters."[88]

Following this high-profile visit, the shah returned to an aroused public, filled with hatred of the West in general and the United States in particular. The resentment crystallized into a political movement. Before the shah had left for the United States, he confronted a demonstration in Tehran led by Mosadeq (the same who had led the fight against granting foreigners oil concessions). The nationalist leader protested against attempts by the palace to rig elections to the 16th *majlis*.[89]

Mosadeq led a crowd of some 2,500 protestors on a peaceful march through the city to the palace, where a small group of the protestors participated in a *bast* (roughly translated, a sit-in) on the palace grounds. Because the shah was about to embark for the United States (and did not want unfavorable publicity to proceed him there), he ordered the palace to keep hands off the poll. The elections were held; they were relatively honest, and, of the deputies elected, eight were from Mosadeq's group, christened the National Front.[90]

Another complicating factor was Britain's decision in September 1949 to devalue the pound. The British had been hoping that the palace could get the Supplemental Agreement through the *majlis* before this was done. First Qavam had stalled; then his government fell. A new, ineffective government did nothing. In the fall of 1949, when the new *majlis* convened, the Supplemental Agreement still had not been approved; only now—with the pound devalued—it was not the same agreement that originally had been concluded.[91]

The Iranians asked the company if it would compensate for shortfalls, and the company said no. To give the AIOC managers credit, they did approach the British government with a request that remedial action be taken. However, the British chancellor of the Exchequer, Sir Stafford Cripps, refused. According to Bamberg, even the Foreign Office weighed in, asking that something be done. The Exchequer was adamant. The Labour government did not feel that it could stand the expense.[92]

This handed Mosadeq's fledgling "party" a made-to-order issue. There was yet another variable that influenced events. A new American ambassador had arrived from India. Henry Grady had the reputation of being an activist, and his appearance in Iran met with widespread approbation by those who saw this as a sign of American sympathy to the country's nationalism efforts.

Grady was well disposed toward the Iranians, particularly toward Mosadeq, with whom he felt the Americans could work. He looked on Mosadeq as a gentleman of the old school, as someone who was not obviously corrupt. Further, he admired Mosadeq's charisma (witness the outpourings of popular support), and he was especially pleased to find that Mosadeq was an inveterate foe of the Tudeh. Last but not least, Mosadeq was no friend of the shah, about whom, as we said, Washington had misgivings.[93]

Thus, the Iranians seemed to have an important American on their side (in the fight that was developing with the British). Indeed, they had another friend in Washington—George McGhee, the assistant secretary for Near Eastern affairs of the State Department.[94] McGhee had been following the buildup of nationalist sentiment in the country, and, as with many other Americans, he feared to see the country "go communist." McGhee urged the British to give way on the 50:50 deal. At a January 1950 meeting with McGhee in Washington, company officials insisted that, to make concessions would "beggar" them. McGhee, an oilman, pointed out that ARAMCO had recovered its total investment in Saudi Arabia after only five years of operation. AIOC had been operating in Iran for 40 years, with production costs under 10 cents a barrel and a sales price between one dollar and three dollars.[95]

Because the British—both the government and company—would not give way, the stage was set for a showdown. This came at the end of 1950. Mosadeq had gotten himself appointed to the newly created Oil Committee of the *majlis*, which was to undertake the preliminary review of the concession. Four of Mosadeq's National Front colleagues also had gained places on the committee, making it a bastion of anti-AIOC sentiment.[96]

In mid-June 1950 Mosadeq proposed what eventually came to be Iran's nationalization law. In his presentation to the *majlis*, he made reference to his personal philosophy of "negative equilibrium." Iran (he felt) should steer clear of entanglements with either Russia or the West. In the past, Iran's approach had been to balance one empire off against another—now appeasing Russia, now Britain.[97]

Mosadeq argued this had brought Iran nothing but grief and that in the future it should avoid entanglements with either. As for Iran's precious oil, the country should develop that itself. In other words, Mosadeq was proposing that Iran embark upon a course of economic nationalism.

The utility of Mosadeq's approach was marked. In Tehran at the time, many elements opposed Britain but differed among themselves on unrelated issues. Mosadeq's negative equilibrium line was broad enough to attract many shades of opinion.

Indeed, Mosadeq made significant inroads to the traditionalist camp when he enrolled the Society of Muslim Warriors into his National Front. This was led by Ayatollah Abol-Qassem Kashani, a bitter foe of the British (they killed his father in Iraq in 1941). Kashani's shock troops had already assassinated several Iranian personalities. Besides giving the Front muscle, the warriors enabled Front leaders (who mostly were affluent cosmopolitans) to mobilize the mob. Kashani was a skilled street orator, and ultimately much of the Front's political clout came from whipping up crowd sentiment in Tehran's broad *maidans* (squares).[98]

Thus, there were Mosadeq, strategically placed on the Oil Committee; several politicians inside the *majlis* who could translate Mosadeq's committee moves into legislation; several journalists whose papers played up Front actions; and now Kashani to whip up crowd sentiment. This last was extremely useful for intimidating *majlis* deputies into supporting Front initiatives.

The British response to this friction (as they called it), was to counsel the shah to appoint a strongman, General Ali Razmara, as the next prime minister and let him shepherd the Supplemental Agreement through. The shah balked, in part because he saw Razmara as a rival.[99]

Razmara had distinguished himself in Western eyes by recovering Azerbaijan from the breakaway republic. He was a national hero. Under importuning by the British and Americans, the shah gave in and called Razmara to be prime minister.

Razmara took over on June 26, 1950, and began to work for passage of the Supplemental Agreement. He went so far as to argue in the *majlis* against nationalization, claiming that it was beyond the capabilities of the Iranians to run such a complex industry as oil.[100]

Ultimately, Razmara's efforts were doomed. On December 30, 1950, the Saudis (following up on the Venezuelans' breakthrough) got their own 50:50 split from ARAMCO. Four days before this revelation, Razmara (perhaps having been tipped to the announcement) had withdrawn the agreement from the *majlis*.[101]

When news of the Saudi coup was announced, as might have been anticipated, a storm erupted. Xenophobes now had something substantial on which to vent their resentment. On March 7, 1951, Razmara was assassinated while on his way to the mosque by a follower of Kashani.[102]

The *majlis* then elected, and the shah appointed, Hossein Ala, but he turned out to be (as so often was the case with Iran) a nonentity, and the contract once more hung fire. Meanwhile, in the *majlis*, Mosadeq spoke in favor of nationalization, and shortly after that the proposal was voted by a badly intimidated *majlis* (in the meantime there had been another assassination).[103]

On April 28, 1951—since no one wanted the prime ministership—Mosadeq's name was proposed, and he accepted; the shah (with great misgivings) agreed to the appointment. Mosadeq had gone from being a lone voice protesting palace corruption, to deputy in the *majlis*, to leader of the nationalization fight, and finally to prime minister. He now had the power of the state at his command, since at this stage of Iran's political development real power resided in the *majlis*; the shah was only Iran's titular head.

LONDON TAKES CHARGE

Once nationalization was voted, the British government dug in its heels, so to speak. It took the negotiations away from the company. This was done openly, with no pretense. The matter was viewed as one of national security.[104] The government's first action was to bring the matter up before the World Court. Iran denied that the court had jurisdiction "in a commercial dispute."

In mid-May came the American reaction to the nationalization. According to Bamberg, representatives of major U.S. oil companies, who up to now had been silent, met with McGhee of the State Department to register their unequivocal opposition to this latest development. They called it "concession jumping." Following this, on May 18, the State Department issued a statement expressing its belief that nationalization was not in the best interests of Iran and warning that Americans would not be permitted to replace the British field-workers.

The Iranians were understandably put off by this. They had assumed that America was an ally. Nonetheless, Grady reassured them of America's continued goodwill. At this stage Washington seems to have been fence-sitting. It wanted to be sympathetic toward Iran because, as stated earlier, it feared a communist takeover. But the intervention of the oil magnates obviously had complicated things.[105]

Once nationalization was voted, the Iranians immediately set about taking charge of what they now considered their property (e.g., they lost no time changing the company's name from AIOC to National Iranian Oil Company [NIOC]). The Tehran government sent a delegation to the fields to inventory assets and to attempt to hire the field managers (Europeans and Americans) away from the company. All refused the offer.[106]

The Iranians then presented the works manager with receipts for tanker captains to sign stating their cargoes were from the NIOC (not the AIOC), and—as might have been expected—the manager refused to go along. At that, the Iranian government passed a so-called sabotage bill, decreeing the death penalty for anyone who interfered with the operation of the works.[107] This was immediately interpreted, both in Britain and in the United States, as provocative, a step toward violence.

In the British House of Commons Members of Parliament (MPs) voted to send the fleet to the Gulf. Britain also contemplated deploying its sole paratroop unit to Cyprus. This proposal greatly alarmed the Americans. The State Department cautioned that an attempt to introduce military units could trigger a corresponding move by the Russians (under the provisions of the 1921 Russo–Iranian Friendship Treaty).[108]

The British pulled back and contented themselves with ordering personnel from the fields to relocate to Basrah in Iraq. They also announced publicly that they considered the oil to be company property and would move to block any effort by the Iranians to sell it on the open market.[109]

Having averted an explosion, the Americans called a conference with the British in which they asked their allies to adopt a pose of conciliation. As in all interactions with the British, the Americans took the line that Iran must not fall to communism, which certainly would be the result (they said), unless the affair was composed.

The British were unimpressed; recriminations followed. The Americans complained that, at the very least, Britain should have offered 50:50. The British countered, saying, in effect, that this was all very well for the Americans; 50:50 had not hurt them; they had the economic means to withstand it.

This was a reference to America's unique tax setup. In the case of Venezuela and Saudi Arabia, the American oil companies had shifted the burden of 50:50 to their government because under American tax laws revenue that ordinarily would have gone to Washington could be diverted to the oil producers.

Britain needed all of the tax revenue it could get; otherwise it would never climb out of the economic slough into which it had fallen. In order for Britain to have granted 50:50, it would have had to find a revenue source elsewhere, and there was no elsewhere.

The Americans may not have liked the line that the British took, but they must have seen its logic. Washington was now in a predicament similar to the sterling controversy. In terms of national interest, Britain was behaving rationally. In system terms, however, the issue was not nearly so clear-cut.

As for the cartel, it was hard to say where it stood. The American oilmen had spoken out against the takeover. But, at the same time, ARAMCO looked to benefit from it. As stated earlier, the company had a lot of oil to market, newly produced in Saudi Arabia. With Iran in turmoil and soon to be shut down, ARAMCO could look forward to taking up the slack. Nor need it worry about harming a fellow cartel member, AIOC. As pointed out in the last chapter, Jersey—when it went into ARAMCO—agreed to buy large consignments of oil from AIOC for a number of years. It also knew (because the cartel shared information) that Royal Dutch and AIOC had an arrangement to cooperate in marketing oil in the Far East.

Still, there was a principle involved. Nationalization was an unambiguous threat to the system. The cartel had survived 50:50, but nationalization was far more dangerous; it was the ne plus ultra of threats.

In July 1951 Secretary of State Dean Acheson induced President Truman to send an American delegation to Tehran to try to arbitrate between the British and Iranians. The British opposed the move, claiming it was "meddling"; it only dragged the matter out, as it fostered delusions on the Iranians' part.[110]

For their part, the Americans argued that the situation was too serious to let ride. Violence had begun to escalate in the oil fields; there were several more assassinations in the capital, and the Tudeh Party—a particular concern of the Americans—was visible on the scene. Therefore, Acheson felt that America must act and he picked to head the delegation Averell Harriman.

THE HARRIMAN MISSION

Harriman was not an oilman, nor technically was he an official of Truman's administration. He was highly placed in Democratic Party circles, having served Roosevelt during World War II as, among other things, ambassador to Moscow and to London. Harriman took with him Walter Levy, onetime petroleum adviser to the State Department. Levy's participation was essential because, as McGhee said, much of the delegates' time in Tehran was spent explaining "the facts of life about oil to Mosadeq."[111]

The hope on the Americans' part was that Mosadeq could be brought around to Washington's view and that he would then be amenable to selling that position to his people. Washington thought some cosmetic solution would do for Iran. Specifically, it foresaw the formation of a management group that would buy oil from Iran and sell it on the international market. Aware of Iran's antipathy toward AIOC, the Americans intended it to play no part in the planned consortium.

Harriman's mission was something of a head-hunting operation, Mosadeq being the candidate for co-optation. Whether the effort succeeded would depend on the Iranian and on how he handled himself in interviews that the Americans would conduct.

Harriman and Levy meant to straight-talk him, passing insider information about how the system worked. This was quite something. Those who were of the system usually kept shut about it; in their view, it was no one's business how it worked. There was a risk here, but evidently Harriman and Levy had taken it into account, or maybe they just saw no other way.

Harriman and Levy spent several sessions with Mosadeq, in which they explained about the cartel and, in particular, about its marketing arrangements. They explained why the Iranians must not seek to interfere in this aspect of the business. Mosadeq wanted to market Iran's oil, setting a price based on the country's requirements conditioned by what the market would bear.[112]

This was the main point that Harriman and Levy tried to get across—*there was no such thing as a market price in oil.* The cartel members set the price themselves, taking into account factors of importance to them, such as how to get the best deal on taxes. The prices, *the actual prices*, the Americans explained, were *arbitrary*, something that the cartel members worked up and then agreed to abide by.[113]

After all the talk, Mosadeq dismissed the Americans' explanations. He would not give in on his key point, that he must be able to handle marketing, and it must be he who set prices. This, the Americans told him, was against the economics of the system. Economics, said Mosadeq, is nothing; what counts is politics.[114]

Well, there you had it—Mosadeq (the Americans were forced to conclude) was hopeless. They had tried. In the end, the old man had stood up for his principles—he was, it seemed, not just a nationalist but something much worse, an autarch. Neither the Americans nor the British were prepared to countenance such a one as that.

Harriman returned to the United States. On his way back he stopped over in London, where he conveyed his frustration to the British. At the same time, he and Levy also vented their irritation about London's behavior. Levy, in a session with the British Cabinet, told them to forget any idea that they might have about the company's returning to Iran. The level of Iranian hatred was intense, said Levy. The best that the British could hope for was a consortium arrangement along the lines that the Americans were proposing. Britain might have a part in that, but only if it behaved more accommodatingly.[115]

The British were impatient of the Americans' admonitions, which they could not dismiss out of hand. The British knew that, were the Iranians to be brought around (to some sort of acceptable compromise), they would have to be bought off, and only the Americans were in a position to do that. This being the case, why were the British not compelled to give in to Washington's demands?

The British had a fallback position. Whereas the Americans feared the breakup of Iran—which would have opened the five northern provinces to the

Soviets, the British were not at all upset by this prospect. After all, had they not struck just such a deal with the old Russian empire in 1907 and lived with it for a number of years?[116] As long as the oil fields were secure, and they could move their oil to market, the fate of Iran territorially was of little concern to them.

Well, then, why could not the Americans have gone along with a carve-up? As long as the British controlled the southern oil regions, what was the problem with Iran's being dismembered? The Soviets would get the northern portion, but what would that entail? An entity too weak to constitute a state.

This is where the Americans' secret agenda came in. They wanted to see the breakup of old empires—British as well as Russian. They wanted that for economic reasons. A unified Iran with an effective nationalist government at its head could become America's trading partner. A *divided* Iran, with no one to keep it stabilized, was of no value as far as the business-minded Americans were concerned.

The Americans also had a geopolitical reason to reject partitioning. They were now involved in a war in Korea, which had developed out of a similar arrangement. North Korea had invaded South Korea. The United States could really not be sanguine about these north–south setups.

So, then, as of 1951 the Americans and British were at odds as to how to handle Iran. What is ironic is that America and the Soviet Union wanted the same thing. Unless one takes the position that Moscow sought to absorb Iran entirely (which the record will not support), Moscow wanted a unified Iran—as a buffer against Western advances north to Baku, the Russians' oil region.

THE END OF THE AFFAIR

We have now progressed to the year 1951, and events, after this, move fast. The British, under prodding by the Americans, agreed to send a delegation of their own to Tehran. Lord Richard Stokes, the privy seal, met with Mosadeq, but neither gave way. The British had by this time made it known that 50:50 was acceptable to them. But 50:50 was no longer of interest to the Iranians, now that nationalization had been decreed.

The British had also agreed, partially, to America's idea of a management company—however, under their interpretation, this new entity would have to be totally owned by AIOC.[117] The Iranians saw through this, refusing even to consider Britain's position. Consequently, the Stokes mission withdrew, and the British moved on another track to force the issue. They announced that they were taking the dispute to the United Nations.

As they had done previously (when Britain took the matter to the World Court), the Iranians rejected the United Nations' right to intervene in what the Iranians claimed was an internal affair. Nonetheless, Mosadeq subsequently announced that he would travel to New York to make Iran's case before the world body.

Mosadeq was always something of a showman, with a good dramatic flare. Coincidentally, television was just becoming popular in the United States, and the old man made a great impression on American audiences. His histrionics were widely appreciated. So popular was he that *Time Magazine* chose him "Man of the Year."[118]

In Washington Acheson and other top officials met with Mosadeq and tried to talk him into accepting the consortium arrangement.[119] Iran was by this time beginning to feel the economic pinch. Iran wanted aid from Washington, which the latter was willing to consider, provided Iran agreed to compromise. Mosadeq seemed to give way on a number of issues. However, in the end problems arose over the question of price. It came down to the following.

The oilmen were asking Mosadeq to accept $1.10 a barrel; Mosadeq wanted $1.75, based on the fact that this was the price that the cartel charged when it sold oil that it received from the producer. But the oilmen countered that $1.10 was the price that they *paid* the producers.

Mosadeq countered that if he accepted $1.10 with a 50:50 split, as was demanded, he would net only $0.65 a barrel.[120] Now that he had nationalized, there had to be more payoff than that.

The American side rebutted that argument by saying that if they allowed NIOC to take $1.75, then all of the other native producers would nationalize, and that would break the cartel. So, in the end, one could say that what set the two sides apart was whether the nationalization would stand.

The Americans evidently believed that Mosadeq could accept 50:50 (which he could have gotten back in the beginning, when the crisis started) and sell that to his people. This was either willfully imperceptive on the Americans' part or just plain dumb.

It underestimated the perspicacity of the Iranian people, who had been following the crisis in all of its ramifications for over three years now. If Mosadeq even attempted to do what the Americans were urging, he most certainly would have been shot.

Effectively, nationalization was doomed. Once Mosadeq opted for it, and the *majlis* passed it, Iran and the companies were on a collision course. All the negotiations back and forth and the interventions by the United States were merely attempts to avoid the inevitable.

The companies would not allow Mosadeq to interfere with the pricing mechanism. They were bound to take whatever measures necessary to balk him in this regard. Inevitably, that meant that the companies must be prepared to use force; the gloves would have to come off.

After Acheson's talks with Mosadeq, the State Department evidently believed that it had brought Mosadeq around. Acheson told the British that he "thought" the Iranian would go for $1.10.

This was delusive, the British believed. A company official declared that the point was not whether Acheson *thought* he had a deal. Did he, or didn't he?

For the future of the cartel and for Britain's ability to go on extracting needed revenue from the company, this fact must be ascertained with definiteness.[121]

FIXING IT WITH THE CARTEL

Acheson, on his own, approached the American cartel members with the proposal that they collectively organize worldwide deliveries of oil. His reasons for doing so were the following.

The Korean War was being fought, and this raised energy demands worldwide; it certainly made continued availability of oil vital to the Americans. Along with this, the United States did not want price rises occurring because of shortages. Recall, the Marshall Plan had encouraged switching from coal to oil by the Europeans. As energy prices crept upward, the poorer European nations were hard hit; thus, the aim of the plan was undermined—to fight communism by improving the economies of free world countries. With this in mind, the Americans wanted the cartel "to restore equilibrium" by pumping extra oil to make up the growing shortfall.[122]

Two things about this move on State's part. First, it amounted to de facto admission by the U.S. government of the cartel's control over world oil distribution. The cartel companies mainly were being asked to undertake the relief mission. Acheson's proposal violated U.S. anti-trust laws.[123]

Now we come to the cartel's real coup, the clever manner in which it finessed the anti-trust action. As alluded to earlier, the Congress and the Justice Department were conducting separate investigations of the international oil industry. This was spurred on, we said, by the sensational FTC report.

When Justice learned that State was proposing that the companies take over regulation of the international oil trade, it immediately objected. Justice Department attorneys argued that it made no sense for one arm of the U.S. government to be inviting the oil companies to undertake actions for which another arm was preparing to indict them.

Acheson may have seen the sense of this, but he did not back down. Indeed, he enlisted support from elements of the Defense establishment—the army, navy, and Central Intelligence Agency (CIA). All averred that, for national security reasons, any attempt to block Acheson's scheme was ill advised.

This put the matter squarely into Truman's hands. The president earlier had gone along with a Justice Department initiative of empaneling a grand jury to hear charges against the companies. In agreeing to this, the government was setting the oilmen up for criminal indictments.

Truman went along with Justice's plan, in part, because he had no love for Big Oil. In his youth, he had tried and had failed as a wildcatter, and this seems to have predisposed him against the large, integrated oil companies.

At the same time, however, Truman was a politician who knew the power of the companies. Engler says that it is unlikely that he would have countenanced

Justice's plan had not Senator Sparkman released a copy of the aforementioned FTC report. Effectively, in deciding to go along, Truman was responding to the furor that the release occasioned.[124]

Ultimately, Truman caved in to Acheson's appeal. Irrespective of any implications that this might have had for the Justice Department's case, it certainly wrecked the Iranians' chances of surviving the British-imposed embargo.

Tehran reacted with fury, accusing the Americans of "stabbing them in the back," which, practically speaking, is what had been done. The only recourse now for Mosadeq was to tell his people to tighten their belts, because from here on there was scant hope of settling the issue painlessly.

The Iranians had been having terrible luck trying to sell their oil, a tribute to the power of the cartel, which—despite the tempting rebates—refused to buy. It was also due to U.S. government intervention—State blocked several attempts by American independents to take the oil.[125]

Eventually, the Italians broke the embargo. They took delivery of a tankerload of oil in mid-February 1952 and then proceeded to sail for home with it. However, the tanker, the *Rose Mary*, got only as far as Yemen, where British frigates forced it into port. Since Yemen was a British colony, it was an easy matter for a British judge to impound the cargo.[126]

Activity such as this kept the embargo functioning, and consequently by 1953, the crisis appeared stalemated. Below the surface, however, some currents were stirring. In fact, the situation in Iran was deteriorating because of developments on a number of fronts.

In February 1952 Britain and Iran broke diplomatic relations. Following that, Britain froze Iran's sterling balances. It then refused to permit essential supplies to be exported to Iran, thus cutting off shipments of such commodities as sugar and steel.[127]

One would have expected Iran to succumb quickly to such rough handling. Perhaps because the country had always been poor, the people could stand it. However, it was not "the people" that Mosadeq had to be concerned about; it was the country's elite. Here, quite large cracks had begun to appear in the solid front of Iran's anti-British opposition. The "families" were unhappy, as were elements of the armed forces.

In anticipation of moves to unseat him, Mosadeq in July 1952 demanded that, in addition to being prime minister, he must also be made minister of defense. The shah would have none of that; he had always retained the portfolio of commander in chief. Were Mosadeq to take over the army, he might purge it of shah supporters. When the shah refused Mosadeq's demand, the old man resigned.[128]

The British were ecstatic. They viewed this as the opening for which they were looking. They would now seek to influence the choice of Mosadeq's successor. The shah eventually chose the aging Qavam ul Sultanah, but as soon as the choice was announced, huge protests broke out in Tehran. The shah had to withdraw the offer and ask Mosadeq to serve both as prime minister and as defense minister.[129]

It appeared that Mosadeq had scored a clear win. Actually, though, his position was compromised. Ayatollah Kashani, always a wild card in the Iranian political equation, unexpectedly distanced himself from Mosadeq. Kashani maintained that, by taking over the Defense Ministry, the prime minister had grown too powerful. As a Shia cleric who despised temporal authority, Kashani could not countenance Mosadeq's aggrandizing himself to this extent. With Kashani's estrangement the climate in Tehran changed, for now Mosadeq had Kashani's commandos to fear.[130]

DOWN TO THE WIRE

While these events transpired in Tehran, Britain worked to forge a joint U.S.–British stand on the crisis. London moved closer to Washington's position. Where the two continued to part company was over the composition of the consortium to exploit Iran's oil. The Americans wanted only token AIOC representation on the body (and that heavily disguised); this was not acceptable to the company (although some within the British government seemed to be leaning toward this as a solution).[131]

Company chairman, Sir William Fraser, was particularly hard-nosed. He accused the Americans of being ready to sacrifice the company for peace. Actually, Fraser and the AIOC board were a large part of Britain's problem—at least as far as the Americans were concerned. Americans who had held discussions with AIOC's board almost to a man regarded Fraser and his colleagues as antediluvian. Truman was particularly outspoken in his criticism, labeling the board a "bunch of imperialists."[132]

Thus, Truman's defeat in the 1952 elections worked in favor of the British. Coincidentally, the Labour Party, too, lost out at the polls. Now the planets were in line for a major policy shift. Churchill, the new prime minister, was determined to take a more aggressive approach to the crisis. During the height of the affair (while he was yet out of office) the Conservative leader had complained that the whole business could have been settled by "a sputter of musketry."[133]

In Washington the new Eisenhower government, too, was indisposed to indulge the Iranians. With men like Charles Wilson (the former chief executive officer [CEO] of General Electric) prominent in the cabinet, this was a much more pro-business administration.

THE PLOT

As far back as 1950 the British had been formulating plots to forcibly overthrow Mosadeq. Now, as the Republicans came to power in Washington, British intelligence approached the CIA's new director, Alan Dulles. Dulles showed interest in British proposals to forcibly remove Mosadeq; however, he counseled patience. The Republicans had to wait until the lame-duck Truman had departed.[134]

The man whom the Americans eventually settled upon to orchestrate the coup was Kermit Roosevelt, grandson of the late president Theodore Roosevelt. Roosevelt went to Tehran in March 1953 to scout the territory. The American found the country dangerously unstable. Earlier that same month, Kashani's toughs had marched on Mosadeq's home, thinking to surprise him (and, one must assume, kill him, had they succeeded).[135]

That had triggered a counterrevolt by National Front supporters, with assistance from the Tudeh. Fierce street clashes had developed, at the end of which Mosadeq was back in control, although not as securely as before.

Roosevelt actually made two attempts to bring Mosadeq down. The first, which occurred on August 15, 1953, succeeded only in humiliating the shah. When the National Front forces rallied against CIA-hired toughs, the shah fled the country, first to Baghdad, then on to Rome. At this point, according to Elm, Washington was set to abandon coup plotting and instead make another try to work with Mosadeq. Roosevelt, however, was not so easily put off.[136]

On August 19 he tried again and this time succeeded, after the CIA had suborned elements of the Iranian army. General Fazlollah Zahadi took over in the capital at 3 A.M., suppressed National Front supporters who attempted to rally to Mosadeq's side, and then put the prime minister under arrest.[137] That was that; the nationalization crisis was over.

THE CONSORTIUM

Immediately after the coup, a number of things happened. For one, the United States extended financial aid to Zahadi—$85 million of mutual security and technical assistance program funds in 1954, $76 million in 1955, and $73 million in 1956. In the first year $1.7 million of these funds was for bonuses to the Iranian army, gendarmerie, and police. This was to tide the new regime over and allow it to pay its troops and anyone else whose loyalty was deemed essential to maintain.[138]

The problem was that, among Iranian rank and file, considerable sentiment remained for the nationalization, and, even though he was imprisoned (and subsequently to be put on trial for his life), Mosadeq, too, retained popular support. So Zahadi and the Western powers had to move cautiously, lest they trigger an outburst by partisanship toward the defunct regime.

As for the Tudeh, which had come out into the streets in support of Mosadeq (but had done so belatedly and so had had little effect), it immediately was purged by the army. Its members were rounded up and thrown into jail. Trials of the leaders were set, and several were ultimately to face the death penalty.[139]

Meanwhile, Zahadi and the shah (the shah wholeheartedly supported Zahadi throughout all of this) had to make a start at dismantling the nationalization.

For that, foreign support was needed. In Washington, Eisenhower tapped Herbert Hoover Jr., son of the former president, who had his own oil consultancy business. He sent him to Iran to see what could be done toward putting matters to rights.[140]

In October 1953 Hoover began a kind of shuttle diplomacy between Tehran and London, trying to work out a settlement that both Iran and the British could accept. The British were quite revived by what had happened. No longer were they dogs in the manger, sullen, peevish, feeling despised and unjustly treated. Now (and this particularly was the case with Fraser), they were cocks of the walk. Their tactics had paid off. They had not given way to the Americans—McGhee and Acheson and the rest; they had not surrendered to the Iranians. Mosadeq was in jail, and the shah was set to make a deal. The British intended to get as much of their own back as possible.

Hoover, who had never been a partisan of the British, tried to disabuse them of their misconceptions. The British could not go into Iran—not officially—because the countries had severed relations. Whatever reports of conditions inside the country that they got came from Hoover. He told them that the Iranians were as antagonistic as ever. Were the AIOC to go back into Iran, there would be renewed violence. The best that the British could expect was to return as part of a consortium, in which there might be some British representation (Royal Dutch, maybe), but not AIOC.[141]

So the battle lines formed—Fraser of the AIOC disputing Hoover, the American emmisary, on practically every point and the Iranians looking to the Americans to be their defense. Previously, the British Foreign Office had been set to abandon AIOC; that, however, was under Labour. Now with the Conservatives back in office, the government was determined to keep the company in Iran. However, first the British had to get physically into the country. On December 5 (much to Whitehall's relief) Iran agreed to restore diplomatic relations, and the British went back—to ascertain for themselves that, indeed, the attitude of the Iranians toward the AIOC was hostile.[142]

Fraser disparaged the reports of British officials on the scene, insisting that an AIOC representative be sent to see for himself. Ultimately this was done, but, in the meantime, Eden convinced Fraser that he should begin planning for the consortium takeover. With much ill will, Fraser sent letters to the CEOs of the cartel companies, including the French company Compagnie Francaise des Petroles (CFP), summoning them to a meeting to be held in London at Britannic House (AIOC's London headquarters).[143]

Jersey was represented by its chief, Orville Harden; Royal Dutch by John Loudon. Winthrop Aldrich, U.S. ambassador to London, called it "the largest and most influential group of private companies ever gathered together." The meeting did not accomplish a great deal, primarily because Fraser persisted in remaining difficult. He laid out the company's proposed settlement, which the Americans thought unrealistic.

AIOC wanted to be restored to its former position in Iran. If this was impossible, it should have the largest share of a consortium. Fraser also wanted compensation from the Iranian government as well as payment from the other participants in a consortium, who would, in effect, be buying their shares from the company.[144]

The Americans pointed out to Fraser that they were at Britannic House at the insistence of their government. In the interim—since AIOC had been kicked out of Iran—they had on their own succeeded in eliminating shortfalls in world oil supplies; they had rerouted transport routes; logistics problems had been overcome. Supplies were holding up well (indeed, there was likely an oversupply). If AIOC did not behave reasonably, the Americans would go home.[145]

The Americans' attitude seems disingenuous. These gentlemen, after all, wore two hats—on the one hand they were representatives of their government (as they said), but they also were in the cartel together (AIOC included). As cartel members, they would not wish to see Iran become a vacuum into which the independent oilmen would rush, making whatever deals that they could and generally upsetting the cartel's pricing system.

Ultimately, the trans-Atlantic shuttle by Hoover resumed, and after further delay an agreement was reached on terms that proved satisfactory to all parties. The high points were that AIOC would take 40 percent of the consortium; Royal Dutch, 14; each of the five U.S. companies, 8; and CFP, 6. (Later each of the five U.S. companies gave up one-eighth of a share so that nine smaller U.S. companies [called Iricon] could be included—this was done to appease the antitrust forces in the United States.)

As to the matter of Iranian compensation, this would be conceded, but at a much lower figure than AIOC had demanded. Fraser expressed himself as greatly disappointed. In fact, the British were made to give way on compensation only after John Foster Dulles, the new American secretary of state, threatened to "rethink" Anglo–American solidarity in Middle Eastern affairs. As Bamberg said, the company by its tactics had brought British–American relations to the brink of disaster.[146]

Iran, for its part, had to accept 50:50, something that it could have gotten all along but that Mosadeq consistently had rejected. It was quite a defeat for them. According to Elm, under the original concession, Iran could claim 20 percent of AIOC's worldwide profits; it lost that in the consortium deal.[147]

The big victor, however, was the cartel, since it kept control over price and marketing. Iran was totally excluded from having anything to do with either of these. The cartel's grip over the industry worldwide remained intact.

The Americans—government and oil company executives—were pleased. Dulles praised Hoover for his remarkable contribution.

The British government positively crowed. In Parliament, R. A. Butler, chancellor of the Exchequer, pointed out that the government's shares in AIOC, for which it had paid £5 million (back in the early 1900s), were now worth over £233 million, following the run-up in prices once the consortium deal was announced.[148]

WHY?

Two aspects of this affair are worth commenting upon. It is important to be aware that the United States never admitted that it had staged a coup. In Washington and abroad, everyone in an official capacity insisted that Zahadi had acted on his own. This was (to hear American officialdom tell it) an indigenous response to a situation that the Iranians felt could no longer be borne.

For years outside Iran, this pretense was kept up; it was not until quite late, when Roosevelt wrote his memoirs and revealed the part that he had played in the affair, that America's complicity was exposed.[149]

This refusal of the Americans to officially countenance the part that they had played cost them later on. It seems legitimate to conclude that the anti-Americanism displayed by the Khomeini regime when it took power (and anti-Americanism is still strong in Iran to this day) grew out of the CIA role in overthrowing Mosadeq. Today, when Americans profess bemusement as to why they are so hated by Iranians, their stance is comprehensible only in light of the the fact that for years they denied that they had acted in this undemocratic fashion.

The other point is that the Tudeh was never the threat that the Americans made it out to be. The party virtually had been wiped out by Reza Shah in the late 1930s. It was only when the Allies took over in Iran that it reemerged. The Soviets freed the Tudeh cadres from prison. The cadres then resumed their organizing activity, mainly in the south in the oil fields. Still, at the end of the war, the British were instrumental in getting Mohammed Reza to crack down again (as if the shah needed encouragement).[150]

So when the nationalization fight erupted, the Tudeh was effectively underground. (Actually it was in a kind of limbo—not completely underground, not overground either.) Then, as the nationalization fight sharpened, the party took a stance of *fighting* Mosadeq. The Tudeh behaved toward Mosadeq as had the Communist Party toward the fascists in Europe before World War II. The European communists were more interested in fighting the socialists than their real enemies (or, at any rate, their effective enemies), the fascists. The Europeans paid for their strategic blunder, as did the Tudeh. The party, after the coup, was decimated.[151]

But perhaps most damaging (to those who take the communist threat seriously) was the failure of the Soviets *to do anything*. To be sure, Stalin died just before the coup occurred, and so the new leadership in Moscow was preoccupied, but in the lead-up to the coup, the Russians never acted, and, over the years, from the end of World War II to the coup, they had plenty of opportunities to meddle, which they neglected.

Viewed from this light, one has to rethink the climate engendered in the United States of anti-communist hysteria. Particularly one needs to reassess the companies' role in exploiting this Red scare.

As brought out earlier, the companies at the time were having to answer anti-trust charges. Rather than defend their actions, they went on the offensive, taking the line that the government's action was helping the communists. The companies painted a picture of a world divided—the communist East locked in combat with the West; and they claimed that the government, by trying to break the power of the oil companies, was assisting the communists because this ultimately would result in a weakening of America's position overseas.[152]

Evidently, this approach was a strong one, because Truman completely caved in to it. The president, although he originally supported the anti-trust action, later on cooled toward it appreciably. Just before he left office, he decided to scrap the grand jury action, making it into a civil suit, something much less threatening to the companies.[153]

After the fact, Truman gave various explanations for his behavior. He claimed, for example, that the National Security Council (NSC) had misled him. He also, at one point, said that he had acted on assurances of General Omar Bradley "that the national security called for this decision" (i.e., that the case be switched to a civil suit).[154]

In any event, once Truman took this step, the oilmen knew that they had won. Then, when Dulles asked them to put together a consortium to insinuate Iran's oil back onto the world market, they viewed this as a means of getting completely free from prosecution. The oilmen insisted that, before they could cooperate, they had to have guarantees from the Justice Department that their cooperation would not later on be construed as conspiracy, that is, the basis for further anti-trust action.[155]

Reluctantly, under prodding from the CIA and the Defense Department, the then-attorney general, Herbert Brownell, gave those guarantees. Still, the oilmen kept on importuning Eisenhower to abandon the anti-trust action completely. Ultimately, the NSC took the matter out of Justice's hands and turned it over to State, which was, of course, the oilmen's advocate in government.[156] Ultimately, the anti-trust action dribbled away to nothing.

NOTES

1. The author is making a distinction between the system and the cartel. The cartel is a formal organization, comprising seven oil companies. The system is the ensemble of arrangements that the seven have worked out to control the oil business, with the aim of aggrandizing themselves. When we say that countries have now become part of the system, we mean that the countries share in the rewards previously reserved for the seven. See Introduction note 3.

2. Henrietta Larson et al., *New Horizons: History of the Standard Oil Company (New Jersey), 1927–1950* (New York: Harper & Row, 1971), 698.

3. David Painter, *Private Power and Public Policy* (London: I. B. Tauris, 1986), 160.

4. Larson et al., *New Horizons*, 705. This was a function, too, of the implementation of the Marshall Plan, which specified, for security reasons, that oil for Europe come from

non-U.S. sources, the idea being that America must conserve its energy in the event of another war.

5. Britain had junked practically all of the wells in Iraq and in Burmah during World War II, fearing that they would be seized by the Axis.

6. Svante Karlsson, *Oil and the World Order* (Totowa, NJ: Barnes & Noble Books, 1986), 68, implies that this was a strategic decision to bring the European economies more closely under the direction of the United States, since coal was a domestically produced commodity (for the Europeans), while oil was not.

7. According to Larson et al. (*New Horizons*, 696–699), the so-called sterling area was made up of countries short of dollars. It included most of South America, scattered British island possessions in the Western Hemisphere, and nearly all the noncommunist part of the Eastern Hemisphere. The British government, because of London's financial position among soft-currency countries, after the war came to occupy a dominant position in most of that world. Through its financial agencies it administered the sterling system. Under it, trade among participating members could be financed and paid for in sterling without prior individual approval for each transaction. With respect to trade with countries outside the system, each one agreed to deposit all receipts—whether from current transactions or capital movements—with the Bank of England and to receive the equivalent in sterling in exchange for deposits to its account. Similarly, the needs of members for currencies of other countries to pay for imports outside the sterling area were met by exchanging sterling deposits with the Bank of England. Says Larson, "[O]f particular importance was the pool of hard currencies—notably U.S. dollars—administered by the Bank of England."

8. Ibid., 706.

9. Of course, Gulf also was affected by this action of the British.

10. Larson et al., *New Horizons*, 706.

11. Painter, *Private Power and Public Policy*, 161.

12. Larson et al., *New Horizons*, 706.

13. The AIOC, the reader should recall, was 56 percent owned by the government of Britain.

14. Larson et al., *New Horizons*, 708.

15. Of the oil produced by the Mene Grande Co. in Venezuela—of which Jersey and Royal Dutch each owned 25 percent and Gulf the remainder—only that fourth representing Royal Dutch's share was classed as sterling. Ibid., 708.

16. Ibid.

17. Painter, *Private Power and Public Policy*, 163.

18. Ibid.

19. Irvine Anderson, *ARAMCO, the United States and Saudi Arabia*, (Princeton, NJ: Princeton University Press, 1981), 185.

20. Larson et al., *New Horizons*, 713.

21. Ibid.

22. Anderson, *ARAMCO, the United States and Saudi Arabia*, 188. The neutral zone was a vast, empty stretch of desert. In the early part of the century, when Britain was the dominant influence in the Gulf, it arranged the borders between Saudi Arabia and Kuwait, and, to accommodate bedouin tribes that roamed back and forth between the two countries, it left undemarcated an extensive stretch of land that later became known as the neutral zone—Saudi Arabia owned half; Kuwait, the other half.

23. Ibid.

24. George Stocking, *Middle East Oil* (Kingsport, TN: Vanderbilt University Press, 1970), 131.

25. Anderson, *ARAMCO, the United States and Saudi Arabia*, 190.

26. Ibid., 187–197.

27. Ibid.

28. There is some question as to who actually came up with this scheme. John M. Blair, *The Control of Oil* (New York: Pantheon, 1976), 197–198, attributes it to an unnamed Treasury official; Anderson implies that it was Jersey (190). Painter also implies that Jersey first raised the possibility of transferring taxes (165). It seems beyond question that the whole thing was set up to benefit ARAMCO; the tip-off was Abdul Aziz' subsequent action in remitting taxes on Saudis whom he had only just made subject to the tax. See later.

29. Burton Kaufman, *The Oil Cartel Case* (Westport, CT: Greenwood, 1978), 24f.

30. For discussion of how Treasury eventually came to approve the deal and why the approval came after the fact, see Anderson, *ARAMCO, the United States and Saudi Arabia*, 195.

31. Ibid.

32. Ibid., 193.

33. Painter, *Private Power and Public Policy*, 171; see also Blair, *The Control of Oil*, 196–203.

34. Anderson, *ARAMCO, the United States and Saudi Arabia*, 195.

35. Larson et al., *New Horizons*, 740.

36. Kaufman, *The Oil Cartel Case*, 50f.

37. Robert Sobel, *The Age of Giant Corporations* (Westport, CT: Greenwood, 1972), Chapters 3, 8.

38. Ibid., 85.

39. Ibid., 123.

40. Ibid.

41. As Sobel says, "[T]he FTC could not complain of loss of competition if a manufacturer of textiles acquired the assets of a chain saw firm." Ibid., 195.

42. Kaufman, *The Oil Cartel Case*, 25.

43. For example, there were the so-called Western agrarians, senators like William E. Borah of Idaho, Gerald P. Nye of North Dakota, Burton Wheeler of Montana, and Joseph C. O'Mahoney of Wyoming, all of whom drew their intellectual precepts from the old populist tradition. Ellis Hawley, *The New Deal and the Problem of Monopoly* (Princeton, NJ: Princeton University Press, 1966), 290.

44. Ibid., 446.

45. Yet in the short term, as we shall see, coal benefited from quotas placed on the importation of foreign oil to conserve the domestic supply.

46. Anderson, *ARAMCO, the United States and Saudi Arabia*, 201.

47. U.S. Senate, *The International Petroleum Cartel, Staff Report to the Federal Trade Commission, Submitted to the Subcommittee on Monopoly of the Select Committee on Small Business* (Washington, DC: Government Printing Office, August 22, 1952).

48. John M. Blair, who helped compile the report, subsequently wrote *The Control of Oil*.

49. Hawley, *The New Deal and the Problem of Monopoly*, 420.

50. Ibid.

51. Kaufman, *The Oil Cartel Case*, 25.

52. Ibid., 26.

53. Hawley, *The New Deal and the Problem of Monopoly*, 442.

54. U.S. Senate, *The International Petroleum Cartel*, 280.

55. Kaufman, *The Oil Cartel Case*, 28.

56. Ibid., 29.

57. Ibid.

58. Ibid., 38.

59. Ibid., 30.

60. Ibid.

61. M. Reza Ghods, *Iran in the Twentieth Century* (Boulder, CO: Lynne Reinner Publishers, 1989), 132. See also L. P. Elwell-Sutton, *Persian Oil* (London: Laurence and Wishart, 1955), 108; and Mostafa Elm, *Oil, Power and Principle* (Syracuse, NY: Syracuse University Press, 1992), 44.

62. Ghods, *Iran in the Twentieth Century*, 132.

63. Elm, *Oil, Power and Principle*, 46.

64. Ghods, *Iran in the Twentieth Century*, 138.

65. The one in Kurdistan is difficult to categorize. There are indications that the Russians had nothing to do with stirring this one up but that the Kurds were simply copycatting the Azeris.

66. Ghods, *Iran in the Twentieth Century*, 136.

67. Ibid., 156.

68. Elm, *Oil, Power and Principle*, 46.

69. Elwell-Sutton, *Persian Oil*, 118–119.

70. Ibid., 119.

71. Richard Freeland, *The Truman Doctrine and the Origins of McCarthyism* (New York: Alfred Knopf, 1972).

72. Venezuela enacted the new income tax law (which effectively gave it the 50:50 split) on November 12, 1948.

73. Bamberg, *The History of the British Petroleum Company*, Vol. II, 324–326.

74. Ibid.

75. Ibid.

76. Ibid.

77. Alan Ford, *The Anglo-Iranian Oil Dispute of 1951–1952* (Berkeley: University of California Press, 1954), 37.

78. Ghods, *Iran in the Twentieth Century*, 111, 204. Elwell-Sutton, *Persian Oil*, 189, calls them the "upper ten," a term that the author has never heard before. They are the same group, however.

79. The reference here is to the Arthur Milspaugh mission, an economic delegation from America that attempted to reform Iran's finances. See Ghods, *Iran in the Twentieth Century*, 134.

80. Elwell-Sutton, *Persian Oil*, 160.

81. Effectively, the Shias believe that allegiance is owed to the Imam, that is, the spiritual head of the community (the Shia equivalent of the Sunni's caliph). The Shias trace a line of Imams from the Prophet's son-in-law Ali down to Muhammad al-Mahdi, who allegedly disappeared about 873 A.D. According to belief, the Imam has not died but is merely hidden and will return; hence, to pay allegiance to a temporal monarch is to obey an usurper.

82. Bamberg, *The History of the British Petroleum Company*, Vol. II, 385–386.

83. Ibid.

84. Ibid.

85. Ibid.

86. Ibid., 398.

87. Ibid.

88. Ghods (*Iran in the Twentieth Century*, 180) notes that Truman became alarmed by Justice William O. Douglas' reports of massive corruption in Iran. Douglas, a world traveler, had visited Iranian Kurdistan and was befriended by the Kurds, making him a great champion of that people later on. Of course, the Kurds were at this time severely suppressed by the Iranians.

89. Bamberg, *The History of the British Petroleum Company*, Vol. II, 400.

90. Ibid.

91. Ibid., 399.

92. Ibid., 400.

93. Ibid., 401.

94. It is interesting that the British seemed to have attributed a lot of the opposition from McGhee and Grady toward their Iranian policy to the fact that both men were of Irish descent. See Elm, *Oil, Power and Principle*, 89; see also G. Garaudy, *Three Kings in Baghdad* (London: Hutchinson, 1961).

95. Elm, *Oil, Power and Principle*, 61, 66.

96. Painter, *Private Power and Public Policy*, 172f. Bamberg, *The History of the British Petroleum Company*, Vol. II, 401.

97. Bamberg, *The History of the British Petroleum Company*, Vol. II, 411; Ghods, *Iran in the Twentieth Century*, 10.

98. Ghods, *Iran in the Twentieth Century*, 10.

99. Elm, *Oil, Power and Principle*, 62f.

100. Ibid., 80.

101. Ibid., 73.

102. Ibid., 80.

103. The minister of education was fatally wounded by a theology student with a grudge against him, according to Bamberg, *The History of the British Petroleum Company*, Vol. II, 416.

104. Bamberg, *History of the British Petroleum Company*, Vol. II, p. 417.

105. Ibid., 420.

106. Ibid., 435.

107. Ibid., 433.

108. Elm, *Oil, Power and Principle*, 124.

109. Ibid., 117; Elwell-Sutton, *Persian Oil*, 255.

110. Bamberg, *The History of the British Petroleum Company*, Vol. II, 438; Painter, *Private Power and Public Policy*, 176.

111. Bamberg, *The History of the British Petroleum Company*, Vol. II, 462; Elm, *Oil, Power and Principle*, 130.

112. Elwell-Sutton, *Persian Oil*, 278.

113. For discussions of Mosadeq's ideas on price, see ibid.; Bamberg, *The History of the British Petroleum Company*, Vol. II, 464; Elm, *Oil, Power, and Principle*, 186; Ford, *The Anglo-Iranian Oil Dispute of 1951–1952*, 115.

114. Bamberg, *The History of the British Petroleum Company*, Vol. II, 462.

115. Elm, *Oil, Power and Principle*, 132.

116. This is a reference to the Sazenov-Paleologue Treaty of 1907 when Britain and Czarist Russia divided Iran into spheres.
117. Bamberg, *The History of the British Petroleum Company*, Vol. II, 444.
118. Elwell-Sutton, *Persian Oil*, 258.
119. Bamberg, *The History of the British Petroleum Company*, Vol. II, 460.
120. Bamberg, *The History of the British Petroleum Company*, Vol. II, 464.
121. Ibid.
122. Painter, *Private Power and Public Policy*, 180.
123. Ibid., 193.
124. Robert Engler, *The Politics of Oil* (New York: MacMillan, 1981), 202.
125. In all cases where State intervened, it argued that America's security was at stake.
126. Elm, *Oil, Power and Principle*, 267.
127. Ford, *Anglo-Iranian Oil Dispute of 1951–1952*, 119.
128. Elwell-Sutton, *Persian Oil*, 309.
129. Ibid.
130. Ibid.
131. Bamberg, *The History of the British Petroleum Company*, Vol. II, 502.
132. Painter, *Private Power and Public Policy*, 173.
133. Daniel Yergin, *The Prize* (New York: Simon and Schuster, 1991), 464.
134. Elm, *Oil, Power and Principle*, 292f.
135. Ibid., 295.
136. Ibid., 303.
137. Ibid.
138. Robert Engler, *The Politics of Oil* (New York: Macmillan, 1961), 206.
139. Ghods, *Iran in the Twentieth Century*, 189.
140. Painter, *Private Power and Public Policy*, 193.
141. Bamberg, *The History of the British Petroleum Company*, Vol. II, 491.
142. Ibid., 495.
143. Ibid.
144. Bamberg, *The History of the British Petroleum Company*, Vol. II, 495.
145. Elm, *Oil, Power and Principle*, 321.
146. Bamberg, *The History of the British Petroleum Company*, Vol. II, 502f.
147. Elm, *Oil, Power and Principle*, 329.
148. Elwell-Sutton, *Persian Oil*, 328.
149. Kermit Roosevelt, *Countercoup: The Struggle for the Control of Iran* (New York: McGraw-Hill, 1979).
150. Elwood-Sutton, *Persian Oil*, 106.
151. Elm, *Oil, Power and Principle*, 332.
152. Engler, *The Politics of Oil*, 211, 215.
153. Kaufman, *The Oil Cartel Case*, 47.
154. Ibid.
155. Painter, *Private Power and Public Policy*, 195.
156. Ibid.

CHAPTER 4

The OPEC Revolution and the Clashes between Iraq and the Cartel

The period we have just looked at marks the zenith of cartel power. When this crisis was playing out, forces were already stirring that would bring the great cartel down or at least so immobilize it that, for a time, its fate would be undecided. The forces predominantly developed in Iraq, for, as determined as the Iranian assault on the cartel may have appeared, it was nothing compared to what took place in Iraq. We look first at the 1958 revolution in Iraq. This is the key to understanding Iraqi society, the Ba'th Party and Saddam Hussein. Saddam and the Ba'th are products of that great upheaval.

We also spend a considerable portion of this chapter looking at Abdul Qarim Qasim, who made the revolution and who was, after Mosadeq, the next popular leader to confront the cartel. Finally, we introduce the topic of the 1973 OPEC revolution, which we further treat in Chapter 5.

1958

The first thing to understand about Iraq's 1958 revolution is that it was complete; that is, everything that is supposed to go on in a revolution took place in this one. The ancien régime was swept away. Indeed, the royal family was gunned down in the palace yard, and the prime minister, Nuri, literally was torn to bits by the mob.

In place of the monarchy there emerged an entirely new system of rule—the first Iraqi republic. Finally, throughout the early days of the revolution and for a number of years thereafter, popular demonstrations kept up. The popular aspect of the revolt, the hallmark of any true revolution, was marked.

To be sure, the revolution was made by the army, but popular elements—in part led by the communists—took over in certain areas.[1] Ultimately, the people were made to relinquish their hold on events; however, this came about only after a long interval, and even after the army had regained control, the people did not stop interfering. The Iraqi experience was almost unique in the Arab world—among Arabs very few revolutions have developed from the ground up.

The leader of Iraq's revolution was Brigadier General Abdul Qarim Qasim. He set himself up to be the sole leader. The people related to Qasim on the basis that he alone personified the revolution. Qasim wanted it this way, and the people seemed comfortable with this setup.

Qasim, however, in electing to rule as the sole leader, alienated many of the so-called Free Officers who made the revolution with him.[2] This made him draw even closer to the people. Qasim went so far as to arm his supporters; he allowed them to form militias, but he prudently kept them on a short leash, as it were. Qasim made the militiamen turn in their ammunition every evening. Qasim's caution seems to have been dictated by fear of the communists, who at the time were the only strong party in Iraq and heavily represented in the militias.

Qasim's hold over the people was never absolute or even approaching that condition. Time and time again, the popular elements broke free and perpetrated some terrible excesses. Iraq in those days was riven with class hatreds—the dispossessed turning on the possessing classes. Whenever the possessors thought that they had found an opening, they struck back with a vengeance.

In great part, this class hatred was a legacy of World War II. Like Iran, Iraq was occupied by the Allies during the war, and, like Iran, the Russians participated in the occupation. They took a weak, much harassed native Communist Party and built it into a formidable aggregation. During the war this party organized among the workers; it also propagandized vehemently against the IPC.

As a consequence, by the time that the war had ended, the party had put down roots. Subsequent attempts by the British and the Iraqi government to extirpate it largely failed. Once the 1958 revolution occurred, the party came into the open, not just in the Arab south but in the Kurdish north. In fact, a bastion of the Communist Party in Iraq was (and is today) the Iraqi Kurdish area.

It is no accident, therefore, that the first truly alarming incidents of violence after the revolution took place in the north. Riots erupted in Mosul and Kirkuk. Qasim, viewing photographs of the Kirkuk riots, is supposed to have exclaimed that the Mongols, in all their barbarity, never perpetrated anything like this: there were lamppost lynchings and car draggings, and supposedly, 40 people were buried alive. Official casualty figures set the deaths at 200; it is likely the actual toll was much higher.[3]

This type of behavior shocked Arab society. To be sure, there have always been outbreaks of violence in Arab lands; but it is indicative of the ferocity of what went on that Arabs generally regarded the violence in Iraq during this period as unusual.[4]

To accommodate the popular elements, Qasim adopted a program of reforms aimed at bettering the people's lot. For example, he reduced rents of rooms by 20 percent, of houses by 15 to 20 percent, and of shops by 10 to 15 percent. He brought down the price of a flat of bread from six to four fils and, commensurately, the price of flour supplied to bakeries, having the government make up the difference.[5]

Qasim limited night work to seven hours and day work—including that of seasonal workers—to eight. He obliged industrial establishments employing more than 100 workers to build houses for their workers. He enforced provisions for social insurance against sickness and unemployment, and, in the first year of his regime, he allowed wage earners to organize and federate in a general union.[6]

It is important to mention this because Qasim's reputation (in the West at least) is other than as portrayed here. He is regarded by Westerners as something of a quack. The fact of his living in the Ministry of Defense, that is, of his having no home outside of it, is viewed as odd.

Much has been made of the fact that he never married, highly unusual for an Arab officer, especially a brigadier. In personal interviews, he was apparently quite off-putting. Supposedly, he would fix one with a wild eye and frequently would rant.

Qasim's personal behavior aside, his reform program had a lasting effect on Iraqi society. The people came to believe that revolutions not only could but *would* function as welfare providers. They came to believe that all good things flowed from the revolution.

The idea was not so far-fetched. Iraq, after all, sits on one vast pool of oil. Through all of the days of the monarchy, benefits from oil were withheld from the people. Qasim redirected the flow, so to speak, away from the elite toward the masses.

Of course, to provide these benefits, he had to confront the oil companies. Where else was he to get the wherewithal to institute his reforms?

NEGOTIATIONS—FIRST ROUND

It did not take Qasim long to open negotiations with the IPC, and, when he did, initially it appeared that he would be reasonable. He sought to clear up minor points that the previous government had been bargaining over when the revolution occurred.[7] For example, he wanted to discuss such things as discounts. The companies claimed discounts to compensate them for selling Iraq's oil. Qasim thought this improper. The IPC companies, as stated before, were integrated organizations—they sold Iraq's oil to themselves. In other words, they were discounting to each other.

Stocking says that the stands taken by Qasim were sound.[8] As far as he could determine, the companies' accounting practices, "if not actually sharp, were not calculated to inspire confidence in skeptical minds."

Once past the minor points, the tone of the negotiations sharpened as Qasim brought up more contentious issues. For example, he wanted raised production levels. Nothing unusual in that, except that, along with it, he wanted 20 percent participation in IPC, and that really was radical. No other producing country had that, and, of course, the companies were not about to give way on this.

Qasim also wanted the companies to give back to Iraq acreage held but not exploited. He had seen other countries wangle lucrative deals by inviting independents to bid on unclaimed acreage. This often lit a fire under the cartel, forcing it to renegotiate previously concluded contracts.

Unfortunately for Iraq, it had no unclaimed acreage; IPC had gotten it all, "by hook or by crook," as we saw earlier. Nonetheless, the companies eventually gave way on this point, but only conditionally—they wanted to release the lands over a seven-year time span, and they wanted to pick the parcels to be surrendered and in what order they would give them up.[9]

It was not that the companies were grasping, that is, unwilling to give way on anything; it was rather that the demands that Qasim made touched systemic concerns. If the companies conceded to Iraq on any one of these points, they would then have had to make similar concessions down the line.

Why did Qasim make demands that, from the companies' standpoint, were impossible of fulfillment? Because he felt that this was Iraq's due. Recall that Iraq was supposed to have had 10 percent participation; that had been part of the original concession agreement, a provision that the companies had chosen to ignore, just as they had ignored restrictions as to how much acreage they could exploit.

Every Iraqi knew that the country had lost out on these points (thanks, in large part, to the communists' propagandizing during World War II). So, for Qasim, the issue was clear-cut—he meant to get the country's own back.

There were also problems with the way that the negotiations were structured. The IPC sent comparatively low-level teams to Baghdad to conduct the talks. Whenever it became necessary to resolve a difficult issue, the company representatives would call a halt while they repaired to London and/or New York to parley. In this way the negotiations dragged on for almost two years.[10]

To give the companies credit, they made several offers to which the Iraqis could respond. For example, they agreed to double oil production. Unfortunately, over the course of the negotiations with Qasim that concession was not fulfilled, in part because of action taken by the sole leader.

In December 1959 Qasim had increased the dues that the companies paid to ship from Basrah. Qasim did this after surveying amounts charged by other ports, including Kuwait and Saudi Arabia; and then he informed the companies of the step that he was about to take. He was at pains not to surprise them.

Nonetheless, the companies responded rashly. They shut down production in IPC's Rumaila field, and they confined production at the Zubair field to 8 million tons a year.[11] They explained that, with increased port dues, it was no longer profitable to ship from the Gulf. As with the discount issue, this explanation did not make a lot of sense. The companies were part of an oligopoly, which meant that they did not have to be concerned with the free market conditions, not as long as they could set whatever prices they wished.

Marr says the companies' action was "insensitive."[12] The suddenness with which the riposte was administered took the Iraqis off-guard. Coming relatively early in the negotiations, it did not inspire confidence.

In any event, unfortunate stands were taken, and some of these created a bad atmosphere. In this instance, the companies' response presaged the breakdown of the talks. In September 1960, without warning, Qasim published the minutes of the negotiations to date, an extraordinary thing to have done; no party to negotiations anywhere had ever done such a thing. Oil-producing states usually prefer to work in secret. That way they can spare themselves embarrassment if they don't get what they want.

Once the minutes were publicized, the climate of the negotiations changed. Pressures on the country team intensified—Qasim had cut off all possibility of retreat. He had laid everything out for the public's view—the positions of the two sides, the main areas of contention. Qasim even went so far as to advise his people where he felt they must not give way.

After this, there was not much hope of a resolution. With the Iraqi people in on the talks, so to speak, Qasim had to play to his audience, and under the circumstances he was not likely to compromise. Still, the principals soldiered on. London and New York sent out a new, more senior negotiating team. Then, in the summer of 1961, Qasim announced that the Iraqi side was closing down. He thanked the company team for coming out and hinted that he would now do what he had to do.

On December 11, 1961, he published Public Law 80, which took back 95 percent of the acreage that the companies had acquired but never exploited. He left them 5 percent, in addition to the fields that they were already exploiting.

This was as close to nationalization as one could get and, as such, another milestone (after Mexico and Iran) in the saga of country takeovers of the oil industry. However, as stated, this was not quite a nationalization. By leaving untouched the already exploited fields, Qasim allowed the companies to go on operating. Still, included in the sequestered portion was the North Rumaila field. The companies had early determined that this one was particularly rich. Losing this must have hurt.

TESTING THE SYSTEM

One wonders why Qasim took this step of sequestering the unexploited territories; after all, he could not exploit them. He had planned for some time to set up a national oil company (the Iraqi National Oil Co. [INOC]), but this existed only on paper. As long as the cartel controlled the marketing of oil worldwide, Qasim had no way of selling his production.[13]

Iran had already shown the futility of pursuing the course that Qasim was preparing to embark upon. At the same time, however, this much can be said about Qasim's tactic—it tested the system by showing up the basis on which it was built. The system was powerful because, as with the state, it claimed a monopoly on violence. With the state, the claim was certified by law; with the system, custom operated.

The system had shown its competence in so many fights, against so many formidable opponents over the years that in the world's eyes it was unassailable. However, a perception like this can be changed. By submitting one's case to hazard, it may fall out that circumstance decides in one's favor.

This was what Qasim did and what eventually happened with the Iraqis. By breaking off negotiations and by taking back the oil lands (which Qasim deemed Iraq's by right), he forced the system to defend itself. The world then was treated to a replay of the Mosadeq scenario. This time, however, the outcome was different.

TIME OF STRESS

Qasim made his decision to reappropriate the unexploited lands in the summer of 1961, and coincidentally the tribe of the Barzani Kurds revolted in the north. In making his announcement (of the reappropriation) to the Iraqi public, Qasim twinned the two events. He scornfully made reference to the Barzani revolt. "The British and their American stooges," he said, deliberately fostered it.[14]

Thus, Qasim put the onus on Britain primarily for stirring up the tribes, a natural response given Britain's past performance—it frequently had resort to such tactics. We saw how they behaved in precisely this way toward Feisal and Reza in Iran.

To be sure, the Barzanis (and many of the other Kurdish tribes) had a grievance. The tribal leaders were all feudalists, like the southern sheikhs, and, like the sheikhs, they condemned the social reforms that Qasim was pressing. In the south, however, the reforms went through comparatively easily. In the north this was not the case, due to a number of factors, including the inaccessibility of the region and the tight control of the chiefs over the tribes.[15]

Still, Qasim was adamant that the chiefs must conform. Particularly, he pursued the land reform, which the chiefs feared most of all. Qasim's land reform was sweeping, although not as severe as that put through by the Egyptians. By December 31, 1961, three and a half years after the revolution, Qasim had managed to distribute 601,949 dunnams (0.168 acre per dunnam) to 10,672 peasant families. It was not a great beginning, but it was a start; however, distributing this much land had been like pulling teeth.[16]

In the north, therefore, the land reform had barely penetrated. Qasim persisted; the chiefs resisted, ever more fiercely. It was hardly surprising that some *agas* (as they were called) resorted to violence. If, in fact, the British suborned the tribes (as Qasim claimed), this might have induced them to take up arms.

One point about this revolt needs clarification—this was not a widespread, *popular* revolt. At best, one or two tribes were involved, and the *agas* primarily were rebelling. We go more deeply into this when we look again at the Kurdish leader, Barzani.

The revolt of the Kurds complicated Qasim's situation terribly. To begin with, he now had to fund military operations. Actually, the fight of the government against the Kurds never amounted to much—some bombing of villages and troop deployments and some skirmishing.

This was not total war, where two sides stake their all on achieving a thought-out military plan. The Kurds, rather, enveloped Iraqi army units in garrison and tried to prevent them from being resupplied, while the government concentrated on keeping open important roads through the region.

Nonetheless, the revolt hurt Qasim by, for one thing, cutting off trade with the north. It also freed the army to go north where officers opposed to Qasim could plot against him. Finally, the army had to be provided with ammunition. Qasim's former policy had been to restrict it to two day's supply. In other words, Qasim lost control of the army at a crucial juncture, and this largely was due to the Kurds.

Thus, from 1961 on (when Qasim broke off negotiations and reappropriated the oil lands) he experienced mounting difficulties managing the country—most seriously, he was running out of cash. Iraq's economy was (and still is) based on oil. It has enormous amounts of oil (in the words of the 1974 U.S. Senate Subcommittee on Multinational Corporations report, its reserves are "fantastic").[17] However, up to this time it had not seen much return, the IPC not being interested in developing Iraq's potential.

According to Blair, in 1948 production in Iran was seven times larger than in Iraq. In Saudi Arabia commercial production did not begin until 1938, but by 1948 it was almost six times more. Adil Hussein says that, during the three years that Qasim was negotiating with IPC, Iraq's oil production showed an annual decrease of 5.1 percent, while oil production in Iran went up 12 percent annually; Saudi Arabia's rose to 9 percent, and Kuwait, too, experienced an increase, to 11.5 percent.[18]

The companies could justify this partly on the basis that Iraq was unstable. But there were years (under the dynasty) when Iraq was a paragon of stability, and liftings remained low. What is even more interesting is a fact brought out by Blair and Rand. As indicated earlier, the British mainly controlled the IPC concession, and they seem deliberately to have concealed the extent of Iraq's resources, not just from the Iraqi government but from their American partners as well.[19]

Rand says that Americans on visit to Iraq were shepherded around by British officials who steered them away from certain areas. The key region, according to Rand (and Blair), was the disputed middle third of the country. Rand says it was a blank, not shown on any oil maps (or few at least) and barely explored.

The implication is (and we will look at this further) that Iraq's resources dwarf those of other countries and may even be more than Saudi Arabia's and that this was kept a dark secret.

But to get back to Qasim's difficulty. He had, as stated, set up this ambitious program of reforms, which, even if everything had gone well, would have been difficult to carry through. Things did not go well. I mentioned land reform—here, Qasim got himself into a terrible muddle.

The peasant proprietors who took over the new lands found that they could not cope with tasks that formerly had been performed by the sheikhs or their estate agents.[20] The government did not have experts available to help out, and, although the peasants displayed great ardor (as Batatu says), this was not enough. Production fell markedly.[21]

The situation was not helped by two successive droughts (1959 and 1960).[22] This further cut down production and, with the cutoff of trade with the north, created a major food crisis.

With such hardship, Qasim needed to sell oil, as much as he could. The companies, since they were still operating, could have helped, but, as mentined before, they were disputing the government's right to select additional land parcels. As long as this went on, the companies were not disposed to be helpful.

The companies also wanted the dispute moved to arbitration, which Qasim refused. The companies dug in their heels, and Qasim, in retaliation, put the reappropriated lands up for bid, hoping to attract independent oil company buyers.

In the United States, Qasim's offer attracted considerable interest, but this was damped down by the State Department.[23] We have more to say later about industry-wide conditions that led independents to covet the properties. (This relates to the activity of the OPEC, discussed in the next section.)

Averell Harriman, the same who had lobbied Mosadeq, orchestrated the campaign to discourage the independents. He met with several top CEO's, men like E. L. Steiniger of Sinclair Oil Co. and James Richards of Standard Oil of Indiana. To each he put the case that it was not in the interest of U.S. business to encourage the Iraqis; if Iraq wanted some relief, it could go to arbitration.[24]

Harriman made this argument despite the fact that the State Department's own lawyers, who had been asked to examine the issue, declared that Baghdad was within its rights to reappropriate the lands. The lawyers suggested that IPC had been following a "dog in the manger policy" and that any thorough airing of the charges in an international court would probably not be in its interests.[25]

In disputes of this nature, the system seemed to trust to the fact that it could outlast its opponents; it had deep pockets, one could say. By dragging out the process, it could hope to exhaust its opponents, which is what happened with Qasim.

Qasim found himself more and more beleaguered. He could not dispose of the reappropriated properties (all of the independents having shied away—some, like Richards, more or less gracefully; some, like Steiniger, under coercion); the oil companies kept Iraqi production to a minimum; conditions in the country worsened (the population becoming more and more restive). At this point Qasim involved himself in a ruinous confrontation with the British over Kuwait.

The Kuwait crisis needs to be treated in context and so is taken up in the last chapter. However, the result for Qasim of raising this issue was to further isolate himself. Arab countries that had reason to oppose the sole leader (primarily this was Egypt) came to Kuwait's defense and in the end forced Qasim to back down.

In 1963 a violent attempt was made to overthrow him.

BA'TH #1

The attempt to overthrow Qasim was a puzzler. In the first place, it was carried out by a relatively small group, the Ba'th Party. Batatu says that, when the Ba'thists moved against Qasim, they had about 15,000 members; however, of these only 830 were "actives."[26] The Ba'th is an extremely hierarchical organization; so, of the total, only a small percent could have been said to have been true Ba'thists—the rest, sympathizers. Along with that, the majority of the active Ba'thists were civilians, and the head of the party, Ali Saleh As Sa'di, was a ghetto tough. Finally, most of the Ba'thists were youths, many no more than high school age.

The attempt came on February 8, 1963. Preceding the event, in December, Ba'thists had provoked demonstrations in the high schools over a comparatively minor incident.[27] Qasim chose to view this as a plot against him and had the Ba'thists rounded up. This seems to have forced the leadership's decision to bring down the regime.[28]

One could see the Ba'thists mounting a demonstration or attempting to assassinate Qasim (which, in fact, they did do; the attempt was made by, among others, Saddam Hussein, who was wounded in a shoot-out, an incident that subsequently has been incorporated into the leader's public myth).[29] But a coup would appear to have been beyond them.

Be this as it may, on the morning of February 8, they assassinated the commander of the air force, a loyal Qasim supporter, as he left his home in Baghdad. Within minutes planes appeared over the Defense Ministry and began to bomb it.[30] Meanwhile, at the Abu Ghurayab garrison a strong tank force, commanded by Ba'thist officers, subjected the ministry to ground attack.[31]

Over the course of the coup, Qasim made several errors. First, he did not correctly assess the seriousness of the situation. Then, when he might have come out of the Defense Ministry with his personal guard and fought in the streets, he remained inside, where he was vulnerable to further air raids.[32]

Finally, Qasim never armed his supporters. The communists and lower-class elements (mainly *shurugis*, mentioned earlier) who came to his aid had to fight with sticks.[33] Other army units (non-Ba'thist) did not take part in the coup, but they did not help Qasim either, an indication of the degree to which he had lost the support of his fellow officers.[34] Eventually, he surrendered and came out of the Defense Ministry, whereupon the Ba'thists killed him.

And so ended his career. Ironically, his demise was not much different from that of the royal family—gunned down in the courtyard of his residence. (A ghastly photo of the crumpled corpse of the sole leader is included in Uriel Dann's book.[35])

The major criticism leveled at Qasim was that he never formed a party. He took too much on himself, whereas, if he had had a party, he might have delegated more. He is supposed to have worn himself out (became paranoid, some said), and that confused his judgment. He made wrong moves, like invading Kuwait.

It is hard to see how Qasim could have formed a party—his vision of the sort of society that Iraq should have was so at variance with what anyone else seemed to have wanted. Few of Qasim's fellow officers shared his zeal for reform. To whom, then, would he have gone to form this putative party?

Arab officers in those days were practically a caste. All over the Middle East they were staging coups. Out of power, they promised much; in power, they generally looked out for themselves. Few turned out to be Nassers or Qasims. All they wanted was to consolidate their gains, so their progeny would be well taken care of.

Perhaps the best epitaph for Qasim is Batatu's. He said that Qasim "did not feed the poor with words, he acted in a tangible manner." In line with this, Qasim had no Swiss bank accounts. When he died, what he had was in the Defense Ministry. After his death, the *shurugis* claimed that he was still alive and would return to them.

In any case, immediately after his death, the Ba'thists began an orgy of retaliation against the communists. They killed, by conservative estimates, upward of several thousand. Why did they do it? Several highly respected sources say that they acted at the behest of the Central Intelligence Agency (CIA).[36] The Ba'thists supposedly worked from lists of communists that the agency supplied them.

Eventually, the bloodletting ceased, and the Ba'thists had to rule; the Ba'thists did not know how to rule. Instead, they co-opted non-Ba'thist officers into positions of responsibility. As president, they chose Col. Abdul Salam Aref, who had made the original coup with Qasim but then had had a falling out with the sole leader. Aref was a Pan-Arabist, but no Ba'thist.

The Ba'thists stayed in power only 10 months, too brief a time to make an adequate assessment of them. One aspect of their behavior, however, should be commented on. One would have expected them (assuming that reports of CIA involvement are correct) to move sharply to the right, once they seized power. Not so. They ended up proclaiming themselves communists or, at least, leftist radicals.

The author has a theory that the Ba'thists were trapped by their constituency. Virtual unknowns, they had to find a way of appealing to the people, and, as stated earlier, the people expected to be taken care of regarding their welfare. So, the Ba'thists really had no alternative but to carry on Qasim's work of passing reforms. In time, they appropriated the program of the communists, who were the most involved in this activity.

The Ba'thists also resembled the communists in another area—they kept up the institution of the popular militias.[37] They became the National Guard. Qasim, as we said, had been supportive, but wary, of this group. The Ba'thists threw caution to the winds. They allowed the militias to mount nightly patrols, in which the militiamen stopped and searched individuals, and, of course, they did not hesitate to use violence—from all accounts, it appears that they positively thrived on violence.

The militias went so far as to abuse military officers, whom they frequently would arrest. This appears to have been what brought about the Ba'thists' demise. The Pan-Arab officers associated with the regime prevailed on the Ba'thist officers to bring them under restraint.

In November 1964, during a meeting of the party's so-called Regional Command, a group of the Ba'thist officers burst in on the civilians, held them at gunpoint, and then drove preselected individuals (As Sa'di included) to the airport, put them on a plane, and flew them to Spain, without passports.

This touched off a revolt in the National Guard. The guardsmen battled the army for a week, an entirely one-sided affair, since the army had the tanks and aircraft. Still, one guardsman-zealot commandeered a plane and dive-bombed the Ministry of Defense, thus wrecking the best aircraft that the Iraqis had.

The passing of the Ba'th was not mourned. The Iraqis clearly were sick of them and of their excesses. Their violence had surpassed reasonable limits. The country seemed to be slipping into anarchy (if, indeed, it was not already there). In this respect the takeover of the military probably was welcomed.

We return to the Ba'thists in the next chapter, when we introduce Saddam Hussein.

THE AREF BROTHERS

With the civilians gone, the military Ba'thists were free to go on functioning in the government, and many did. However, Aref, who was not himself a Ba'thist, clearly mistrusted them, and so gradually he maneuvered them out of positions of influence. Finally, the most respected of the Ba'thist officers, Ahmad Hasan Al Baker, withdrew from the regime, and with that the Pan-Arabists were wholly in charge.

Aref immediately sought to effect the merger with Egypt. Interestingly, Nasser dissuaded him. The Egyptian leader had just survived a setback with Syria. The latter had broken away from the Arab Union after traditionalist elements inside the country balked at implementing Nasser's socialist reforms.

Nasser advised Aref first to socialize Iraq, and then the merger might follow.[38] But Aref was not at all enamored of socialism. He was a traditionalist himself, and thus he allowed the country to drift.[39] It seems likely that ultimately he would have taken the country back into some sort of relation with the West.

In fact, he made a start in that direction by giving back all of the reappropriated lands to the IPC. Not baldly, just like that; rather, he worked out a deal with the Qasim-created Iraqi National Oil Co. (INOC) whereby it and the IPC would cooperate to develop the lands.[40] Abdullah Tariki, the grand old man of OPEC, castigated Aref for selling out to the oilmen over this, and, in Baghdad, six Pan-Arabist cabinet members quit on hearing the news.[41]

Aref never completed this deal. On April 13, 1966, he died accidentally in a helicopter crash. His brother, Abdul Rahman Aref, then was appointed by the army in his stead, and essentially he carried on in the same vein as his brother; that is, he attempted to ameliorate relations with the West (and, by extension, the oil system).

Before he died, Abdul Salam had appointed a civilian, Abdul Rahman Bazzaz, prime minister, who had instituted something called "prudent socialism." This seems to have been an attempt to move the country away from the directed economy and reestablish private enterprise.

Abdul Rahman Aref was no more successful than his brother in trying to deradicalize Iraq. The program worked out with the oilmen, whereby the IPC would be let back into the reappropriated fields, proved impossible to implement. In part, this was due to internal politics—the disposition of the reappropriated territories became a political football, with various factions lining up on one side or the other. Along with that, hope of coming to terms with the cartel died once the 1967 Arab–Israeli War broke out.

Immediately after the war, Aref introduced a slew of measures inimical to the IPC. He turned over all exploration rights in the rich North Rumaila field to the state-controlled INOC, granted to the French concern Enterprise de Recherches et d'Activites Petrolieres (ERAP) an exploration and development contract for central and southern Iraq (because of France's support of the Arabs in the 1967 war), and finally entered into an agreement with the Soviet Union to furnish technical assistance and drilling in the North Rumaila field and to help in marketing the oil produced by the national company.[42]

Aref's actions were almost certainly driven by anger at the West for having sided with Israel. He had to fear for his regime had he not acted—the Pan-Arabist officers were wrought up over the war. At the same time, the main reason would appear to have been economic. Iraq desperately needed to achieve some sort of resolution of its fight with the companies.

Just before the Arab–Israeli War broke out, Syria had shut down the pipeline through which Iraqi oil was conveyed to the Mediterranean. The Syrians wanted the IPC to pay an increased tariff. The IPC refused, and the dispute dragged on for months, during which Iraq got no revenue.

When the dispute finally was settled, the Iraqis entered into a dispute of their own with the companies, demanding compensation for the revenue lost. The companies claimed a *force majeure*. This dispute then dragged on for several more months until it was finally settled.

Much has been made of the fact that Iraq turned to the Soviet Union; this probably should not be overemphasized. They also made overtures to the French and the Italians. The Russians simply were the first to pick up the offer.

In any case, despite his attempts to salvage his regime, Aref's days were numbered. On July 17, 1968, the Ba'thists struck again. As apparently was the case with the first Ba'thist coup, outside forces were involved. Batatu claims to have been told by Aref that the oil interests bankrolled the coup (through the CIA). The interests were angry over his having awarded a contract to ERAP and having called in the Soviets to develop the North Rumaila field.[43]

The companies' "tool," as Aref described him, was a member of the palace guard (a clique of officers close to Aref), Abdul Razzaq an Nayef. Nayef was the head of the intelligence network. He co-opted Abdul Rahman ad Daud, the head of the Republican Guard, supposedly Aref's protectors. A third officer, Sa'dun Ghaidan, commander of a tank regiment attached to the Republican Guard, brought the Ba'thists into the plot.[44]

According to Batatu's account, the Ba'thists did not learn until just before the coup that Nayef was involved and then thought of backing out, as they did not trust him. They went ahead, and, once the coup succeeded, they ousted both Nayef and Daud.[45]

In control, the Ba'thists turned on the oil interests with a vengeance. They not only implemented all of the anti-IPC measures adopted by Aref but added to them. For example, they worked out barter arrangements whereby countries from the Soviet bloc took the oil and in exchange provided Iraq with commodities and expertise. They also nationalized the Kirkuk field, which up till then had been spared (although this nationalization was not completed until 1975).[46]

Again, as was the case with the first Ba'thist regime, it is hard to reconcile this behavior. How could individuals who were so professedly anti-communist and who apparently at one point had connections to the CIA have acted so inimically toward the oil companies?

It seems that they wanted the oil. They wanted it on their terms; that is, they wanted to have sole control over it (just as Mosadeq had wanted), and that they could not have until they had solved the sales problem. They could seize the oil but not sell it—as long as the cartel had a lock on the world market.

The radical measures adopted by Aref promised a way out for the Ba'thists. By bartering to the Soviets, they got a guaranteed market. But—and this is important, as it affects the later outbreak of the Gulf War—they also got infrastructure development. The Ba'thists brought in Eastern bloc technicians to build up their fields. The reader should be aware that, unlike Iran and Saudi Arabia (and even Kuwait), Iraq had no very sophisticated oil field facilities, because the IPC had consistently stinted them on this.

At any rate, as we will see, this kind of behavior was characteristic of the

Ba'th. Frustrated at not being able to find a way out of an impasse, they would frequently adopt the most uncharacteristic line of attack. In this case, they wanted to build up their oil industry; the oil system balked them, so they, the arch anti-communists, did a deal with the communists. A pretty daring maneuver, given the state of the Cold War in those days.

At the same time, however, it will not do to overestimate their "accomplishment." A lot of the Ba'thists' success can be set down to dumb luck or at least to an accident of timing.

The Ba'thists nationalized the IPC holdings one year before the OPEC revolution; there could not have been a better (for them) time to do it. When the smoke of that crisis cleared, the Ba'thists were—so to speak—sitting pretty. They had eliminated the oil companies, and so they now controlled production and, with the price of oil tripling and quadrupling, were free to do pretty much as they pleased.

An interesting sidelight to this is that Saddam Hussein conducted the negotiations with the Soviets. He had gone from being a foot soldier in the revolution to the head of something called the Follow-Up Committee, created by the Ba'thists to manage oil affairs. Saddam was by now on his way to taking over the party; at this stage he was number two, behind the Ba'thist president, Ahmad Hasan Baker.

OPEC

We are now ready to look at the great trauma of international oil, which came with the rise of OPEC and the challenge of the Fourth Arab–Israeli War.

The conditions that undermined the oil system began to mature in the 1930s, when, as the reader may recall, the majors went along with a U.S.-imposed tariff on oil, the aim of which was to keep prices high so that hard-pressed independents could stay in business.

After that the cartel companies invested heavily in overseas properties, specifically in the Persian Gulf, where by 1938 they had acquired many richly producing fields. After this, as we said in Chapter 2, the Gulf became the center of gravity of the oil business.

The consequences of the shift (away from the Western Hemisphere) need to be fully comprehended. By building up facilities in one area, the cartel companies got control of the production end of the business. Previously, they had been concentrating on marketing as a means of eliminating competition; they had been divvying up the marketing regions among themselves, agreeing not to compete in certain areas. The new strategy was different. The companies perfected the installations in Iran and Saudi Arabia (but particularly in the latter). They made them so technologically advanced that there was nothing to match them anywhere.

Thus, the cartel companies could calibrate demand to supply. Whenever conditions in the market changed, the companies could respond by opening or closing the tap in the Gulf. It was nothing for them to ratchet up production several hundred thousand barrels a day and, correspondingly, to push production down.

In this way the cartel companies made themselves shockproof, and that opened the way to long-term planning. Assured of a firm grip on the market, the companies were not afraid to invest, and thus a kind of dynamic was built into the system. Because conditions could be kept stable, more and more money could be invested, and this made things even more stable.

Meanwhile, developments were being watched by noncartel companies in the United States. Several thought that they saw openings for themselves in the new setup.[47] What attracted them most were the conditions under which oil was produced in the Gulf region.

Once the tariff went into place, the price of oil inside the United States rose correspondingly. For a long time there was not much to be made of this. But as conditions in the Gulf grew more and more stable, the noncartel companies were motivated to throw some money in, seeking to cadge concessions. Once gained, these proved tremendously lucrative because the oil, as mentioned earlier, in some areas practically leaped out of the ground.

The costs of production were next to nothing. The interlopers, therefore, found that they could absorb the U.S. tariff *and* the costs of transportation *and still* make a profit.[48]

The first firms to take advantage of this were Getty, Standard Oil of Indiana, Standard Oil of Ohio, Continental, and Atlantic Richfield. The movement, however, really took off after the settlement of the Iran crisis, because then, as we saw in the last chapter, a number of smaller companies (the Iricon group) were let in on the restructured AIOC concession.[49]

As outsiders started coming in, the cartel saw that it was losing its edge. However, it was not the cartel companies primarily that suffered, but rather the smaller independents that operated back in the United States—the original wildcatters and such in Texas and Oklahoma. They were selling oil at the artificially high tariff-supported price and now were being undercut by cheap oil being brought in by Getty and the rest, primarily from the Gulf region.

The cheap oil first appeared along the eastern seaboard of the United States, but, eventually, it penetrated as far inland as western Pennsylvania. The independents were nothing if not well organized, plus they had a geostrategically significant base in the American Southwest. They got congresspeople from this area to agitate for oil quotas.[50]

President Eisenhower resisted, but the pressure proved too much for him. Finding it impossible to withstand powerhouses like Sam Rayburn and Lyndon Johnson, the president tried to temporize. He first called (in 1954) for voluntary quotas, which did not work. In 1957 he made the quotas mandatory, but with significant loopholes that diminished their effectiveness.[51]

Finally, in 1959 Eisenhower imposed full quotas, which remained in effect for 14 years.

Now the cartel truly began to hurt. Firms like Getty and Bunker Hunt (of Hunt Brothers Oil), when they found that they could not dispose of their oil in the United States, dumped it on the spot market, where it was quickly snatched up by Europeans and Japanese.

A word about this institution of the spot market. It was a setup for disposing of oil at the margin. If a refiner had excess production he could not accommodate, he would offer it for sale and a potential buyer would pick it up at a discounted price. This essentially was what was happening here. However, as we shall see, the spot market takes on a different aspect during the 1973 OPEC revolution when it literally becomes the center for oil sales worldwide.

In 1959 this spot market activity had a dual effect. One, it tightened the hold of oil over the international energy market. Up to this point, the Europeans had been mainly coal consumers. But now they and the Japanese, lured by low prices, swung decisively over to oil.

The second result was that prices continued their slide. The gap between the posted and the spot market price of oil widened significantly. If the majors wanted to compete, they had to close this gap, which meant cutting the posted price, and this they were reluctant to do.

In the 1940s the ARAMCO companies, to accommodate the demands of the Saudis for more money, hit on the scheme of having Riyadh tax them.[52] They then went to Washington, where they complained of "double taxation." Washington (thanks largely to the friendly intervention of the State Department) agreed that the companies needed tax relief and so had exempted them from paying taxes on their overseas profits.

That was a signal coup for the companies—however, to make it work, they had had to declare their profits "upstream," at the point of production. (As stated earlier, the cartel comprised integrated firms that, since they controlled every aspect of the business, could assign profits wherever they wished.)

Once the decision was taken to make upstream the profit-producing sector, everything became built around that. Subsequently, when the oil-producing states negotiated 50:50 profit-sharing agreements with the cartel, these were predicated on levels of production; and profits from production were based on the posted price.

To cut the posted price would cause harm to the oil producers, particularly countries like Iran that had Five-Year Plans to keep up. But, in fact, there was not a country that would not have protested price cuts, since they all, by now, had become imbued with the spirit of nationalism.

The CEOs of the majors knew that they should not cut. They knew that once they did, in the words of one of them, "all hell would break loose"; still, in their eyes, cuts were inevitable, as the situation was growing chaotic.[53]

The spot market had become the locus of international trading, superseding the contractual deals worked out by the cartel members. The overseas independents (Getty, and the rest) were heavily involved in this market, and now the Russians, too, were coming on-line. Finally several national oil companies—like Italy's state oil company, Azienda Generali Italiana Petroli (AGIP)—were showing interest.[54]

On August 8, 1960, Monroe Rathbone, president of Exxon (the new name of Jersey Standard), cut the posted price by an average of 10 cents per barrel. According to Sampson, this was a unilateral move; Rathbone did not inform his fellow cartel members of it. Sampson says that, on hearing the news, Harold Snow, president of British Petroleum (the new name of the Anglo-Iranian Oil Co.), wept.[55]

He well might have—the cut sparked the formation of OPEC.

The two men most involved in setting up OPEC were Perez Alfonso and Abdullah Tariki, the former a Venezuelan, the latter a Saudi. The founding country was Iraq. (The first meeting of the core group of OPEC states—Venezuela, Iran, Kuwait, Iraq, and Saudi Arabia—was held in Baghdad in 1960; the convenor was Qasim.)

OPEC was an idea long overdue. If there was an oil company cartel, why not one for oil producers? Alfonso and Tariki had been pushing this for years. Nothing had come of it, even though relations between the companies and producers were growing increasingly strained.

Too many obstacles stood in the way of its realization. Most difficult was the apparent incompatibility of the potential members. How could the shah of Iran sit down with the president of Iraq, particularly when, in the eyes of the former, the latter was a regicide?

Another problem was location. Venezuela was on the other side of the world from the Persian Gulf, and, of course, jet travel was not as accessible then as it is today.

Because of these and other handicaps, OPEC, after its initial meeting in 1960, effectively went nowhere—until in the late 1960s something occurred to light a fire under it.

LIBYA

A new oil province of the Middle East, developed after World War II, was the Maghreb, in particular, Libya. In the 1950s the then-king of Libya, Idris, opened his country to oil prospectors.[56] He did it in such a way as to discourage the cartel from coming in; as he said, he did not want to become another Iraq.

The king encouraged small, noncartel companies like Occidental. In fact, Armand Hammer's company was one of the first to go into Libya, along with Bunker Hunt's group.

Immediately, Occidental and the others struck oil that was "sweet," meaning low in sulfur. This was a plus because of the growing environmentalist movement in the United States—low-sulfur oil is less polluting. Another advantage of Libyan oil was its location. Libya sits on the north coast of Africa (the

Maghreb), just across from Europe. Oil from there does not have to transit the Suez Canal (which was still closed after the 1967 war) or be hauled round the Horn.

The rush was on to develop not just Libya but the whole Maghreb region.

Then, in 1969, Libya was hit with revolution, which brought Mu'ammar Gadhafi, then a captain in the Libyan army, to power. Gadhafi and the young officers surrounding him determined to control their country's oil resources (just as Mosadeq had done and Saddam after him). They set about renegotiating existing contracts, and they did it in a most ruthless manner.

Gadhafi singled out Occidental, totally concentrated in Libya (and thus dependent on it), and presented Hammer with an ultimatum—either he agreed to a price rise, or he would have to cut production, the aim being to progressively work away at him, cutting him more and more until he capitulated.

Hammer appealed to Ken Jamieson, the new chief executive of Exxon, for aid. He asked for oil at close to cost (which he could then sell to his customers and thus keep himself in business).[57] Jamieson was prepared to offer replacement at the normal price for third parties; beyond that he would not go. At that, Hammer caved in, and, as might have been expected, within no time all of the other companies operating in Libya went along.

Then the sleeping giant, OPEC, stirred. OPEC had been dominated up to this time by the conservative states like Saudi Arabia. Now all of the OPEC members perceived the advantages of militancy, and so in December 1970 in Caracas, Venezuela, the OPEC countries met to unveil a manifesto. It called for, among other things, a minimum acceptable tax on profits, a demand for higher posted prices, and a call to eliminate company discounts.[58] If these (and other measures) were not agreed by the companies, the manifesto declared, the countries would unilaterally enact the changes.

Now the action shifts to the corporate headquarters of the majors, where the CEOs sought to coordinate their response. They were not about to capitulate to the likes of Gadhafi; however, they were savvy enough to know that beating him would not be easy. The companies decided on a strategy. They would call for negotiations with OPEC as a single entity; that is, they would insist on negotiations cartel to cartel. They would not enter into bilateral deals one on one, where the Libyans could whipsaw them.[59]

This seemed a foolproof approach. If the OPEC cartel went along, then the companies' bargaining position was enhanced. On the other hand, if the radicals in OPEC balked at adopting a common front, this would split the organization, and that, too, would help the companies.

The only thing that could undermine the strategy was if one or more of the conservative OPEC countries (i.e., the nonradicals) balked. Unfortunately, this is what happened. Iran refused to accept this arrangement, and, what is more, the shah made a strong case to Washington for not doing so. Nixon acceded to the shah's demands.

Thus, the oilmen were surprised when they got to Tehran and were told by the shah that their approach was inoperative. Apparently, Washington had not bothered even to inform the oilmen of its decision to back the shah. Caught unawares, the oilmen were forced to back down. To take a unified position, they had to get clearance from the Justice Department—colluding on prices, remember (as far the United States was concerned), was against the law.

The negotiations went ahead on the shah's plan and turned out as the companies had feared. In bargaining sessions first in Tehran, then in Tripoli, the companies, after agreeing among themselves to hold the line at an increase of $0.15 per barrel (the countries wanted $0.54), agreed to $0.30, escalating to $0.50 by 1975.[60] Effectively, the OPEC countries had leapfrogged them.

Why did the U.S. government not back the companies? Writers like Odell and Rand think that there was a conspiracy.[61] They believe that the companies had made up their minds beforehand to accept a price rise and that the United States supported their stand. But why? Why would they do that?

Because (as Odell and Rand construe it) a price rise would have put more money into the companies' pockets. It would also have narrowed the gap between the posted and spot market price, which would hurt the independents, and a higher price would assuage the hunger of the producers for higher royalties; in effect, it would get the producers off the companies' backs.

As for the United States, it was tired of paying a high price for oil while the rest of the world was getting it cut-rate. At the time, Washington—for domestic reasons—did not feel that it could cut the tariff, but, as long as the tariff stood, oil in the United States was going to cost more.

The arguments of Rand and Odell on the surface look good, and probably some of what they say is true. Where the argument breaks down, however, is that, along with everything else, the companies lost control of the price-setting arrangement. Whoever controls price controls the system. Under no circumstances would the cartel members have wanted to see control pass into the hands of the OPEC countries. The fact that it did meant significant loss for the companies.

There is another weakness in the argument—the companies' predicament was not over after Gadhafi acted. The shah next determined that he must have what Gadhafi had gotten, and maybe a little more. In other words, the oilmen now had to endure another leapfrogging session.

Finally, all accounts say that the oilmen were furious over what had been done. Reacting to the news that Washington had sided with the shah, George Piercy of Exxon is supposed to have remarked, "This whole exercise is silly as hell [i.e., the exercise of the oilmen going to Tehran to negotiate]."[62]

What was going on? If this was not all an elaborate charade, as Rand and Odell seem to believe, what was behind the U.S. government's decision not to stand behind the companies?

The answer, it would appear, is bound up with the Fourth Arab–Israeli War.

THE WAR AND THE U.S. RESPONSE

According to congressional testimony, Nixon was forewarned that the Arab oil embargo was about to come off. King Feisal called top executives of ARAMCO to an audience on May 3, 1973, and told them that the Arabs were set to attack Israel. Feisal was being called on to use the oil weapon (he said) as part of the Arab strategy.[63]

On May 23 Feisal summoned the same lot of executives, plus the heads of ARAMCO's parent companies, and repeated his warning. Nixon must correct America's biased attitude toward Israel, or else it would lose everything, he claimed.[64]

After that, the executives returned to Washington, where they passed the warning to the White House and also to the State and Defense Departments.[65] Nothing happened.

In other words, the system had broken down. The individuals on whom Feisal had counted to look out for his interests could not get through to Nixon; or, if the word was passed, the president was not sufficiently impressed to act on it.[66]

We have to view this occurrence in conjunction with the business of the shah, of his undercutting the companies' strategy. There is no doubt (at least as far as the author is concerned) that the State Department failed the oil companies. Not once but twice.

For years, the State Department was the agency that looked out for the cartel in government. It protected it against the Justice Department, and, whenever the companies had a particularly tricky piece of business to transact, they went to State.

However, in 1973 the State Department was in the throes of a great upheaval. Henry Kissinger (who was then national security adviser) was feuding with the secretary of state, William Rogers, over who was going to direct foreign policy. Kissinger ultimately won out, and Kissinger was no friend of the Arabs, whereas he was a friend of Iran through his Chase Manhattan Bank connections.

It would seem that the companies lost out because their friend in government was indisposed to protect them, now when they most needed him to act. Along with this, the White House itself was in disarray. Nixon was under extraordinary pressures at this time, having to fend off charges of improper behavior over Watergate. Along with that the public mood in the United States had turned ugly over Vietnam. Finally, the economy was not performing at all well. In other words, the government was facing crises on a number of fronts and may not have felt that it could concentrate on oil problems.

In any event, the system broke down, and there were many repercussions from this. But for our purposes one thing was crucial—thanks to the collapse Iraq beat the rap, so to speak. Iraq was (until OPEC blew) sure to be punished by the oilmen; they could never forgive it for doing what it did. Baghdad had not only taken something that the oilmen believed was theirs by right but also sought to protect itself from retaliation by doing a deal with the Soviets.

In the eyes of the companies, this was an unpardonable crime, and now, it appeared, the Iraqis were going to get away with it. Clean away, because the cartel was too preoccupied with trying to recoup after the OPEC revolution to take vengeance.

Nonetheless, the crime certainly was registered in New York and London; the men of honor could afford to wait, to bide their time. They would get their own back, sooner or later.

What the author is suggesting is that Iraq's coup of nationalizing the IPC fields became a factor later on in precipitating the confrontation with the United States. Saddam Hussein and the Iraqis, by taking the action that they did in 1972, put themselves beyond the pale, so to speak. They became, in the eyes of many powerful figures, marked men. This would explain why, as the 1990 confrontation moved to a resolution, Saddam found himself so alone and why, when he tried to defuse the clash, he was consistently rebuffed.

But here we are getting ahead of our story. To wrap up the 1973 crisis—after Libya's coup, OPEC determined to push up prices to what the members felt was a reasonable level. They were well launched on that course when, coincidentally and apparently unknown to any of the OPEC countries (except Saudi Arabia), the 1973 war erupted. Certain parties in OPEC then saw an opportunity to achieve what previously had been unthinkable—to actually take control of the pricing authority, which they now proceeded to do. The shah and the Venezuelans led the revolt—between them these two ran the price up to $11.65 per barrel (from less than $3), an increase of 300 percent.

The fact that the shah led the revolt was a particularly cruel blow to Washington. The shah, America's friend, had now turned out to be the number one hawk of OPEC.[67]

Is that to say that the Arab countries were not the villains? There really were no villains or heroes in this business. A revolution was occurring, and, as happens in such situations, some were set to benefit, some to be hurt.

As Odell and Rand have pointed out, the companies were not in bad shape after the event. They clearly benefited from the price run-up, especially those in Saudi Arabia, which managed to retain a close relationship with Riyadh, continuing to market Saudi oil.

At the same time, in another regard the companies lost. Starting in 1973, with the OPEC revolution, the oil-producing states took control of production. This was not called nationalization but rather "participation."

In most cases, the move to participation started out slowly, with the producers taking back only 60 percent of the production.[68] Eventually, however, they took it all.

The companies were caught between a rock and a hard place. If they fought the takovers while the OPEC crisis was going on, they almost certainly would have been excluded from buying oil when it was bringing the highest prices from the consumers.[69]

By agreeing to go along, the companies locked in the fantastic profits, but forever after their relation to the producers had changed—the producers ruled, so to speak, because the latter now had control of the pricing mechanism.

The OPEC countries certainly were not hurt. The world's consumers and, with them, the government of the United States were made to suffer.

In the case of the United States the damage was not immediately apparent, because much of OPEC's profits found their way into America's banks. But, in fact, the United States *was* hurt systemically, and that is what we look at in the next chapter.

NOTES

1. The best history of the Iraqi Communist Party is Hanna Batatu's book, *The Old Social Classes and the Revolutionary Movements of Iraq* (Princeton, NJ: Princeton University Press, 1978). The treatment of the communists' role in the coup is quite thorough.

2. He also alienated Nasser. Nasser had been hoping that Qasim would defer to the Egyptian leadership of the Arab world. By setting himself up as sole leader, Qasim was signaling that he was above parties—including Nasser's Pan-Arab party; hence, he wanted to be his own man.

3. Batatu, *The Old Social Classes*, 888.

4. One really does sense that, as in France, the lowest element of the population (in France, the *sans culottes*; in Iraq, the *shurugis*) had gotten completely out of control. See ibid.

5. Ibid., 841.

6. Ibid.

7. A good account of Qasim's dealings with the IPC is in David Hirst, *Oil and Public Opinion in the Middle East* (New York: Frederick A. Praeger, 1966), 76f.

8. George W. Stocking, *Middle East Oil* (Kingsport, TN: Vanderbilt University Press, 1970), 244f.

9. Hirst, *Oil and Public Opinion*, 96.

10. Ibid.

11. Ibid., 90.

12. Phebe Marr, *The Modern History of Iraq* (Boulder, CO: Westview Press, 1985), 173.

13. Qasim had made provision for such a company but had never gotten round to setting it up. It was not until the later Aref regime that this was done.

14. Hirst (*Oil and Public Opinion*) says that the way in which Qasim phrased his declaration implied that the oil companies were behind the Barzani revolt.

15. The control of the Kurdish *agas* over their tribesmen was much harsher than that of the sheikhs. Among the Kurds there existed a whole class of so-called *mishkin*, who were really serfs. See Batatu, *The Old Social Classes*, 9.

16. Stocking, *Middle East Oil*, 235.

17. Blair, *The Control of Oil*, 84.

18. Adil Hussein, *Iraq: The Eternal Fire* (London: Third World Center for Research and Publishing, 1981).

19. Christopher Rand, *Making Democracy Safe for Oil* (Boston: Little, Brown, 1975), 191f.

20. Majid Khadduri, *Republican Iraq* (London: Oxford University Press, 1969), 152f.

21. Ibid.
22. Ibid.
23. Blair, *The Control of Oil*, 86.
24. Ibid.
25. Ibid.
26. Batatu, *The Old Social Classes*, 1010.
27. This was an instance of official favor to the son of the army officer who headed the infamous court that tried the remnants of the old regime. The Ba'thists provoked an uproar, and the students walked out of classes. The Slugletts say the 1963 coup was "a texbook example of its kind: detailed planning, close coordination with sympathetic officers, who were to seize key military and communications installations, the killing of the head of state and his entourage and the nomination of a 'military figurehead.' " Marion Farouk-Sluglett and Peter Sluglett, *Iraq, since 1958* (London: I. B. Tauris, 1987), 83. Of course, this begs the question of how these inexperienced youths could mount such a sophisticated operation.
28. Details in Khadduri, *Republican Iraq*, 188f.
29. Saddam was shot in the leg, then dug out the bullet with a penknife while still escaping in the getaway car.
30. Khadduri, *Republican Iraq*, 188.
31. Ibid.
32. Ibid.
33. Batatu, *The Old Social Classes*, 976.
34. Ibid.
35. Uriel Dann, *Iraq under Qassem* [*sic*] (London: Frederick A. Praeger, 1969).
36. Batatu says that Hasanein Haykal, a confidant of Nasser, was told by King Hussein of Jordan that the CIA supplied lists to the Ba'thists of which communists to kill. The Slugletts expand on this, saying that they were told by someone in the U.S. State Department that Saddam Hussein and other Ba'thists made contact with the U.S. Embassy in Damascus sometime in the 1950s. Finally, the Penroses say that, although they did not believe that State Department was involved in the coup, they are not so sure about the CIA ("with its obsessive fear of communism"). Batatu, *The Old Social Classes*, 985; Farouk-Sluglett and Sluglett, *Iraq, since 1958*, fn. 3, 297; Edith Penrose and E. F. Penrose, *Iraq, International Relations and National Development* (London: Ernest Benn, 1978), 288. Of course all this is hearsay; apparently there is no smoking gun.
37. The communists first developed the militias, and indeed the concept has survived in Iraq, where there is still a Popular Army, although it is much diminished in prestige. Batatu, *The Old Social Classes*, 1011.
38. Ibid. 736.
39. Khadduri, *Republican Iraq*, 215.
40. Stocking, *Middle East Oil*, 259f.; see also Hussein, *Iraq: The Eternal Fire*, 64f.
41. Stocking, *Middle East Oil*, 265.
42. Batatu, *The Old Social Classes*, 1066f.
43. Ibid.
44. Ibid., 1073f.
45. Ibid.
46. Ibid.
47. Effectively, now the industry in the United States was broken down into three components—the independents (i.e., companies that depended on outside supplies for

more than 70 percent of their oil); large, integrated firms (like Standard Oil of Indiana) that were not one of the so-called Seven Sisters; and the Sisters.

48. Anthony Sampson, *The Seven Sisters* (New York: Bantam Books, 1973), 170f.

49. Ibid.

50. Ibid., 172.

51. Blair, *The Control of Oil*. The loopholes enabled oil to come in from Canada and Mexico. This was done supposedly for national security reasons, but it angered the Venezuelans.

52. See Chapter 3.

53. Sampson, *The Seven Sisters*, 188.

54. For the story of Enrico Mattei, the head of AGIP, and his fight with the Sisters, see P. H. Frankel, *Mattei: Oil and Power Politics* (New York: Frederick A. Praeger, 1966).

55. Sampson, *The Seven Sisters*, 189.

56. Rand, *Making Democracy Safe*, 84.

57. Sampson, *The Seven Sisters*, 252f.

58. Ibid., 256f.

59. Ibid., 268f.

60. Ibid.

61. Peter Odell, *Oil and World Power* (London: Penguin Books, 1974); Rand, *Making Democracy Safe*, 257–258.

62. Yergin, *The Prize* (New York: Simon and Schuster, 1991), 581.

63. "The Oil Companies in the Crisis," in *The Oil Crisis in Perspective*, ed. Raymond Vernon (New York: W. W. Norton, 1976), 183.

64. Ibid.

65. Ibid.

66. James Akins, who was then U.S. ambassador to Riyadh, claimed that neither Nixon nor Kissinger was interested in oil at this time. "You couldn't get anybody to focus on it," he said. "Everyone thought the price of oil was coming down forever. Everyone thought there was a permanent glut." Jeffrey Robinson, *Yamani: The Inside Story* (New York: Atlantic Monthly Press, 1989), 80.

67. George Lenczowski, *Middle East Oil in the Revolutionary Age* (Washington, DC: American Enterprise Institute, 1976), 26.

68. The 60 percent figure came about because of tax complications. The American companies derived the tax advantages from the U.S. government based on their retaining at least 40 percent control.

69. At an early stage of the crisis, the shah—to see what the traffic would bear—offered Iranian oil on the spot market. It fetched $17 a barrel, a 600 percent increase over the posted price.

CHAPTER 5

Second and Third Shocks and the 1987 Reflagging

We said in the introduction that systems, as we defined them, were coercive arrangements.[1] They are worked up to perpetuate control over some sort of exploitative activity by a select group. Implied is the fact that the group is able to protect itself against interlopers.[2] The system members, in other words, have to have the capability of using force successfully to keep others from poaching on their preserve.

In the last chapter we said that, with the OPEC revolution, the international oil system faltered, because its members could not avail themselves of protection that they had thought assured.

The Nixon administration, which had the capability to act, did not do so. We asked, Why not? We looked at the behavior of Kissinger, of the State Department, and, finally, of Nixon himself.

We did not look, but perhaps we should have looked, at the oil companies. They certainly were implicated in the breakdown. Why could not they have forced the issue, that is, brought pressure to bear to make Nixon act? Their peculiar situation may have inhibited them. Whatever they did—in the issue-raising line—was risky, since they constituted a cartel, something illegal under U.S. law. The public, as, we saw, was not at all sympathetic to them and, in fact, was prone to become violently antipathetic toward them, if aroused.

Shortly after King Feisal gave his warning to the oil company executives, Chevron (the new name of SOCAL) tried to make an issue of America's tilt toward Israel. It ran a press campaign on the West Coast taking the Arabs' side and warning (in line with what the executives had been told by Feisal) that, should America go on favoring the Jewish state, this would jeopardize U.S.

interests. That triggered a countercampaign against the oil companies by the American–Israeli Political Action Committee (AIPAC), and Chevron soon backed off.

One could also indict Feisal. Why did he wait so long to pass his warning? Had he acted sooner, the companies might have found some more subtle (and effective) way of bringing influence to bear on the White House.

To look into this question is beyond the scope of this book. It would be an interesting topic to research, but it would take us quite a ways off the track.

We want instead to look at steps that Washington took to try to reclaim control of the situation. Effectively, it forged a special relationship with the Saudis in which protection was offered, and there was a mechanism worked up to assure the Saudis that such protection could be counted on.

In this chapter we see how this special relationship worked out. It exposed a lot of hostility, both in the United States and abroad, from interests opposed to U.S. involvement with the Arabs. The outbreak of the Iran-Iraq War also greatly complicated the issue.

SPECIAL RELATIONSHIPS

Once the oil producers got control of production, *they* were then able to set prices, and, price setting being the alpha and omega of the oil business, it was now a producers' show, so to speak, after that.

America was effectively shut out of it, but, as we shall see, it was soon able to influence the process. America co-opted the Saudis, who, among oil producers, were the most independent and powerful. Once they were won over, the Americans could then rest assured of having a say, even a crucial one, in how much oil would be produced and thus what the oil price would be set at.

The old mechanism for keeping control of oil production and for setting prices had been the posted price arrangement, which the oil companies had contrived to suit themselves and to placate the producers. The new mechanism that the United States now developed (to co-opt the Saudis) was the special relationship.

The United States offered to draw the Saudis into its worldwide security net, and the basis of this maneuver was arms transfers. America allowed the Saudis to have some of the most up-to-date weapons that it produced. The Saudis would buy them, of course.[3]

The reader may ask, What was so good about that? If the Saudis had to *buy* the arms, were they not doing the *United States* a favor? Not so, because it was not the *use* value of the arms that counted; it was their *exchange* value.

What had held the Arabs back for so long from developing ties to the United States? For one thing, it was the fact that the United States was not much interested in the Middle East, in general, and the Arabs, in particular. The area was never important for Washington, at least not in an official sense.[4] Washington was content to leave it to the oil companies to manage affairs in this part of the world. It would intervene in emergencies, as happened in Iran in 1953. But once the difficulty was taken care of, the U.S. government happily withdrew.

Another reason for American chariness to get involved was the Israeli lobby. The American Jewish community could make difficulties for an administration perceived by the community as drawing too close to any one of the Arab states.

Arms transfers got around the necessity (and difficulty) of having to craft a formal alliance between Arabs and Americans. The transfers delivered all of the benefits of treaty ties but were less vulnerable to attack by such agencies as AIPAC.[5]

For example, the arms sales invariably stretched out over a period of years, meaning that the Saudis could look forward to regular interaction with the Pentagon. The weapons systems sold were complex, and, consequently, Saudi officers could not be expected to master them overnight; they would have to attend military schools in the United States. In this way networking with Americans could be carried on.

More networking opportunities could be had in official Washington and in the nether reaches of the United States. In Washington the Saudis could enter offices where arms contracts were administered. In cities where arms were manufactured, the Saudis also were welcome. Local contractors became their constituents, undertaking to lobby Congress at their behest. The manufacturers did so hoping to have the contracts renewed, a necessity for the companies' profitability and for the prosperity of the regions where the arms were produced.

Most important, perhaps, the U.S. government itself was indebted to the Saudis. These were not boutique weapons that were being sold, arms specifically designed for third-party states. They were the very weapons that America depended on for its survival. The Saudis, by financing production (to a significant degree), relieved American taxpayers of having to do so.

In other words, the special relationship reassured the Saudis that America would not abandon them, because it appeared so plainly to be the fact that it needed them.

One could argue that it was not necessary for America to become involved with the Saudis at all. Why did the United States have to get tied up with the oil producers? America had oil. Not as much as formerly, but, had there been a serious effort made to conserve, it might have become self-sufficient.[6]

This brings up the problem of who initiated the special relationship between America and the Saudis. The author's view is that it probably was the Saudis, although the Americans, once the matter was broached, were only too willing to go along.

The 1973 war left the Saudis in something of a bind. Up till then they had been advantageously positioned among the Arabs. After the 1967 war the Saudis took over as paymasters of the so-called confrontation states (Egypt, Syria, and Jordan). Since they held the purse strings, their counsel was sought; their advice was followed. Even under Nasser, the Egyptians were loath to cross the Saudis.

But what happened after 1973? Influence among the Arabs reverted to the states that had actually fought Israel; Saudi Arabia's influence thus declined perceptibly. Moreover, once Sadat elected to ally Egypt with the United States through formal ties, this, too, diminished the Saudi role. Egypt now could look to the United States for financial support—it could play off Washington against Riyadh.

Hence, it seems likely that it was the Saudis who sought closer ties to Washington, and Washington—for all of the reasons given—was happy to oblige.

THE SPECIALNESS OF THE SAUDIS

Starting in 1974, we see an upsurge of arms buying by the Saudis.[7] Whereas, before, they had kept their spending down (according to the Stockholm International Peace Research Institute [SIPRI]), by the late 1970s they were the number one arms buyer in the Middle East; ultimately, they supplanted the shah.[8]

Initially, a good portion of the Saudis' expenditure was on infrastructure—airfields, roads, storage facilities, that sort of thing.[9] This required the importation of numerous foreign workers and Americans to manage them, since it was American contractors mainly who were being employed.[10]

Penetration of Saudi society by Westerners upset many Saudis, who took seriously the injunction—operative until then—that non-Muslims be kept away from the Holy Places.[11] That there was concern about this is evident from the many violent occurrences during this period—the Grand Mosque seizure, the assassination of Feisal, and the seizure of the OPEC delegates in Vienna.[12] This last most likely was not the work of disgruntled Saudis.[13] Still, it shows how anger over the Saudis' strengthening ties to the United States spread throughout the Arab world.

Another factor influencing the Saudis' move to the side of the United States was increasing polarization among the Arabs. As Sadat concluded his separate peace with Israel, the Arabs condemned him, and all parties had to join in the attacks. The Saudis are never happy frozen into a public stance from which there is no easy retreat. To have courted closer U.S. ties at the same time that the Arabs were pressing them to become more outspokenly anti-Zionist would have been characteristic of them.

The kingdom of Saudi Arabia had at this time an insubstantial population base (probably no more than 3 million).[14] Thus, the Saudis were no match for the Israelis, who, even though they were not much more populous, nonetheless were better fighters than they. As for Iran, with the shah in charge it seemed not to present a danger. Still, certain policies of the shah gave pause to Arab states like Saudi Arabia.

And then there was Iraq. After its 1958 revolution, Iraq moved into the camp of the Soviet Union, or so it seemed. Moreover, the Ba'thists were the most rabid in their opposition to Israel and support of the Palestinian cause. As noted earlier, this kind of extremism made the Saudis uneasy.

All of these security considerations aside, something else determined the Saudis to draw close to the United States. Starting in 1974, they had enormous amounts of petrodollars to recycle. With their small population, they could not absorb all of the money that they were making. New York and London being the financial capitals of the world, it was logical to direct their money there.

Inevitably, the more that the Saudis invested in the West's economy, the more that the leadership came perforce to think as Westerners think. The concept of stability, of great importance to Americans, was not something that appealed to Arabs. It was otherwise for the Saudis, however—a stable world was one in which their investments would be safe.

To be sure, not all Saudis approved of this warming toward the United States. According to Terzian, Crown Prince Abdullah lobbied hard for a cutback in oil production—from 10 million barrels a day to no more than 5 million.[15] Such a move would have distressed the Americans, inasmuch as it would have adversely affected their economy.

Evidently, the Saudi leadership appreciated this, because the proposal was never seriously considered. Harming America's economic position would harm that of the Saudis as well. Rather than do this, the Saudis kept production up, a course that won them numerous enemies within OPEC.

In 1974, immediately after the price quadrupling, oil sold for $10.84 a barrel.[16] Then, at the OPEC meeting in Vienna the following year, this was raised to $11.46, and to $12.70 at the end of 1977.[17] These were all modest increases, or at least they were so seen by the OPEC hawks—the Iranians, Iraqis, Algerians, and Libyans.

That the prices did not go higher was thanks to the Saudis' keeping them down. In 1976 the contest between OPEC doves and hawks became so heated that the organization adopted a two-tiered price structure, the Saudis (and United Arab Emirates) refusing to go along with the higher price advocated by Iran.

The hawks imputed political motives to the Saudis' unwillingness to raise prices; they called them "tools" of the Americans.[18] This view of the hawks is understandable, but, in the author's view, probably not tenable. The Saudis acted for self-interested reasons.[19] They looked on OPEC as an instrument of their national policy. Were the organization to become too radical, the industrialized states surely would work to destroy it. This seems to have been the Saudis' perception and great fear.

Kissinger, right after the OPEC revolution, instituted the International Energy Agency (IEA), an organization of OECD countries that he hoped would become a consumers' cartel to oppose OPEC. The IEA, among other activities, lobbied for conservation measures to be undertaken throughout the West, but particularly in the United States.[20]

Holding the OECD countries together on oil policy was not an easy proposition for the Americans. Ofttimes their own policies made problems among the other OECD states. For example, the Europeans (and Japanese) suspected the special relationships that Washington was cultivating—not just with the Saudis but with the Iranians as well.

The relationships were seen as attempts by Washington to aggrandize itself by creating bilateral deals that would assure America access to oil at discount prices. According to Robinson, Kissinger supposedly told the shah that America could tolerate higher oil prices but wanted Iran to continue making arms purchases; implied here is a quid pro quo.[21] Assuming that the account is accurate, it raises an interesting point.

The arms that the shah (and now the Saudis) was buying were superinflationary. To pay for them, the monarchs were going to have to maximize revenue, and this perforce would lead them to push oil prices even higher.[22]

Is this not contradictory? It would appear to be so. We hold off discussing this aspect of the situation, however, until we have had a chance to probe a little more deeply into America's relations with the shah.

CO-OPTING THE IRANIANS

One of the things that the United States lost in 1973 (with the OPEC revolution) was expertise on the Middle East.[23] Before the crisis, the United States relied on the oil company executives to look out for matters in the Gulf, the only area that Washington was half interested in (after Israel, of course, which was a sui generis case). The assumption of U.S. policymakers seems to have been that America's interests and those of the oil companies were identical.[24]

After the crisis, the oilmen became, effectively, paid retainers of the oil sheikhs. ARAMCO became the marketer of the newly created Saudi national oil company. To be sure, for the oilmen this was a comedown—previously *they* had controlled the Saudis' oil production. Now they simply put what was produced onto the market.

At the same time, however, with the price of oil rising astronomically, the oil companies profited handsomely from their special relationship with the sheikhs. This was not a setup that they would likely cast aside. Effectively, a tie was forged, based on mutual interests. As we said, economically, all of this made sense, but it does not detract from the fact that now the oilmen were more allied to Riyadh than to Washington.

In the same way, America lost out in its relationship with the British. For years it had taken British involvement with the oil producers for granted. This was only natural since, from World War I on, the Middle East was Britain's sphere.[25] But, then, in 1971 Britain withdrew, protesting that it could no longer afford to keep up its commitment to this part of the world.

Thus, in the space of only two years—first with the defection of the oil executives, then with the withdrawal of the British—Washington lost the support of individuals and agencies that really knew the region.

After Britain's departure, the United States ought to have taken an active interest in the Gulf, proclaiming that fact to the world; in other words, taken the area over as its sphere from the British. But Americans were not about to do this—in large part, because of difficulties that they were then encountering over Vietnam.

That business in Southeast Asia had turned out so badly that no American president would want to contemplate another such involvement. Nixon particularly was not up to it, having gotten himself into such difficulty at home.[26] A surrogate had to be found who would guard the Middle East—or, at any rate, the Gulf.

The Saudis could not do it. The Americans already were protecting them. Israel would have jumped at the chance, but that would have sabotaged all of America's (and the West's) interests in the area. Really, there was only one candidate, and that was the shah.

THE AMBITIOUS SHAH

When we looked at the shah in Chapter 3, America had restored him to his throne. For this, he was grateful. However, almost immediately he began importuning President Eisenhower for aid. He wanted economic assistance and arms.[27]

With the latter, he proposed to stabilize conditions inside his country and also (he said) to defend the West against the Russians. President Eisenhower found this latter idea absurd and said as much in letters to the shah.[28]

Eisenhower's reaction the shah found hurtful. As we will see, the shah was a prickly character, easily wounded where his *armour propre* was involved. The shah confessed himself baffled by the behavior not just of Eisenhower but of Eisenhower's successor, Kennedy.[29]

Kennedy rebuffed the shah as severely as had Ike. He advised him to reform his country, do something about the rampant corruption there, and stop thinking about weapons. Like Eisenhower, Kennedy felt that the shah's priorities were muddled.[30]

We have, then, a ruler who, in the period from 1953 through the early 1960s, is looked down on by the Americans but who, by 1972, has so far recovered as to have received this remarkable offer of becoming America's surrogate.[31] It does not make a lot of sense, especially as we know that just one year later, in 1973, the shah turned on the Americans, driving the price of oil upward when Washington was striving to keep it down.

Why were Nixon and Kissinger able to look on the shah with such favor in 1972, when Nixon's predecessors could barely tolerate the man?[32]

In the interval—between 1953 and 1972—the shah's public image had undergone a refurbishing, a consciously directed campaign performed by Iranian and American publicists; and this was done largely in response to events that took place in Iraq.[33]

THE SHAH AND THE KURDS

When the Iraqis overthrew the monarchy in 1958, and when they subsequently reappropriated the oil lands in 1961, influential circles in the West saw Iraq as "going communist." That opinion was shared by the sheikhs of the lower Gulf. For a time, no country in the Middle East was as isolated as Iraq. The isolation increased once the Iraqis signed a Friendship Treaty with Moscow in 1974.

Even the radical Arab states like Egypt and Syria mistrusted the Iraqis. About the only ally that they had was the Palestine Liberation Organization (PLO), because, among Arabs, the Iraqis took the fiercest stands against Israel.

It was this universal mistrust of Iraq that the shah exploited to rebuild his image. He offered his country as a base from which the Iraqi Kurdish leader Barzani might carry on his revolt. In effect, he opened his border to the Kurds, allowing them to move back and forth, an arrangement that is crucial for a landlocked guerrilla movement such as this.

The author is not aware that the shah did anything more for the Kurds; he assumes that he did not actually provide funds for them. However, money to support the revolt would have had to come from somewhere. (Except in unusual circumstances, the Kurds do not fight unless paid.)

Whatever the shah did, it was welcome in certain quarters in the West. Practically all of the instability with which Iraq was plagued from 1960 onward was due to unrest in the north. (What we are saying is that if the oilmen did not outright connive to obtain this result, they certainly had reason to applaud it.)

The shah made another calculated move. He took increased revenue from oil sales and spent it on weapons. Until the early 1960s the United States had been *giving* the shah arms—not a great many, in fact, the minimum that could be gotten by with and then just to placate him.[34]

But then after the IPC shut down in 1963, production in Iraq shifted to Iran. This had the effect of boosting the shah's revenues. He took the extra cash and spent it on weaponry, mainly from the United States.[35] For the United States, the purchases could not have come at a better time.

In 1961 Washington switched from giving away arms to trying to sell them. In that year, it created the office of International Logistics Negotiations (ILN) to promote the sale of America's military hardware. Along with that, the Pentagon developed the Military Assistance Credit Account to guarantee financing for the sales from American banks.[36] This account grew to munificent proportions, thanks to a special procedure whereby the credit was repaid to it, not to the Treasury—in effect, this was a revolving fund.[37]

The Congress, which knew nothing of this special procedure, found out about it in 1967 and cut it off, which adversely affected the Pentagon's arms-selling activities.[38] Why did the Congress do this? Because in the late 1960s–early 1970s growing numbers of Americans disliked the Pentagon. According to John Lewis Gaddis, because of opposition to the Vietnam War, the Senate in 1971 almost passed an amendment that would have reduced America's commitment to NATO by half.[39]

At this juncture the shah made his offer to Nixon to buy arms—and not just a few arms but many; and he stipulated that these must be the most up-to-date systems. One can see why Nixon would have jumped at this opportunity. Let Congress cut off the Pentagon's credit. Nixon would finance America's defense establishment with arms sale to the shah.[40]

By 1975, according to Sampson, the Congress was alert to the fact "that America was forging a new kind of commitment to the Persian Gulf based on arms sales," not just to the shah but to the Saudis and to some of the lesser sheikhdoms.[41] This triggered a revolt on the part of the Congress, which now demanded a say on what weapons could be sold to whom. It got this with the passage of the 1976–1977 Arms Export Control Act.

We are getting somewhat ahead of our story here. The point is that America's perceptions of the Middle East underwent change at this time. Before 1972 the whole region (except for Israel) was of little importance to it; now that no longer was the case. The Gulf gained because wealthy oil producers resident there had the means and the willingness to buy American arms.

HOW IT WORKED OUT

The shah's army was barely competent. It had taken part in just one significant military engagement, to put down the insurrection in Oman in the late 1960s and early 1970s. British officers seconded to the Omani army, who had observed the Iranians' performance in this instance, were not impressed.

Then, in 1971, the Iranian army seized three small islands in the Strait of Hormuz, the possession of one of the emirates, which itself was practically a nonentity. (The emirate did not even possess an army.)

In 1974 the Iranian army came near to fighting Iraq (and we have something to say about this in a moment), but that, too, turned out badly.

From a military standpoint then, the shah's army was not up to a great deal, and consequently it is remarkable that Nixon would have tapped it for such an assignment.

One suspects that America's designation of the shah was pro forma. It wanted the Gulf to be seen as part of the West's appanage. It would not take over the protection duties there itself. By appointing the shah, it indicated its concern for the region without having to make sacrifices.

This attitude on the Americans' part was somewhat casual; the shah's view of the setup differed considerably from this. He took the surrogate role seriously. Indeed, he embarked on an arms-buying campaign that was, by any standards, excessive. From 1972 through 1976 the shah bought $10 billion worth of U.S. arms, including sophisticated surveillance devices.[42]

The purchases disturbed the Pentagon generals, who expressed their concern to Nixon.[43] They complained that not only did the shah buy weapons that were too sophisticated for his forces, but he bought far and away too much; in some instances he seemed to be needlessly duplicating purchases.

The president and Kissinger took the line that the shah should be indulged. In effect, they gave him carte blanche where weapons buying was concerned. By 1972 the Vietnam War was going badly, which caused the doves in Congress to redouble efforts against the Pentagon, and thus the urgency to sell arms had increased. In addition, after the 1973 OPEC revolution America's balance of payments was seriously disturbed, and arms sales to oil producers were seen as a way of redressing it somewhat.

Hence, the White House was not concerned about the good sense of what the shah was doing. Indeed, the generals' arguments that the Iranian army was incompetent to use the weapons, far from influencing Nixon to hold back, probably was a goad to sell more. If the army could not use the arms, it could not get into trouble with them.

At the same time, however, Nixon's policy caused strains with the Arabs. The shah did not disguise his expansionist ambitions—he meant to turn the Gulf into an Iranian lake,[44] and this was not a program that the Arabs could support. Not just the sheikhs but all the Arabs mistrusted the shah. Not only had he taken those three small islands from an Arab country, but he had declared an irridentist claim to Bahrain (another Arab island).[45] As part of its plan of withdrawal from the Gulf, Britain had sought to include Bahrain in the United Arab Emirates (UAE), a unitary state based on the old Trucial Coast arrangement. The shah refused to sanction this, because, he said, Bahrain was Iranian.

The shah had also, as we have just discussed, inserted himself into the Oman civil war, in effect, extending Iran's reach to the furthest extremity of the Gulf. That action provoked Baghdad into supporting the Omani rebels.

Washington should probably not have gotten so deeply involved with the shah if it intended to keep up good relations with the Arabs. That it could not see problems developing along this line would appear to show ignorance. Washington in those days saw everything through the optic of the Cold War. All Gulf states, with the exception of Iraq, were anti-communist; the Iranians were arch anti-communists; ipso facto, the Iranians and the sheikhs should be friends.

As for the Iraqis, Iran's weapons purchases confronted them with a dangerous threat. The shah was actively promoting an anti-Ba'th strategy. Baghdad had no doubt that, ultimately, it would have to defend itself against Iran. The Iraqis stepped up arms purchases of their own, using their newfound oil wealth.

The Gulf, then, in the mid- to late 1970s, became the vortex of an arms blizzard; the whole area was awash with guns. Now all that was wanted was a war, and that was not long in coming.

THE LAST BARZANI REVOLT

In 1972, when Nixon appealed to the shah to protect U.S. interests, the Iranian talked him into financing the Barzani revolt. The shah had been supporting the Kurds since 1961. By 1972 the revolt was about to peter out. Saddam had made an offer that Barzani felt obliged to accept. It was better than any that the Kurds had been offered to date.[46]

The shah, then, teamed up with the Israelis, who, like the shah, desired to keep the war going.[47] The Israelis and the shah talked Nixon into giving Barzani $16 million worth of weapons (which the Israelis had taken from the Arabs in the 1967 war). These would be transferred to the Kurds on condition that they recommence fighting.[48]

It seems legitimate to speculate that the oil companies were involved here. The timing is certainly suspect. In 1972 the Ba'th announced its intention of nationalizing the IPC; the same year, all of these forces undertook to revive the Barzani revolt. If it was not the threat of nationalization that spurred this activity, what then?

In any event, over the objections of some of his closest advisers, Barzani accepted the deal, and the war recommenced.[49] It soon turned into a debacle for both the Kurds and the United States.

First of all, the shah's security apparatus SAVAK practically took charge of the fighting. SAVAK agents, reorganized into a paracommando group called Parastin,[50] replaced Barzani as the effective commander.

Barzani had always been a successful guerrilla fighter. A man with a reputation of playing his cards close to his chest, he had managed to maintain an autonomous stance in the Middle East. Under the influence of SAVAK, however, he made deplorable blunders.

Militarily, he stopped waging a positional war (at which he was adept) to fight what was more of a war of maneuver (about which he knew comparatively little).[51]

Then he abandoned his erstwhile reserve on the political front. Whereas in the past he had been careful to maintain good relations with practically all parties outside Iraq, now he alienated not only the Arabs but the Russians. In an extraordinary interview with a freelance journalist, he made the most damning statements. For example, he practically revealed that he was getting arms from the Israelis, and he said that he would be willing to let foreign oil firms into Kurdistan to exploit the fields, were he to win his fight with Baghdad.[52]

This upset the Russians mightily. The history of Barzani's involvement with Moscow is beyond the scope of this study. Suffice it to say that, at crucial periods in the career of the Kurdish leader, the Russians befriended him. Until 1972, Barzani had been careful not to impose on this friendship, but now he threw it away, in effect, as the Soviets practically withdrew their support. The reaction of the Arabs not just to Barzani but to the Americans' role in the affair was, if anything, worse.[53]

The Arabs asked, What have we gotten ourselves into? The United States had turned over the Gulf to the shah, ostensibly to become our protector. The shah's first action had been to collude with the Israelis to rekindle the Barzani revolt. Barzani, a man whom we have all along regarded as sensible, had abandoned restraint and made these incredible statements. How had we, the Arabs, not been compromised?

At this point the Iraqis and Iranians declared a truce. They agreed to compose their long-standing differences, in other words, put an end to the war.

WHAT HAPPENED?

The Barzanis had not fared well in the fighting. They had been pushed back to the border and thus obviously were in need of assistance, which could have come only from the shah. He would have had to commit his forces, that is, take a direct part in the war.

From the ferociousness with which the Iraqis fought, it was clear that they would not give way. That meant that the Iranians' commitment would have had to be total. Was the shah up to that?

First of all, he would be fighting for the Kurds—to an Iranian, this was an inane proposition. One did not promote Kurdish nationalism, not when—as was the case with the shah—one had millions of discontented Kurdish subjects who would have loved to revolt if they thought there was a hope of succeeding,[54] and, of course, if Barzani won his fight, that hope would have been demonstrated.

Along with that, this was (by now) 1975. Money from the OPEC revolution was streaming in. Why should the shah involve himself in a potentially ruinous war when he had better ways of spending his windfall?

There was another consideration. Both Iraq and Iran are what are known as high absorbers. That means that, as oil-producing states, they have enormous demands upon them and can absorb almost any amount of cash (this largely is due to their having large populations). They, therefore, tend to favor policies that drive prices up.

The so-called low-absorbing states, like the Saudis, do the reverse; and the United States and the rest of the OECD countries back the low absorbers.

So, then, after the OPEC revolution, Iraq and Iran, longtime enemies though they were, found that they had strong economic interests in common—they needed to push up prices, against the wishes of the sheikhs and of the West. There thus was a practical reason for the shah and Saddam to get together.

Evidently, Saddam felt the same way, because he grasped at the shah's offer. In return for tangible concessions (Saddam had to relinquish half the Shatt al Arab, an enormous sacrifice for him), the shah agreed to renounce support of the Kurds.[55]

So the deal was concluded at the 1975 OPEC Conference in Algiers. It was one of the more surprising turns of events of the post–World War II era, something on a par with the Arabs' declaring war on Israel in 1973.

Practically every commentator on the agreement underrates its importance. It is treated with a kind of embarrassed dismissiveness, as though the shah had had a lapse.

But this was no aberration. The deal struck with Saddam held for as long as the shah held onto power. There is no hint that either of the two men was less than scrupulous in fulfilling his obligations.[56]

But, one could say, how about Russia? The shah supposedly was anti-communist. How could he make a deal with what many believed was a Soviet client? In fact, Iraq was moving away from the Russians during this period. Saddam had actually initiated a purge of Iraqi communists.[57] He sponsored other changes, having the effect of moving Iraq closer to the West.

By moving to the center, Saddam made it possible for the shah to reconcile with him, and yet it seems likely that, even had the Iraqis not changed, rapprochement would have occurred. As long as their interests on oil were allied, it was folly for these two not to get together.

From 1973 on (within the circles of OPEC) and from 1975 in the security arena, the Iraqis and Iranians worked in tandem. Both became foremost hawks in OPEC, and both espoused the position that Gulf security should be left to the littoral states. This latter was an extremely controversial position; it frightened not only the West but many of the Arab oil producers.

It is interesting to see the changed treatment accorded the shah in the Western media at this time. The shah was now more and more being taken to task by Western reporters; he found himself involved in numerous, quite testy exchanges. One is typical. Asked about his policy of pushing prices up, he said that for years the West had exploited the oil producers. It was time for a change, he said, and, he intimated, he was prepared to bring such change about.[58]

WHAT HAPPENED TO THE SHAH?

Why did the shah lose out so spectacularly? The author feels that his strategy was defective—it did not match means to ends. The shah wanted to make Iran into a first-rate power, and this required having a first-rate military, which, in turn, meant one that was technologically sound.

There were not enough competent technicians in Iran to accomplish this result. The shah's way of getting around this was to import technicians who would operate the advanced weapons systems that he bought.[59]

He also imported teachers to train the unsophisticated Iranians. But this latter task was immense, the Iranians being so terribly backward. The population at the time was 80 percent rural. The shah ought to have eased back on his weapons buying or at least have taken steps to stop importing foreigners.

Given the intense hostility of Iranians for Americans, after the 1953 Mosadeq overthrow, the shah ought to have taken heed; he was sailing into dangerous waters. Indeed, when Iran's economy stumbled (as it did in 1978), resentment boiled over.[60] The clerics and *bazaaris* exploited popular hostility by raking up the Status of Forces issue.[61] Once that issue was joined, things deteriorated rapidly.

The question, then, was, Why did the shah not simply inform the Americans that he was overcommitted in the weapons-buying line and that he would have to rest on his oars, so to speak?

In the author's view, this was never a possibility. Effectively, the shah had put himself in a box. He had styled his army along modern lines; that is, he made it into a carbon copy of that of the United States. It was only from the United States that he could get replacement parts, not to mention new systems.

Washington was not interested in the judicious shaping of Iran's military to make it a first-rate fighting force. It was primarily set on exploiting the shah's penchant for arms purchases so as to keep expense for arms production in the United States down.

In other words, the shah's only usefulness to the United States was as a purchaser of arms. Had he stopped doing that or even scaled back appreciably, Washington would have valued him less, and, remember, the shah's army was—as stated earlier—untested. He was therefore in need of protection, if not from the Russians (the author thinks that threat has been overstated), then from his own people. Arms display was a way of cowing the populace.

Harking back to the matter of arms purchases being superinflationary, one could say that this destroyed the shah. Every year, the price of the systems went up, leaving it to the shah to find the means of continuing his purchases. He could not do it, and so, ultimately, he lost out.

In 1978 on a visit to Washington, the shah said that oil prices should come down; effectively, he reversed field. Immediately afterward, he was overthrown. It's interesting to speculate that this announcement had something to do with the overthrow—until he made it, his credentials as a nationalist were sound.

Sophisticated Iranians would have perceived the implications of the shah's announcement, that it was a capitulation to the United States.

THE SECOND OIL SHOCK

The shah's overthrow, besides bringing to power an austere, religiously based regime in Iran, triggered the event that subsequently has become known as the Second Oil Shock. Before we discuss the Khomeini regime and the activity that led to the Iran–Iraq War, we should look at this next disruption of the world economy. How America reacted and what it did (and did not do) have great bearing on the outbreak of the Gulf War.

We are now five years past the OPEC revolution, and, in a certain sense the world has been on a roller-coaster ride. Oil prices that went through the roof in

1973 were held down in 1974 and 1975, partly because of a worldwide recession and partly due to the exertions of the Saudis. After that (through 1977 and into 1978) prices hovered in the vicinity of $12 per barrel. Comparatively speaking, this was not a lot, but, in the United States, it was thought to be so.

With the initial run-up in oil prices an attempt was made in the United States to find scapegoats. The Arabs were targeted, but along with them, the oil companies, too, were indicted. Congress (through the Church and Jackson Committees) ran a series of highly publicized investigations, out of which came several legislative reforms.

Among the changes agreed on was a cutback in the depletion allowance (which reduced the tax on oil production). Also cut back was the companies' foreign tax credit (the so-called golden gimmick). There were efforts made to roll back oil prices. There was even a movement toward divestiture, that is, the breaking up of the integrated firms into separate entities.[62] Still to come were the imposition of a windfall profits tax and decontrol of oil prices.

All of these changes weakened the position of the cartel. To be sure, in financial terms, the companies were doing well. Their profits had skyrocketed as a result of these successive oil shocks, and, as stated, they retained ties to the most important producers, becoming their marketing agents for downstream operations.

But the very fact that they had not been hurt financially worked against them. An aroused Congress accused them of making money off the crisis, while the rest of the country suffered.

What the Congress overlooked or refused to consider was that the companies now were reduced to the status of traders. Once the oil producers either nationalized (as did Iraq) or demanded participation (as did Saudi Arabia), the companies then had to give up equity.[63] The spot market became the focus of activity. The character of the oil business changed. The Congress, however, continued to view it as dominated by the so-called Seven Sisters. It failed to perceive that the cartel, in effect, was in a holding pattern; or, put another way, it was somewhere in limbo.

It is hard to say definitely what happened to the cartel as a result of these successive crises. Its power, if not destroyed, was certainly impaired. Evidence of this is what happened on the legislative front in the United States. The American cartel companies would never have permitted themselves to be stripped of so many legal privileges had they retained their former strength.

As for the British companies, they certainly lost out. Iran was one of British Petroleum's most valuable properties. The Iraq Petroleum Co., in which Britain held the controlling interest, retained properties in Qatar and the UAE, which it now sought to develop, by way of compensation. But, of course, this only exacerbated the already vexatious problem of excess capacity.

Some of the companies sought to cover themselves, as it were. They moved into other fields. For example, Mobil (the new name of Socony-Vacuum) even went so far as to purchase businesses outside of oil. Most, however, played to their strength—they established positions in oil-related fields, such as the petrochemical industry.[64]

At the same time, however, one cannot say that OPEC took over from the cartel, that is, appropriated the old system to keep it running. The OPEC countries do not seem to have given much thought to the concept of regulation, and this is part of the reason that the Second Oil Shock proved so devastating.

The Second Shock was triggered by the shah's overthrow. As soon as this occurred, the conviction grew among oil consumers that the Second Shock was merely the prelude to a third. Countries like Japan (highly industrialized and oil-deficient) made the most extraordinary efforts to sew up supplies, and this had the effect of driving prices even higher. They went to astronomical heights, reaching up to $40 a barrel in May 1979 (i.e., from roughly $12; *or from $3*, if one wants to go back to pre-OPEC revolution days).[65]

This was how oil behaved under free market conditions. Between 1974 and roughly 1977, the Saudis had tried to keep prices down. Now, with the Second Shock, prices took off, and not the Saudis or anyone else could have prevented this. Too many exogenous factors had come into play; one agency could not control them.

Also contributing to panic was the failure of Washington to foresee the shah's overthrow or to make provision for it when it came. This was another instance of elite failure. The U.S. policy-making establishment missed the boat completely, even though there were indications of what was in store. Indeed, a long-running oil field strike led to the shah's being overthrown.[66]

Why were not the Americans sensitive to these forces? Preoccupation with Arab–Israeli peacemaking had something to do with it. This was an intense period of negotiation, brokered by the Carter administration. Washington's attention was focused on this to the exclusion of practically all else.

The policymakers' focus on peacemaking may have appeared correct to Americans. The Arabs could not see it that way, at least not the Arabs who dwelt in the Gulf. To them, this was yet another lapse on America's part, an appalling one, and they reacted accordingly.

EFFECTS ON THE GULF STATES

The effect of the Khomeini revolution on the Arab states of the Gulf was intensely disruptive. All of the Arab regimes were Sunni, while Khomeini, an Iranian, was Shia. The two sects have a long history of antagonism going back to the time of the Prophet.

Moreover, Khomeinism was a particularly aggressive movement. The ayatollah deprecated the sheikhs and did not attempt to hide his animosity toward them. Moreover, Khomeini actively strove to arouse their Shia communities to revolt. The Arab states of the lower Gulf all have significant Shia enclaves,[67] and all of these minority groups are discriminated against. Within months after

Khomeini took power, anti-regime revolts by Shias had erupted in Saudi Arabia, Kuwait, and Bahrain.[68]

However, Khomeini's main target was Iraq, where the Shias constitute a majority.[69] Practically from the first, the Iranian leader lashed out at Iraq's leader Saddam Hussein, against whom he harbored a personal grudge.[70]

Also a factor was the location in Iraq of the two holiest shrines of Shiadom, Najaf and Karballa, and one of the largest Shia communities outside Iran was in Baghdad, Qasimayn.

Khomeini reached out to his Iraqi coreligionists, appealing for an anti-Ba'thist revolt. The Ba'thists are notoriously insecure. They worry constantly about their legitimacy. They tend, when challenged, to react with the utmost ferocity. Now they were greatly agitated, as they sought to withstand the propaganda barrage from Tehran.

The Ba'thists worried from another, geopolitical angle. Iraq has only 16 kilometers of coastline. Its main window to the world is through the Gulf. Khomeini, on coming to power, appropriated all of the shah's irredentist claims. Most worrisome—from the Ba'thists' perspective—he sponsored Bahraini guerrillas. Bahrain, as a glance at a map will show, stands athwart Iraq's lifeline to the Indian Ocean and beyond.

But what seems to have angered Saddam most was Khomeini's interference with the Kurds—the Iranian leader recharged that old battery. After Mulla Mustafa Barzani was defeated and had died in exile, his tribesmen—led now by his two sons, Massoud and Idris—came to live in Iran. In 1979 Khomeini used the Barzanis to brutally repress a revolt of Iranian Kurds, and afterward he promoted a new Kurdish revolt inside Iraq.[71] The Barzanis were his agents for this.

Saddam had made extraordinary sacrifices to get peace with Iran. Now, as far as the Iraqi was concerned, Khomeini had abrogated the 1975 Algiers Agreement. The Iranian sought to destabilize Iraq by aggravating ethnic and religious tensions within the country.

By June 1980 the Iraqis and Iranians had begun trading artillery barrages across the frontier, and finally in September 1980 Iraq officially declared war.

IRAQ'S REASONS

One factor that almost certainly influenced Iraq's decision to fight was America's stance on the Gulf, which crystallized after the Second Oil Shock.

Again, as in 1973, Americans sought scapegoats, and once again they targeted the Arabs.[72] There followed an outpouring of mean-spirited articles and television documentaries labeling the Arabs as culprits. The campaign was tinged with bigotry.[73]

The most disturbing aspect of it (from the Arabs' perspective) was loud and persistent demands to occupy the Gulf. From the start of the run-up in prices, the Western media were filled with appeals to take over the Gulf.

The appeals were so strident that Ahmed Zaki Yamani, Saudi Arabia's oil minister, threatened that an attack on the fields would invite retaliation—the Arabs would sabotage them.[74]

The Americans' anger would perhaps have been understandable had it come in December 1979, after the Soviet Union invaded Afghanistan, or in November of the same year, when the Iranians seized the U.S. hostages. But coming *before* the two events, it seemed a blatant attempt to dispossess the sheikhs, on what grounds it's hard to imagine.[75]

In any event, a takeover of the Gulf by the Americans was not an idea that appealed to the sheikhs, and it certainly did not please the Iraqis.

The sheikhs had to question their relationship with the United States. After all, the arms buying was supposed to facilitate ties between the two peoples. An "ally" who takes over one's property is no friend, no matter on what pretext he does it.

The Americans' behavior appeared more bizarre after the hostage seizure in Tehran. The Iranians humiliated the United States, and thus one would have expected this to provide a pretext for military action.

Instead, Washington did nothing. (Actually that is not true—it mounted that ultimately futile and in some respects ridiculous Desert One Operation.) It appeared that, whereas the United States talked loudly about occupying the *southern* Gulf (i.e., taking over Arab lands), it would not contemplate a move in the north. Why? There was too much risk—not from the Iranians but from the Russians. Moscow, under a 1921 treaty with Iran, claimed the right to invade, should foreign troops enter the territory of its southern neighbor.[76]

To anyone who knew of this treaty, Washington's behavior was understandable, but to the sheikhs, the failure was doubly damning. One, it appeared to give the lie to earlier promises (by Nixon and Kissinger) that Washington would protect them, and along with that, it confirmed fears that Washington was anti-Arab.

To be sure, right after this, Carter authorized the formation of the so-called Rapid Deployment Force, later to become Central Command (CENTCOM). This seemed to show that America finally was taking the area seriously. However, even after CENTCOM was formed, it languished; among the so-called unified commands, it was the runt of the litter.[77]

All of this throws light on Iraq's invasion of Iran. Iraq took action that America could not take because Washington lacked the will. To be sure, the Iraqis acted for self-interested reasons, but one should not discount the larger implications of what they did.

Saddam, before he moved, promulgated an Arab Charter, which stipulated that the littoral states should protect the Gulf. He produced the charter after Oman called on the United States, England, and France to patrol the Gulf waters. When the Iraqis made their announcement, Oman withdrew its request, and four of the six Gulf states subscribed to Saddam's proposal.[78]

This would suggest that Saddam's motives in taking action were much more complex than they have been made to seem. Yes, he wanted to discommode the Iranians and, so to speak, take them down a peg. Plus he wanted to aggrandize Iraq by getting back that portion of the Shatt signed away under the Algiers Agreement.[79] But he also wanted to preclude the United States from coming into the Gulf, and in this he had the backing of the sheikhs, who did not want their part of the world to become an arena of superpower rivalry.[80]

It is not tenable to claim that Saddam's decision was not supported by the Gulf Arabs.[81] He may not have cleared it with them, but they surely were warned as to what he was contemplating.

This was an extraordinary period, in which actors did not adhere to assigned roles. We saw how the shah and Saddam composed their feud of long standing. Now the sheikhs and the Iraqis were drawing close.

Driving this latter movement was the breakdown of the protection mechanism discussed at the beginning of the chapter. No one was sure who was protecting the Gulf. Defense Secretary Weinberger on a tour of the Gulf made offers of U.S. assistance, but these came coincidentally with the campaign in the United States to scapegoat the Arabs for the oil price rise.

Hence, there was an opening for Iraq. Given the climate of the times, that Saddam would exploit this vacuum seems understandable.

We have barely discussed the peace process, but, of course, this, too, was affecting the Arabs. Sadat had just signed a separate peace with Israel, which undermined the Arab front. Iraq, formerly on the sidelines of that war, now moved to center stage. Indeed, Baghdad orchestrated Cairo's expulsion from the Arab League.

We spoke earlier of the awkward position in which the Saudis found themselves, when Sadat began his courtship of the West. Until then they, as the Egyptians' principal bankroller, had some leverage on them. Once the United States agreed to supply Egypt with arms and economic aid (in return for signing the peace treaty), the Saudis' influence in Cairo died.

The Saudis and the rest of the Gulf sheikhs needed protection and really they had only two choices—Iraq or the United States. The United States, whereas it might have acted decisively at this juncture, found itself prevented from doing so by powerful domestic constituencies that effectively tied the hands of the Reagan administration.

Nonetheless, because of the way in the which the Iran-Iraq War developed, Washington eventually was forced to take on the role of the sheikhs' protector, and that led it directly into confrontation with Baghdad in the Gulf War.

IRAQ IN THE WAR

All evidence points to the fact that the Iraqis expected the conflict to be a short one. They wanted to acquire territory, some of which they felt had been promised them under the Algiers Accord and never been delivered. They also wanted to deflate the Islamic revolution, which was inspiring such unrest.[82]

To these ends, they moved into Iran in force on September 22. Their advance was a slow one, in keeping with tactics learned from the Soviets. But it would also appear that the army was restrained from making a too swift advance by the leadership in Baghdad. Saddam and his fellow members of the Revolutionary Command Council (RCC) sought to keep the operation controlled; they did not want it to turn into a full-scale war. By moving slowly and taking (and inflicting) minimum casualties, they evidently hoped to be able to move to the negotiation stage with Iran as quickly as possible.

The Iraqis also seemed to have believed that there would be a coup against the clerics, staged by remnants of the shah's army. The clerics, on taking power, had initiated a purge of the old military. There had already been at least one attempt to rebel by the shah's former commanders, which had been crushed.[83] Iranian dissidents who had fled to Iraq assured the leadership that the Iranian army was ready to try again; all that was wanted was a catalyst.

The Iraqi army, then, was limited in its objectives—to seize and hold onto land around the Shatt al Arab. Nothing more was expected; nothing else would have been welcomed. If the clerical regime fell, that was to the good; if it was able to preserve itself, that, too, was acceptable. However, in the latter case the clerics would have been humiliated. This appears to be what the Iraqis really were aiming for—to destroy the ayatollah's charisma.

The operation, while initially successful (in that by October 24 they had captured Khoramshar), was ultimately a failure.[84] The leadership can be faulted with a number of mistakes; most glaringly, it would appear that it overdid the control element—it tried to micromanage, which is almost always fatal.

Saddam ought never to have insisted that casualties be kept down. He ought never to have responded to repeated appeals from the United Nations for a cease-fire (since this checked the army's advance). Finally, he ought never to have gone to war without first having worked out his endgame. By the end of October, Iraq's army had advanced some 65 kilometers inside Iran, captured Khoramshar, and invested four other large cities. At that point, Saddam announced that the Iraqi army, inasmuch as it had achieved all of its goals, would now halt operations. Implied was that Saddam was ready to entertain overtures from the clerics; there were no overtures. So the situation was in limbo. What to do? The Iraqi leadership had no answer to this, other than to restate its original directive—hold in place and do not take casualties.

Conversely, the Iranians ingeniously switched strategies. Up to the ill-fated (for the Iranians) Battle of Suzengard, the Islamic Republican forces had been fighting a traditional, quasi-modern type of war, using tanks, mainly. After Suzengard, after the crushing defeat inflicted on Bani Sadr in that engagement, the Iranians switched to a wildly unconventional war wherein masses of infantry were hurled at the Iraqi forces with the objective of overwhelming them.[85]

Which they did—not at first, but eventually. Iran's population is three times that of Iraq, meaning that Tehran could afford to be prodigal with lives. Moreover, as pointed out, Iranian society is predominantly rural; hence, it is unsophisticated, and Iranians, if properly appealed to, can be motivated to seek martyrdom.[86]

The human wave tactic (which the Iranians adopted) proved ideal under conditions that the Iranians faced, inasmuch as it compounded the dilemma of Iraq's commanders. How were they to hold their ground without suffering too many casualties and minimize casualties of the enemy *when the enemy was bent on achieving martyrdom for itself while destroying as many of the Iraqis as possible*?

By September 1981 Iraq's line began to crumble. Significantly, the first fissures appeared in the so-called People's Army units, comprising professional Ba'thists, men who had been put into uniform and sent to the front to stiffen the ranks of the mainly Shia regulars (whose loyalty was much in doubt).[87]

The Popular Army men were not soldiers, nor were they commanded (in most cases) by men who were. Officers and men alike could barely cope with the forms of traditional warfare. The unique, frightening, human wave attacks predictably unnerved them.[88] Once the Popular Army broke, the regulars had to fend as best they could.

This unanticipated (and wholesale) reverse forced Baghdad to accept defeat—to the extent of recognizing that it could not hold on in Iran any longer.

By May 1982 the Iraqis had fallen back to their side of the border. That this was a great defeat for them is inescapable. The Iranians claimed that they had killed and wounded some 25,000, compared to a loss on their side of 15,000. The killed figure is probably exaggerated. However, the figure of 7,000 Iraqi prisoners is probably correct, while Iran probably lost around 1,000 prisoners.[89]

The prisoner count is what most tells against the Iraqis. Past a certain point, it would seem that the Iraqi effort simply fell apart; men surrendered in droves. Ten Iraqi brigades, composed of 25,000 troops, were badly mauled; seven of these were Popular Army components.[90]

In the previous chapter we postponed discussion of the Ba'th Party; here is the point to take it up. For, in the author's view, the defeats of 1980–1981 can be attributed to the composition of Iraqi society under the Ba'th.

THE BA'TH

In a manner of speaking we now review the bidding on the Ba'th. What do we know about it? First, its origins are mysterious. The party gets its start in Iraq in the 1950s and draws its membership mainly from the Shias.[91]

This in itself is extraordinary. The Shias were virtually bereft of leadership, at least a leadership that would guide them in the way of political involvement. The Shia clergy exhorted their congregations to keep clear of politics; the people were expected not even to vote.[92]

Along with that, the first converts to Ba'thism were poor, probably with a strong admixture of *shurugis*. For Shias to have gone against their priests is interesting, but that *shurugis* should have attempted to influence politics is phenomenal. The widest possible gulf existed between the wealthy Shias and the masses.[93]

In such circumstances, the wealthy would not merely have disowned, but have sought actively to destroy, the fledgling party. Yet the party did form, and it hung on, howbeit in an isolated condition, with no support, we assume, from the larger community.

In power, the Ba'thists proved themselves contrarians. First they carried out the dreadful pogroms (discussed earlier) against the communists, which would seem to confirm rumors about CIA collusion. Then immediately after, they appropriated the communists' reforms and professed themselves radicals in the communist mold.

This so upset traditionalist Pan-Arab officers (who, along with the civilians, had made the coup) that they stripped the civilians of their posts, expelling many from the country.

In 1968, the Ba'thists returned to power, with (if reports are to be believed) the help of the CIA, although this time the agency did not deal directly with them. Rather, it conspired with Cols. Nayef and Dawd, who in turn co-opted the Ba'th without informing the agency. Once the coup succeeded, the Ba'thist turned on Nayef and Dawd and deported them (which must have been extremely embarrassing for the Americans).

The Ba'thists immediately went on yet another rampage; this time, however, included among the victims were Jews.[94] This created an international furor, in which the Ba'thists were stigmatized as the successors of the Nazis.

In some respects one can compare the Ba'th to the fascist parties of Europe. For example, as with the Europeans, it drew membership from the lower classes.[95]

It, too, is socialist and nationalist (although, in professing Pan-Arabism, it technically advocates a form of supranationalism). The Ba'thist are violent, and as with fascism, they adhere to the *fuehrer prinzep* (leader principle). The Iraqis' leader was, initially, Sa'di, then Baker, then Saddam Hussein.

Saddam was a much less complex figure than Hitler, and he was nowhere near the theoretician that Mussolini was. At the same time, however, he was not—as often characterized—merely a thug. Saddam's contribution to the Ba'th was his espousal of so-called party methods. This was his description of a repertoire of techniques borrowed from the Staatssicherheit (Stasi), that is, East German State Security.

In the mid-1970s, when the Ba'th cooperated with the Russians, many barter deals were worked out between Baghdad and the East Europeans. The East Germans agreed to instruct Iraq's security forces in their intelligence operations in return for oil.

The Stasi showed the Iraqis how to mold a superrepressive security system, using methods that were relatively easy to assimilate. Saddam served as the conduit for the information exchange. He vetted the new techniques, and under his direction Iraq became the most totalitarian state in the Middle East.

Statistics show that by 1978 the number of Iraqis on the public payroll was 662,000, and of this number 151,000 were working with the Interior Ministry, hence involved, one way or the other, with the intelligence apparatus (in Arabic, Mukhabarat).[96]

That was Saddam's major contribution to the formation of the post–World War II Iraqi state. Along with that he indulged in activities that were thuggish, and it is for these that he has since become notorious.

He attached himself to a military man, General Ahmad Baker, who became his patron; and then he assisted Baker to survive in the cutthroat environment of the post-1968 coup. At that late date Iraq was still going through the throes of the 1958 revolution.

In the revolution the entire upper echelon of the military was destroyed, leaving only junior officers, none of whom had a power base. To advance, the officers backstabbed each other, literally, and Saddam took part in these maneuvers. He uncovered a number of plots (real or imagined) in which he implicated officers deemed threatening to Baker.[97]

By 1979 Saddam had not only eliminated most of Baker's enemies but managed to ease Baker himself into retirement. As a consequence, the civilian (who had never had any military experience) was able to take power *as a civilian.* For an Arab society, this was a remarkable feat. Moreover, Saddam surrounded himself with civilians, making his regime a determinedly civilian one.

Through the security apparatus the Ba'thists kept tabs on everything that went on in Iraq; any hint of disaffection was dealt with. At the same time, for those who toed the line, the living was good; materially, conditions in Iraq were excellent. After the 1972 oil nationalization, the standard of living for the Iraqis soared. Marr points out that under the republic the increase in annual consumption of food was significant, going from $47.64 in 1958 to over $159 in 1975.[98]

One could say that the Ba'th, as an organization, was a marvel of discipline and control; however, it had very little popular support. It kept itself in power by distributing rewards from the sale of oil and by creating a society where to be not of it meant that one was reduced to pariah status.

We are now ready to take a look at how all of this affected the Ba'th's behavior in the early days of the fighting.

BA'THIST MISTAKES

The Ba'thists did not understand war, and yet they made it. Why? For them, war was a necessary next step by which to further the nation's advance.

It's probably correct to say that the Ba'thists did not believe that they were going to war when they did it. The Ba'thists probably thought (as did the Americans in Kosovo) that they were carrying out an operation. The Iraqi army was tasked with a specific assignment—to take a limited amount of territory around the Shatt. An affair so circumscribed could not be regarded as war, or so the Ba'thists seem to have felt.

This would explain their curious tactics—the slow-moving ponderous advance of the very first days, the repeated halts, and, finally, the unabashed efforts of Saddam, toward the end of the invasion, to broker a cease-fire, under practically any terms that the Iranians cared to offer.

Saddam was in a position analogous to that of the shah in 1975, when the latter had to decide whether to expand the war with Iraq, knowing that, were he do so, he might easily find himself trapped.

The shah was fortunate, in that he had a pragmatist (Saddam) to deal with. But Saddam had a religious zealot to confront. Where Saddam failed was in not perceiving that, for the Iranian clerics, the war had its uses. In the first days of the Islamic Republic a fierce struggle developed between the liberals of Barzagan's faction and the clerics.[99] The war served to mobilize popular support for the clerics against Barzagan and against Barzagan's successor, Bani Sadr.

Hence, the clerics never thought to end the hostilities until the intramural fight in the capital had been wrapped up in their favor. After that, the full weight of the Revolutionary Guard Corps and *basij* was thrown at the Iraqis, with the results that we know.[100]

To conclude, then, the performance of the Iraqi Ba'th in the opening days of the war revealed the immaturity of the regime. It presided over an atomized mass of humanity. Lacking coherence, the mass should have decomposed when the war went badly. Yet it did not. Why not?

The Iranians showed themselves as immature as the Iraqis. After having successfully driven Iraq's forces to the border, they should have sued for peace (and exacted reparations, which the Saudis and other Gulf sheikhs would have paid).[101] Instead, Khomeini decided to liberate Jerusalem.

This awakened dissent in the ranks of the Iranian military, many of whose members had had enough and wanted to go home. The Iraqis, fighting on their home ground and heavily dug in in front of Basrah, decisively repelled the Iranians' attempts at penetration. Three times (in June 1982) the Iranians advanced, and three times they were beaten back with heavy losses. Iraq claimed that it had killed 27,000 Iranians, at a loss to itself of only 5,000.[102]

Even then the clerics refused to put an end to the war. They retreated to recoup and try again the following year. Both sides in this war—being well supplied with oil money—could afford to keep it going. It is estimated that Iran expended 42 percent of its national resources financing its war effort, and spent far less than Iraq.[103]

This was an entirely new situation, where two Third World countries invested fortunes in weapons buying to perpetuate a war that the superpowers would have liked to see ended. To be sure, there were so-called client wars in the Middle East before (and we talk about one in a moment). But they were not so long-lasting. The Iran–Iraq War went on for eight years.

The situation was embarrassing to the superpowers. They had created a system whereby arms could be supplied to client states and with which the clients could be trained to perform. But, despite the powers' insistence that they could control the use of these arms, this was not the case.[104]

ISRAEL AND ARMS

We now need to make an important connection. We need to discover why, in 1984, the United States, without warning, abandoned its stance of neutrality and opted to back Iraq in the war. Given the depth of hostility to Iraq among important elements of American society, it is extraordinary that this policy shift occurred.

To understand why it did, we must go back two years to 1982, to Israel's invasion of Lebanon. This event triggered the Americans' policy change; moreover, it set in train a string of events that culminated in the Gulf War.

We spoke earlier about special relationships between both the Saudis and Iranians with the United States. These were not the first such arrangements that the United States had. Israel had a similar deal for quite a while. As is usually the case with such affairs, the Jewish state was not pleased to see its setup replicated.

Israel tried in every way to prevent arms transfers to Riyadh from being effected. One approach was to get the U.S. Congress to veto the transfers. Another was to attach conditions to them. Eventually, Tel Aviv hit on the plan of allowing the transfers to take place, with the provision that, whatever the Saudis got, the Israelis would get also.

This particular quid pro quo was worked out in 1983. President Reagan agreed, as he put it, to preserve Israel's "qualitative edge"; that is, America would supply weapons to the Jewish state based on materiel received not just by Riyadh but by all the Arabs. Even weapons that Iraq got from the Russians would be included in the tally.

This deal benefited not just the Israelis but the whole American arms industry. It handed the industry what amounted to a windfall. The arms makers could now look forward to dependable contracts that the American government would subsidize, because, under special legislative arrangements that Israel enjoys, it does not have to pay for the aid that it receives.[105]

Arms production, as Keynes has pointed out, is a form of pyramid building, in that it can act as a multiplier, a public relief scheme to provide perks to certain groups in the society and, in the process of doing so, perk up the whole economy.[106]

It is not likely that any of this was in Reagan's mind when he made his commitment to Israel; he almost certainly did it to appease a powerful and potentially disruptive constituency at home. However, in doing what he did, he opened a Pandora's box, as we will see.

LEBANON

The deal to guarantee Israel's weapons "edge" came in February 1982. Four months later Israel invaded Lebanon. This was supposed to be a limited operation, to punish the Palestinians. The latter were based just over the Lebanese border, whence they conducted fedayeen attacks on Israeli settlements. In fact, the Israelis had a much more ambitious plan—to go all the way to Beirut and, if possible, force a change of government on the Lebanese, installing one that would ally with the Jewish state.

To do this, the Israelis had to engage in hard fighting, harder than at any time in their past. What had prevented the Israelis from waging such all-out war up to now was cost. To fight for days, using up enormous amounts of weapons and ammunition, was beyond their means.

Now, however, thanks to Reagan's pledge, they could count on being resupplied. What is more, they would get the replacements free, because, as we just said, they did not have to repay the aid that was being rendered.

Reagan's concession had the unanticipated result of allowing the Israelis to fight a type of war that formerly had been beyond their means. Further, this was a style of war that was new to the Middle East. The Israelis took weapons drawn to the specifications of the U.S. military and meant to be used against regular armies, and they used them against paramilitary groups (like the Palestinians) and civilians. It is estimated that the Israelis killed well over 10,000 Lebanese civilians in the 1983 war, not all of them, by any means, guerrillas.[107] Effectively, the Israelis aped the tactics of the Americans in Vietnam—they made no distinction between combatants and civilians and, in the process, destroyed considerable civilian infrastructure.

In effect, the Israelis were driven to this because of constraints on their activity. They needed to get the operation over before international pressure forced them to desist, and they needed to do the job with a minimum of casualties on their own side, for otherwise the Israeli people would have rebelled. With these extraordinarily lethal weapons supplied by the United States, the Israeli generals felt they had the means to overcome difficulties.[108]

ANGERING THE SHIAS

In invading Lebanon and driving on to Beirut, the Israelis had to overrun the Lebanese Shia enclave on the border. The Shias are one of many sects in Lebanon and by far the most handicapped. To begin with, they are poor, but they also are disadvantaged because the area in which they reside (on the border) was appropriated by the Palestinians, who used it as a staging ground for their attacks.

This meant that whenever the Israelis retaliated against the Palestinians, the Shias were caught up in the fighting and naturally suffered casualties. However, as the Shias believed that the Israelis would finally, once and for all, rid them of the Palestinians, they rejoiced to see the invasion.

Subsequently, however, the Israelis settled down to occupy Shia territory, and they exploited the Shias by, among other things turning the Shias' land over to their (the Israelis') clients the Maronite Christians. At that the Shias turned against them. As the Palestinians had done, they fought to drive the Israelis from their territory.

AMERICA IN LEBANON

Washington reacted to the Israeli invasion of Lebanon with dismay. It immediately sought to get the Israelis out of the tiny Arab state. Ultimately, this necessitated the stationing of American troops in Lebanon as supervisors of a truce (which the Americans had established). However, the American intervention was handled badly; in the eyes of the Arabs it came to appear that Washington favored Israel, and this eventually turned most Lebanese sects against the Americans.[109]

So it was not long before American marines stationed in Beirut became a target of the sects. On October 23, 1983, a suicide bomber from the Shia community drove a truck into the marine compound in Beirut and blew himself up, along with some 300 U.S. Marines, the worst atrocity that the U.S. military had suffered since the end of the Vietnam War.

The bombing touched off a debate in the U.S. government—George Shultz, then secretary of state, advocated reprisals; Caspar Weinberger, the defense secretary, took a contrary stand, saying that America should get out of Lebanon. In Weinberger's view it was not worth further loss of life.[110]

Weinberger won out in this instance. The Americans soon departed Lebanon, a most humiliating experience. But, matters then further deteriorated as the Shias now began to kidnap American expatriates in Lebanon. They refused to let them go and taunted the U.S. administration for its inability to recover the unfortunates.

To be sure, America was impotent to move against the terrorists, but this did not mean that it was completely stymied. Washington could get revenge on the Shias' patron, Iran.

AMERICAN NEUTRALITY

Since the start of the Iran–Iraq War, the United States maintained a pose of neutrality, despite the fact that it really ought to have backed Iraq. Once the Iraqis stabilized the front and indicated their willingness to observe a truce, they ought to have been encouraged.

A truce under those conditions would have meant no victor, and having the war end without an obvious shift in the balance was preeminently in the U.S.

interest. Moreover, a negotiated cease-fire would have had to be purchased, which would have meant getting the sheikhs to finance the deal. This would have made Iraq indebted to the moderate Arabs and would also have attached strings to the reparations that Iran was receiving.

However, so many interests in the United States opposed opening to Iraq that the administration dared not make a move in that direction. The American Jewish community would have fought it, as would the friends of Iran (of whom there were surprisingly many, particularly among the liberals). Finally, it is likely that America's Cold Warriors would have objected, since Iraq, in their eyes, was an ally of the Soviet Union.

Inability to gain Washington's support initially did not trouble the Iraqis. However, once the sheikhs cut back on their aid to Iraq (after the setbacks of 1982), that attitude changed.[111] Baghdad was then forced to go to Europe in search of loans. At this point the Iraqis discovered that they could not get by without the support of the Americans.

TARIQ AZIZ TALKS WITH SHULTZ

Sometime in 1983, Tariq Aziz, Iraq's deputy prime minister, met with Secretary of State George Shultz. We do not know where the meeting was held or who requested it. However, based on what was discussed, it is likely that the approach was made by Iraq.[112]

Aziz wanted the Americans to stop criticizing Iraq's performance in the war. American opinion, at this time, was not supportive of Baghdad, and this showed up in the press, where, Aziz claimed, stories about the war uniformly took the Iranians' side.

Aziz had a theory that what appeared in the American press reflected administration thinking, at least in the foreign affairs realm. To an extent, this is true; certainly, it was the case in regard to this war.[113]

According to Aziz, deprecating articles in the U.S. media affected the European bankers. They would not loan to Iraq when daily in America (and in Britain) articles appeared claiming Iraq was a loser.

Aziz says that in the first meeting Shultz professed indifference to Iraq's plight and insisted that Washington was not influencing press coverage. However, a second meeting was held in the fall at the United Nations, and here the Iraqi claims to have noted a change in Shultz's attitude.

By the end of the year, media coverage in the United States had grown much more sympathetic, which Aziz interpreted as a *volte face* on the administration's part. Indeed, shortly after this, Washington tilted decisively toward Iraq.

What had happened in the interim between the first Aziz–Shultz meeting and the shift in press coverage at the year's end? The Marine Corps barracks bombing in Lebanon.

The bombing hit the Reagan administration hard. Reagan had gotten himself elected on a platform of making the United States "stand tall again" after Vietnam and Iran's seizure of the American Embassy. Now, here were the Iranians encouraging their clients the Shias to kill and seize as hostages American military personnel and expatriates in Lebanon.

Initially, Reagan proclaimed that the Shias would not force America to "cut and run." But five days after he made this statement, he ordered the marines to "regroup" offshore, and, of course, once offshore, they sailed away.

After this, it did not make sense for Washington to go on being neutral in the Iran-Iraq War. The balance of power between Iraqis and Iranians was evenly distributed, and Washington, by supporting Iraq, could have pushed the combatants to a negotiated settlement, which, as we said, was preeminently in America's interest.

The problem was to sufficiently motivate Reagan so he would risk the ire of those anti-Iraq forces in the United States. Evidently, the extreme humiliation visited on the United States by Iran and the mullahs' imprudent behavior (in taunting Reagan) drove the administration to act, which is to say that Washington's tilt to Iraq was driven by a desire for revenge. Thus, it seems legitimate to suppose that had Israel not drawn Washington into a confrontation with the Shias, America's policy on the Iran–Iraq War would not have changed.

SUPER ETANDARDS

Once the United States changed policy on the war, it moved on several fronts to help the Iraqis. It backed United Nations (UN) Resolution 540 for a negotiated end to the fighting (the same that Iraq supported and Iran rejected). It also mounted Operation Stanch, lobbying its allies to cut off arms supplies to Iran. Of a certainty, the United States facilitated Iraq's loan requests. Not that U.S. banks took them up; rather, Washington did not oppose the Europeans' granting them.[114]

Far and away, however, the most fateful step that it took was to give up blocking the transfer of Super Etandard fighters to the Iraqis. This move set in train a whole raft of consequences, of the most far reaching importance. The background to the affair is this.

Iraq had purchased the aircraft from France in 1983, intending to use them against ships calling at Iranian ports.[115] The fighters were perfect platforms for delivering Exocet missiles, which Iraq also had purchased from the French.

Iraq needed the planes to interdict Iran's oil traffic. At this time Tehran was selling quite a bit of oil, compared to Iraq. The Syrians had cut Iraq's pipeline to the Mediterranean in 1982, and that left Baghdad with but one line through Turkey. Meanwhile, in the Gulf, the Iranians kept watch to interdict Iraqi shipping and also to stop foreign ships trying to call at Basrah.

One could say that the Super Etandards were Iraq's "silver bullet strategy." Locked into a static defense along its border with Iran, it hoped to force an end to the war by crippling its foe's economy. Of course, the Iraqi army could have taken the offensive and ended the war that way, but, for good and compelling reasons, this was not an option.[116]

At any event, in 1983 Iraq proclaimed an exclusion zone in the northern Gulf, declaring that it would strike at foreign ships calling at Iranian ports. It also threatened to attack Kharg Island, Iran's main shipping terminal.

At this the United States intervened to prevent the transfer, claiming that it did not want Iran to shut the Straits of Hormuz (which Tehran had threatened to do if the planes went into action). This stand by the Americans was illogical. Had Iran done this, it would have put itself in the fix that Iraq already was in (of having no way to get its oil to market).

Nonetheless, until 1984 Washington professed to believe that this was a threat, and, try as Iraq might, it could not get it to relent. After the second Shultz meeting, however, Washington decided to lift its objection, and the planes were delivered.

The move made immediate difficulties, but in a quite unexpected quarter. Apparently, the British were asked to intervene by the Kuwaitis and Saudis to stop the transfer. A quite startling move, considering that the sheikhs were supposedly backing the Iraqis in the war.[117]

In fact, the sheikhs were concerned that, were Iraq to go after Iranian shipping, Tehran would target ships plying the waters of the southern Gulf by way of retaliation. This is precisely what happened. However, it was not at all a simple process. The mere fact of Iraq's targeting Iranian shipping was not enough to cause this significant escalation.

Something else occurred, in the OPEC arena. Iran and Saudi Arabia were caught up in a dispute over pricing, and that, on top of Iraq's marauding, is what did it.

We intend to look at this business in detail, since it is what got Washington directly involved in the Gulf, an involvement the Americans had been straining to avoid ever since Britain pulled out of the region back in the early 1970s.

IRAN VERSUS SAUDI ARABIA ON OIL

OPEC's union up to the decade of the 1980s seemed blessed. The members had disagreements, but usually over administration of prices—prices could not be too high, as that would discomfort one lot of producers; too low, another. Clearly, however, among all parties there was confidence that a profit would accrue and that revenue would remain ample. It was taken for granted that demand would hold up.

In 1981 the expectation changed, and for the first time the OPEC producers had to confront a sharply curtailed demand for their product. What led to this—for OPEC—distressing turn of events?

The run-up in price of 1979, followed by the further rise in 1980 (because of the outbreak of the Iran–Iraq War), reinforced tendencies at work among the industrialized countries, first of all, a tendency toward conservation. Practically all the OECD states had initiated conservation programs, which, three years after the Second Oil Shock, had begun to take effect. Along with that, the inflation that the Second Shock had triggered created a worldwide recession, and, as a consequence of that, the industrialized countries had less reason to spend money on oil.

These two factors mainly contributed to cutting down demand for oil worldwide.[118]

There was, however, a further complication. When the Second Oil Shock hit (followed by the outbreak of the Iran–Iraq War), consumers foresaw that there might not be an early end to the price rise. Companies (and here we are mainly talking about those formerly associated with the cartel) began buying oil for stockpiling purposes.[119] Countries like the United States and Japan also did this, but the big buyers were the companies.

Stockpiling when prices are climbing is extraordinary; usually, it is the other way around, and this is because stockpiling tends to be costly. In the early 1980s it was supercostly because of something else that was going on.[120]

The U.S. Federal Reserve chairman Paul Voelker, in an effort to stem inflation in the United States, had been driving up interest rates.[121] The higher they went, the more the dollar appreciated and the more return businesses could get by investing at the higher rates. Thus, opportunity costs for storing oil became prohibitive.

At the same time, by late 1981 it began to be apparent that the Iran-Iraq War was deadlocked. Hence, no major crises were anticipated. Companies (and countries) began unloading oil that they had acquired.

So here we have two developments working counter to each other—the stockpilers of oil are dumping it on the market just as the OPEC producers have come to realize that they have more than they can sell. Together these factors put significant strain on OPEC, exacerbating cleavages in the institution.

OPEC from its inception was divided into two factions—the so-called low absorbers and the high. "Absorb" here stands for the ability to sop up money. A low absorber is a country, like Saudi Arabia, that, because of its small population, finds it difficult to absorb a lot of money. With high absorbers (countries like Iran) it is just the reverse—with huge populations, they need all the money that they can get.

In 1981 the Saudis, along with the other low absorbers, were happy to see demand for oil fall off, as they felt that this would help to move prices down. The high absorbers, however, absolutely refused to let this happen, and they made their objections plain.[122] Indeed, Iran claimed that, for it, a price decrease would be ruinous; it could not finance the war.[123]

Thus ensued a period of wrangling, which ended in 1982, when, at the 61st Conference of OPEC held in Geneva, the price was set at $34/b (down from $40/b). This concession was wrung from the high absorbers by the sheikhs. Such a bitter contest it was that few believed that the price would hold.[124]

Why did the high absorbers capitulate? Since the run-up in prices in 1979, the ex-cartel companies had opened new fields in the United States (Alaska) and in Britain and Norway (the North Sea). Russia also had opened new fields in Siberia, and the Mexicans, too, had brought new fields on-line.[125]

The non-OPEC companies (and countries) had developed fields that formerly would not have been efficient to exploit; but now, with oil prices rising, the new fields could easily be made profitable. At the same time, the companies felt compelled to extract as much oil as possible as fast as possible, to amortize what for them had been a considerable investment.

At any rate, by 1982 the non-OPEC producers were pumping so much oil that they threatened OPEC's lead in sales; indeed, the OPEC producers were about to become marginalized. By the summer of 1981, OPEC production had plumbed its lowest level in 10 years. Its members were producing just 21.5 m b/d, compared with 31.4 m b/d in 1977.[126] The non-OPEC members benefited from their ability to cut costs. OPEC producers had a set price to which they had to adhere; non-OPEC companies could always discount.

Thus, the basis of the fight (between non-OPEC companies and the OPEC countries) was economics—one set had interests that the other could not abide. In the case of the former cartel companies, their interests had undergone change as soon as they lost their equity. Where formerly they had taken their profits from upstream operations, now it was downstream where they made their money. To profit from selling product, one must get crude cheaply; the non-OPEC companies wanted the lowest possible prices for crude, while OPEC (as it had to accommodate the high absorbers among its membership) wanted prices to remain reasonably high.

Aware that demand for oil worldwide was down, companies like Exxon (the new name for Jersey) and Royal Dutch and British Petroleum (the new name for the AIOC) saw no reason that they should pay a high rate, and therefore they determined to force a price cut. They settled on Nigeria as the most vulnerable OPEC country to attack. In other words, they had determined to break OPEC discipline. Nigeria was a likely candidate on which to apply pressure, since it had no industry outside oil; it had 70 million people to support, and its government was unstable.[127]

The companies went to Lagos and, in effect, threatened that, unless it agreed to sell at below the OPEC-agreed-upon price, the companies would take their crude from elsewhere. They could do this because all the companies were involved in the North Sea. North Sea oil and Nigerian oil are practically the same; plus, the British and Nigerian producers sell to the same market.

The Nigerians went immediately to the Saudis to report the pressure that they were under, and this forced the latter to take action. Nigeria was an OPEC member, and, were it to capitulate, OPEC's whole carefully crafted price structure would collapse. Price control would then pass out of the organization's hands; the spot market would take over (which, of course, was what the companies wanted).

The Saudis and Kuwaitis went to the companies and threatened that, unless they took from Nigeria at the OPEC price, *they* would cut *them* off. We said earlier that the ex-cartel companies marketed the sheikhs' oil downstream. They thus did not dare risk losing their favored status. Hence, the companies soon backed down.

At the same time, however, they did not give up. Having failed with the Nigerians, they trained their sights on Britain. There were as many as 40 licensees operating in Britain's North Sea, but three of the lot were prime, so to speak—British Petroleum, Shell, and Esso, a subsidiary of Exxon.[128] These three now began to pressure the British government.

To understand how the British government figures in this, one has to understand how the North Sea concessions were arranged. When the fields first were opened (in the early 1970s), Britain offered favorable terms. At the same time, it was careful to safeguard its position. It created a national oil company, with which the licensees had to deal. The British National Oil Co. (BNOC) retained the right to purchase 51 percent of whatever oil the companies produced, *at a price that it set.* Since BNOC had no refining or marketing facilities, it then sold that oil back to the producers.[129]

As long as demand for oil stayed up and prices were high, the arrangement worked to everyone's satisfaction. But once demand fell and price began to slide, problems developed. BNOC had from the first been asking the officially declared OPEC price. After the turndown, this price was no longer acceptable to the Big Three (Exxon, Royal Dutch, and BP), and, in 1983 they insisted that it be reduced.

Hearing that the British were likely to give in to the companies' demands, Saudi oil minister Zaki Yamani flew to London for talks with the government. It was in the government's interest, he argued, to continue coordinating with OPEC; otherwise, there would be a price war.

Evidently, Yamani was persuasive; a compromise was worked out. The British lowered their price, marginally, and the OPEC nations, at a meeting, held (significantly) in London, agreed to cut theirs—to $29.50. After some suspense, the two major producers in the North Sea, Shell and BP, went along (Esso, in protest, pulled out), and that enabled prices to firm up. They stayed firm into 1984.

RENEWED TENSION

While the deal (between OPEC and the British) produced stability for a time, it was not fated to last. The problem was demand—it did not revive, and so many of the OPEC states began to cheat. They overproduced on their quotas, offering special deals; in a word, they aped the tactics of non-OPEC companies.[130]

Once more the OPEC price structure seemed doomed; probably it would have been had it not been for the Saudis, who, in 1983, agreed to play the swing producer role for the organization; that is, they agreed to adjust their production in such a way as to ensure that OPEC's overall quota was maintained.[131] In 1983 the OPEC quota was 18 m b/d, and the Saudi share was 7.5 m b/d. With the Saudi decision to play the swing role, it reduced its quota to 7.0 m b/d, bringing the overall quota down to 17.5 m b/d.[132]

This decision of the Saudis was quite significant, inasmuch as it converted OPEC into a true cartel, something that it had not been since the companies lost control in 1973. OPEC had been accused of being a cartel heretofore, but such accusations were baseless; it was not until Saudi Arabia agreed to control production by adjusting its oil quota that OPEC took on the status of a true cartel.

The Saudis' decision was welcome to the other OPEC members, but the move did not constitute a permanent fix. Cheating went on, and, among the offenders, Iran was an outstandingly bad case.[133] Needing cash to finance the war, it flaunted OPEC rules. Indeed, Iran became a pirate in the OPEC lake. Discounting prices shamelessly, it aimed to sell 3 m b/d, twice its quota.[134]

All this came out of the Saudis' hide, so to speak. They had to keep on reducing and reducing so the overall quota would not be breached. Why would they do it? Mainly they did it because they feared Iran.

The reader should know that the Iranians despised the Saudis. Saudi Arabia is the bastion of Wahhabiism, a variety of Islam that Khomeini could not abide. By keeping oil prices reasonably high, the Saudis sought to conciliate the Iranians, something that did not please Iraq, but as long as Riyadh continued to bankroll Iraq's war effort, Baghdad could not complain.

In any case, the Saudis were bound not to let OPEC succumb and were willing to sacrifice to prevent this from happening. However, as time passed, and Iran's cheating did not diminish, the Saudis found themselves approaching the limit of what they could endure. In 1981 they were making $113.2 billion in oil sales; in 1982 they were down to $76 billion; to $46 billion in 1983. It was predicted that the Saudis would soon have to start dipping into their reserves to cover expenses.[135]

By late 1985, with Iran (and others) still cheating, the Saudis were earning only $26 billion on their oil—selling only 2.5 m b/d, less than half their quota. The country had started to run a rare budget deficit, and foreign reserves were having to be drawn down.[136]

At this point, Britain announced that it was scrapping the BNOC. It would forgo setting prices and would abide by whatever production decisions that the companies felt necessary. Evidently, the companies' pressure had paid off.

Margaret Thatcher (who had just been elected) made the decision. A staunch conservative, Thatcher had never liked the BNOC arrangement and apparently decided to end it. News of Thatcher's action brought the Saudis into play once more. Yamani repeated his warning about a price war. This time, however, Thatcher proved unyielding, and thus a fight became inevitable.

SHOWDOWN

It soon became apparent that the Saudis had been planning for this confrontation for some time; they had their strategy ready. Riyadh had innovated a scheme called netbacking, which assured buyers of their crude oil a profit.[137] The companies pounced on the deal as soon as it was offered, and almost immediately, the Saudis began selling huge volumes of crude, enough to make up what they had lost through lower prices.

The Saudis could do this, of course, because they had the world's most technologically efficient plant, the same that ARAMCO had built up over the years. By means of these exceptionally fine facilities they could calibrate supply to demand. It was nothing to the Saudis to up production by several hundred thousand barrels; and, just as easily, they could take it down again—all in very short order.

Of course, putting their new strategy into effect meant, for the Saudis, having to abandon the swing role. Riyadh sought to convince its fellow OPEC members that in the long run what they were doing would prove beneficial, as it would force the non-OPEC producers (like Britain) to coordinate with the OPEC members. However, the hard-liners in OPEC—Libya, Algeria, and particularly Iran—were not mollified. They wanted to cut OPEC production so as to prop up the price.

The low-absorption countries would not have it, and so the new strategy, called "market share," went ahead.

Perforce, all of the OPEC countries now began pushing netback deals. Once this free-for-all commenced, prices dropped like a rock. West Texas Intermediate went from $31.75 a barrel at the end of November 1985 to $10. Some Persian Gulf cargoes sold for as little as $6 a barrel.[138]

It had previously been assumed that a natural price for oil existed, below which it could not go. The new market share strategy put an end to that idea; effectively, this was the start of the Third Oil Shock.

THE SHOCK TAKES HOLD

When the Third Oil Shock hit, no one expected that it would work in reverse, that is, drive prices down. At first President Reagan, himself a staunch conservative, was delighted with the result. It appeared that the Saudis and smaller sheikhdoms were coming over to the supply side. Instead of trying to coordinate production as a cartel, they were going to give the market a chance.

Reagan had more reason than that to be happy. Inflation, which had been skyrocketing in the United States, fell with the movement of oil prices downward. Business picked up as America began to move out of the recession. At the same time the horrendous deficit that Reagan had triggered to pay for his grandiose arms buildup (about which more later) was pared. These were all dividends, one could say.

Unfortunately, there were also costs. For example, America had been making headway with conservation; that movement died. The domestic oil industry, which had taken off in 1979 and then slumped after 1981 (when it became clear that demand would not revive), became practically moribund. Companies that rented out drilling equipment, alternative heating firms, banks in the Southwest, independent oil companies—all faced extinction.

Another aspect of the business, however, proved extremely troubling, particularly to the Reagan administration, which supposedly was determined to make America militarily strong again. With the price of oil going through the floor, so to speak, and domestic producers finding it impossible to remain in business, the United States was now having to face the prospect of becoming dependent on foreign oil.

This problem was compounded, one could say, because of something else that occurred—with oil prices as low as they were, few companies were willing to prospect for new oil; it simply did not make economic sense to do it. This meant that already existing fields became at a premium, and this effectively handed OPEC a new lease on life. For the Americans this was ironic, since their president had repeatedly claimed that he would like to see OPEC eliminated.[139]

By 1986 deficits from the price war clearly outweighed the dividends, and Reagan's vice president George Bush announced that he was going to the Gulf to talk with Saudi ruler King Fahd to see if he couldn't get him to ease off a bit.[140]

Had Reagan, the great market defender, become an interventionist? The president was asked this question by the press, and he replied that he shared the vice president's concern that cheap oil, if it led to increased dependence on foreign supplies, could have serious national security implications. At the same time, Reagan reaffirmed his faith in the free market.[141] What did this mean? It's hard to figure. One could say that the president was talking out of both sides of his mouth.

As well he might. As noted earlier, America's domestic oil industry was dying. In April, when Bush went abroad, the price of oil was down to $9 and headed lower. The independents could not operate at such a low price.[142]

Bush, who was planning to run for president after Reagan's term was up, saw his main constituency drying up; hence, he was bound to reverse the price trend or at least give the appearance of making an effort to do so.[143]

Reagan, who did not want to lose the Southwest for the Republicans, was loath to stop his number two; at the same time what the vice president was doing so flagrantly compromised Reaganomics that it could not but cause consternation at home.

There was an outpouring of anti-Arab polemics in the press once again. The line taken advocated imposing a tariff to keep the price of domestic oil up, and let the "oil sheikhs" suffer (this was the propaganda line). This argument, while persuasive to some sections of the society, went against the whole thrust of U.S. policy since World War II, which was to avoid protection and push for free trade.

Meanwhile, overseas the price war was having an unanticipated affect—non-OPEC countries were lining up on the side of OPEC. First, Mexico, then Russia, then Egypt, then Oman, and finally Norway all indicated interest in price co-ordination.[144]

Thatcher and Great Britain were the lone holdouts, but after so many non-OPEC countries had succumbed, there was really little that Thatcher could do to affect the outcome. In the end she was forced to give way. In September the British prime minister visited Norway, and while there Norway's prime minster, Gro Harlem Brundtland, announced that the Norwegians would cooperate with OPEC. Thatcher said nothing—her way of signifying, evidently, that, as far as Britain was concerned, the fight could end now.[145]

At virtually the same time, King Fahd announced that the Saudis would no longer look out for market share; they would go back to coordinating with their fellow OPEC members and such non-OPEC states as were of a mind to co-operate. At the next meeting of OPEC, in Geneva, the members agreed on an overall quota of 16.8 m b/d, which got the price up to $14, and, according to the king, OPEC was aiming for $18 a barrel.[146]

With all OPEC countries signifying support and with most non-OPEC countries having publicly indicated their willingness to go along, the oil market now firmed up.

AMERICA COMMITTED

America, whether it wanted to or not, was now in the predicament of Britain after World War I. It needed oil. It had oil, but clearly it had passed its peak of production. With the domestic oil industry becoming moribund, the situation was not likely to be corrected. The United States would have therefore to depend on sources outside its sovereign control.

Britain, faced with this predicament in the early 1900s, had moved to the Middle East, where it had found oil, first in Iran, then Iraq. Subsequently, it had set up an oil lifeline to the Gulf, which it declared itself prepared to defend.

America would now be forced to do likewise; but for the United States the problem was additionally complicated. Americans had gotten used to having oil at cheap prices. This meant that Washington would have to find some means of ensuring that prices would be kept down. To do that, it had to work with OPEC, since, as the Saudis had just demonstrated, without OPEC concurrence production could not be regulated, and production was the key to setting price.

The outcome of the Third Oil Shock must therefore be seen as a clear win for Riyadh. It had succeeded in maintaining OPEC's relevance. How the organization behaved affected the international economy. The United States could not ignore this fact, or, rather, it would do so at its peril.

THE REFLAGGING

In December 1986 Kuwait asked both the United States and the Soviet Union to protect ships calling at Kuwait ports.[147] The requests came after the tanker war had heated up. The Iranians, abruptly and without warning, had started striking shipping belonging to, or involved in, commercial dealings with the sheikhs.

The Iranians, of course, had been threatening to do this. Still, the move is somewhat puzzling. In effect, the Iranians played into the hands of the Iraqis, who, since 1983, had been trying, as they called it, to "internationalize the conflict," that is, force intervention by the Great Powers.

It appears that the Iranians were desperate, as a whole host of things were going wrong. First of all, there were the revelations of Iran-Contra, which we take up in the next chapter. Iran's strongman leader, Rafsanjani, had been badly embarrassed by these, since, in entering into negotiations with the Americans, he appeared to be flaunting the line of the Imam.

Along with that, the tanker war by the Iraqis was taking a toll. Moreover, thanks to the Saudis' activity in driving oil prices down, the shipping losses were keenly felt. Given all of these setbacks, Tehran apparently decided to escalate, even though the risks of so doing were great.

In August 1986 a Liberian tanker, calling at Kuwait, was hit; in September two more, and an additional two in November.[148] After appealing for support from its fellow Gulf Cooperation Council (GCC) members (and apparently not finding satisfaction), Kuwait decided to call on the superpowers for protection.

The Russians accepted with alacrity and leased three Soviet ships to the Kuwaitis and provided escorts for them. The Americans, after initially indicating that they would comply, dragged their feet. The manner in which the Kuwaitis had framed the requests, for the Americans, posed problems.

From America's point of view, it would have been preferable had the Kuwaitis asked the United States alone, not the Russians. Washington evidently felt that, by joining in an operation with Moscow, the United States would, in a sense, be legitimating Soviet penetration of the strategic Gulf.

Why had the Kuwaitis stipulated both superpowers in their appeal? It would appear that they did not trust the Americans to comply were they to have been solicited alone. Kuwait had just undergone a bruising confrontation with the Congress over arms. The latter, responding to the urgings of AIPAC, defeated a Kuwaiti request for Stinger missiles. In 1980 the Saudis had made an appeal for AWACs (aerial surveillance craft), and AIPAC nearly killed that. In 1977 a Saudi request for F-15 fighters squeaked through only because of Sadat's assassination.[149]

Evidently fearing that, were they to ask just the Americans, they would lose out again, the Kuwaitis made an approach to Moscow as a kind of fail-safe.

GREAT DEBATE

In May 1987 the Iraqis, by accident, hit the U.S. *Stark* with an Exocet missile. The deaths of 37 Americans unleashed a veritable storm of disapproval, both in the Congress and in the American media against the proposed reflagging.[150]

Opposition came fully out into the open as the Congress insisted on having a say in the administration's decision to intervene.[151] The Cold Warriors claimed that America, by agreeing to protect just Kuwaiti ships, was proposing to take Iraq's side in the war.[152] The neoconservatives also were opposed, for much the same reason.

It would be wrong, however, to leave the impression that opposition came only from the Right. Some liberal senators like Sam Nunn of Georgia also were antagonistic.[153] Unfortunately for the administration, the reflagging was one of those issues that disaffect a range of interests. Nevertheless, Reagan held firm, which could not have been easy, as he was just then defending himself over Iran-Contra.

Reagan justified his action on the basis that, if America did not act, the Russians would gain a foreign policy victory.[154] To a degree, this was true. But that argument—which under less emotionally charged circumstances might have carried weight—did not begin to mollify the opposition in this instance. It looked for a while as if the issue would be tied up in endless debate.

Then, in July 1987 Iranian pilgrims to Mecca unleashed a demonstration against the Saudis, the United States, and Moscow.[155] The Saudis had always insisted that politics be kept out of the hajj. In flaunting this prohibition, the Iranians knew that they would invite trouble. But their anger at the Saudis was intense.

To quell the disturbances, the Saudi police fired into the crowds, killing some 400 Iranians.[156] Tehran was furious over this, accusing the House of Saud (the hated Wahhabis), of all manner of perfidies.[157]

The Saudis, however, fought back, an uncharacteristic response for them; usually, they do not allow themselves to be dragged into high-profile confrontations. In this instance they did. In fact, the Saudis were so outspoken that the quarrel very quickly escalated.[158]

In this way Washington was forced to become involved. By coming out so strongly against the Iranians, the Saudis raised the prospect of an expanded Gulf War in which they and the Kuwaitis would become belligerents, and this, of course, would have had worldwide repercussions.

The effect on the economy would have been devastating. Recall, for a moment, some of the consequences of the last oil shock. In 1986 the Continental-Illinois Bank collapsed (this precipitated the largest bank run in world history); the domestic oil industry in the United States went into a serious decline (producing a protracted depression in America's Southwest); Mexico defaulted on its bank debts; and the conservation movement died in the United States (with all of the ecological disasters that that entailed).

These are developments in the Western Hemisphere only. In Europe the failure of reform in Russia can be linked to the events of 1986 (petroleum is Russia's biggest foreign exchange earner; once the price collapsed, Moscow could not fund its development plans).

There were numerous crises in the Third World. For example, in Cairo, the Egyptian police mutinied when, because of the price collapse, the government could not afford to pay their wages. The Egyptian army had to be called out, and, in the ensuing confrontation, the army raked the mutineers with machine-gun fire from helicopters.

Having experienced all this in the mid-1980s, the Reagan administration was not about to risk yet another upheaval, which would certainly come about if Saudi Arabia and Kuwait got drawn into war with Iran.

What seems to have forced Reagan's hand, however, was movement on the part of the Europeans. Initially, many Europeans had refused to support the reflagging because of misgivings about the way the United States had "cut and run" in Lebanon. But, once the disturbances erupted in Mecca, objections vanished. A great flotilla was assembled of more than 200 warships. The Iranians were soon overwhelmed.

Nonetheless, they did not stand down, not immediately. There was the embarrassing incident of the USS *Bridgeton*, which struck an Iranian mine.[159] Minesweepers were needed; however, the United States did not have any. They had to be gotten from the British. Then, after several more mine incidents, the U.S. Navy, by way of retaliation, blew up an offshore oil rig owned by Iran.[160]

In the author's view, the importance of the reflagging rests in the fact of its having generated a great debate in the United States over whether the Gulf was vital to America's interests. The issue quite clearly was decided in favor of its being so.

That settled it. America was now in the Gulf, more or less formally. After this it would get only more and more deeply involved. In effect, Washington had taken on the Gulf as its sphere, replacing London in that capacity.

At the same time it was unfortunate that Reagan was not more forthcoming with the American public as to what was at stake here. His insistence on maintaining that America was going to Kuwait's aid to forestall the Russian penetration of the Gulf was pure pettifogging. The Russians were coordinating with Washington throughout the whole affair.

Washington acted because it really dared not do otherwise. After the Third Oil Shock, the prospect of instability in this crucial part of the world could not be entertained. However, by taking the approach that he did, Reagan left the people with the impression that America's intervention was somehow tied in with the Cold War, and this, as we shall see, affected how Americans reacted to the Gulf War when that developed four years later.

NOTES

1. See Introduction.

2. We are using protection in the American sense of the rackets where gangs sell protection to businessmen who may need it but, then again, may not. In any case, for the protector not to be forthcoming with his protection when needed is a sign of weakness impugning the ability of the protector and calling the whole relationship into question.

3. In 1961 the Pentagon established the office of International Logistics Negotiations (ILN), which became the center of U.S. arms sales. In 1964 ILN's director, Henry Kuss, was promoted to the rank of deputy assistant secretary of defense as a result of his success in boosting weapons sales. This marked the beginning of America's shift to all-out weapons sales. Prior to that, under the Military Assistance Program (MAP), America gave away military equipment at the rate of about $2.2 billion a year. See U.S. Senate, Committee on Foreign Relations, *Arms Sales and Foreign Policy* (Washington, DC: Government Printing Office, 1967).

4. Evidence of this is NSC-68, the strategic blueprint for the United States in the post–World War II era. The document mentions the Middle East only once in passing and then as an area that must be safeguarded, but only after Europe and Asia. Also America entered into no formal alliances with any Middle East state. It tried, under Dulles, to promote the Middle East Defense Organization (MEDO) to fight communism, but when Nasser demurred, claiming Zionism, not communism, was the Arabs' enemy, Dulles backed off. He then toyed with the idea of joining an expanded Baghdad Pact but shied away there also; America became an associate of the pact but not a full member. Finally, there was the Eisenhower Doctrine in 1957, which turned into a fiasco and which American policymakers afterward preferred to forget. Ernest May, ed., *American Cold War Strategy: Interpreting NSC-68* (Boston: Bedford Books of St. Martin's Press, 1993). On the Baghdad Pact, see John Ashton Nigel, *Eisenhower, Macmillan and the Problem of Nasser* (London: Macmillan, 1996), 39f.

5. On the indirect benefits of arms sales to the buyer, see John Stanley and Maurice Pearton, *The International Trade in Arms* (London: International Institute for Strategic Studies, 1972), 72f.

6. Although at this time the belief was widespread throughout the United States that America was self-sufficient in oil, this was barely the case. Since just before the OPEC revolution, the United States had been importing a greater and greater percentage of the oil that it used. According to testimony before the Congress in 1977, in 1975, 30 percent of domestic consumption came from OPEC, and it was expected that the figure would rise to 50 percent by 1985. U.S. Congress, Exxon Corporation to the Subcommittee of Energy of the Joint Economic Committee the U.S. Congress, *Energy Independence or Interdependence: The Agenda with OPEC* (Washington, DC: Government Printing Service, January 13, 1977).

7. The special relationship may be said to have been formalized in June 1974, when Prince Fahd signed a military and economic cooperation agreement in Washington, and immediately after that Nixon visited Riyadh. Ian Skeet, *OPEC: Twenty-Five Years of Prices and Politics* (Cambridge: Cambridge University Press, 1988), 120.

8. Abbas Alnasrawi, *Arab Nationalism, Oil, and the Political Economy of Dependency* (Westport, CT: Greenwood, 1991), 114, says that in 1974 Saudi Arabia's expenditure on weapons was $2.6 billion, or 7.5 percent of the value of Saudi oil exports. By

1985 that amount had gone up to nearly $23 billion and more than 88 percent of oil exports. Also, according to Alnasrawi, in the period 1970–1975, when Saudi arms imports averaged only $.3 billion, the United States supplied 51 percent of those arms. The U.S. share increased to 79 percent during the period 1975–1979. Actually, the Saudis' arms-buying trajectory had a slow liftoff. Until the early 1970s the Saudis had no sizable armed forces. However, following their dismal performance in the war with Yemen, they commissioned a number of studies from the United States to develop a modern military establishment. The arms buying takes off in 1974 and climbs steadily after that. See Michael Brzoska and Thomas Ohlson, *Arms Transfers to the Third World: 1971–85* (Stockholm: SIPRI, 1987), 6, 20.

9. John Daly, moderator, *Arms Sales: A Useful Foreign Policy Tool?* (Washington, DC: American Enterprise Institute, 1981), 5.

10. It is also important to point out here that, as late as 1979–1980, the Saudis were considering hiring the Pakistanis as mercenaries. In other words, they had no effective army.

11. This is an injunction that goes back centuries. One has merely to think of the narratives of Capt. Richard Burton and Charles Doughty, famous travelers who smuggled themselves into Mecca in disguise.

12. Robinson claims that the young prince who killed Feisal did it for political motives. The author of the present work was the prince's teaching assistant while he was attending Berkeley. Having to mark his papers, he got to know him fairly well. He was not radical in the pro-PLO sense, but he was violently anti-Israel. See Jeffrey Robinson, *Yamani: The Inside Story* (New York: Atlantic Monthly Press, 1989), 144–145.

13. For the hostage taking, see ibid., 152f.

14. The kingdom, on occasion, claims up to 20 million. It probably has no more than 7 million, and there is cause to believe it is lower than that.

15. Pierre Terzian, *OPEC: The Inside Story* (London: Zed Books, 1985), 261.

16. This was the posted price; the price that the shah got by putting his oil up for public auction was far higher, $17.30.

17. Yergin, *The Prize* (New York: Simon and Schuster, 1991), 646.

18. For an account of sharp clashes between the Iraqis and Libyans and the Saudis over politics, see Terzian, *OPEC: The Inside Story*, 246.

19. The Saudis continually expressed the fear that, were the price to become too high, the West would accelerate exploration for new fields, which, of course, is what occurred with the British and Norwegians in the North Sea and the Americans in Alaska.

20. Yergin, *The Prize*, 626f.

21. Jeffrey Robinson, *Yamani: The Inside Story* (New York: Atlantic Monthly Press, 1989), 118. See also V. H. Oppenheim, "Why Oil Prices Go Up," *Foreign Policy*, No. 25 (Winter 1976–1977), 24–57.

22. In regard to weapons being superinflationary, see Peter Ellis Jones, *Oil: A Practical Guide to the Economics of World Petroleum* (Cambridge: Woodhead-Faulkner, 1988), 47. Each year, he says, more and more barrels of oil were necessary to purchase a tank or fighter aircraft.

23. There does not appear to be any doubt that the U.S. government was considerably alarmed and temporarily at a loss about how to react when the oil companies went over to the side of the producers and undertook to administer the embargo. See the 1975 report on Multinational Oil Corporations and U.S. Foreign Policy in *Report of the Subcommittee on Multinational Corporations of the Senate Foreign Relations Committee*, January 2, 1975.

24. Mira Wilkins, "The Multinational Oil Companies," in Raymond Vernon, *The Oil Crisis* (New York: Norton, 1976), 166; also the *Report of the Subcommittee on Multinational Corporations.*

25. In 1956, of course, the British involved themselves along with the French and Israelis in the disastrous Suez War. After that, Britain's star began to sink in the Middle East. First it lost Egypt, but gradually it lost the Gulf as well.

26. Namely, Watergate.

27. Gary Sick, *All Fall Down* (New York: Viking Penguin, 1986), 16f.

28. Ibid.

29. The shah was warning about a putative Russian thrust to the Indian Ocean through Iran and putting Iran forward as the rampart that would block any such move. That Dulles and Eisenhower, who had apparently been sold on the so-called warm-water ports theory, would ignore the shah's warnings seemed incomprehensible to the Iranian.

30. To give the shah the benefit of the doubt, he may not have been so misguided. After all, in the 1950s, when he began appealing for weapons, he had little cash—the oil industry was very much controlled by the companies then, and they gave the shah as much money as they thought warranted. In order to borrow from Western banks, he would have had to convince them that his regime was secure. What better way to do that than to build a strong military that could guarantee survival?

31. The offer was made by Nixon during a stopover in Tehran in December 1972 on the way back from China. Nixon is actually supposed to have appealed to the shah to protect him.

32. To be sure, a lot of the reaction of these two presidents was conditioned by the desire to practice some austerity. Says Lekachman, "In pursuit of fiscal austerity, the Eisenhower Administration started bravely enough. Assisted by the Korean peace dividend, the President in 1954, 1955 and 1956 pushed the level of the federal expenditure down from 1953's $58 billion to $47.5, $45.3, and $45.7." Robert Lekachman, *Inflation* (New York: Vintage Books, 1973), 12. Kennedy somewhat let up on the austerity, but not a great deal. Both men feared running a budget deficit.

33. Barry Rubin, in his *Paved with Good Intentions* (Oxford: Oxford University Press, 1980), is particularly good at chronicling the ups and downs of *New York Times* coverage of the shah. By 1966, according to Rubin, the *Times* had reached the conclusion that Iran under the shah was one of the success stories of the Middle East (119).

34. The United States stopped giving Iran weapons in 1969, after having discontinued economic aid two years earlier. Lewis Sorley, *Arms Transfers under Nixon* (Lexington, KY: University Press of Kentucky, 1983), 112.

35. Evidently, this trend was set in 1969 on a visit of the shah to the United States, where Nixon indicated that the United States would be pleased were Iran to become the dominant military power in the Persian Gulf. Ibid., 113.

36. Arms trading today is essentially an activity of governments rather than private companies. Therefore, if the transfers are to be made, government financing has to be arranged, hence, the importance of this credit account. See Stanley and Pearton, *The International Trade in Arms*, 85f.

37. Ibid., 88, 116.

38. Gaddis discusses the extreme antipathy in Congress for arming for defense. See John Lewis Gaddis, *Strategies of Containment* (Oxford: Oxford University Press, 1982), 322.

39. Ibid., 320.

40. In purely practical terms, the shah's offer was a godsend. Faced with the prospect of decreased funding, the Pentagon's strategy has always been to try to save as many projects as possible by spreading the available moneys as thinly as possible. This raises the unit cost for each system produced to unacceptably high levels. The shah, by guaranteeing to buy a certain proportion of the systems, enabled the Pentagon to boost the unit-cost ratio. See Joanna Spear, *Carter and Arms Sales* (New York: St. Martin's, 1995), 23.

41. Anthony Sampson, *The Arms Bazaar* (New York: Viking, 1977), 284.

42. M. Reza Ghods, *Iran in the Twentieth Century* (Boulder, CO: Lynne Rienner Publishers, 1989), 261.

43. Ibid.

44. Sampson, *The Arms Bazaar*, 285.

45. Sorley, *Arms Transfers under Nixon*, 113; also Stephen Pelletiere, *The Iran–Iraq War: Chaos in a Vacuum* (Westport, CT: Praeger, 1992).

46. Basically, the Kurds got the appointment of a Kurdish vice president; the establishment of Kurdish as one of two official languages; and representation of Kurds in government, army, police, legislature, and the universities in proportion to their number. See Stephen Pelletiere, *The Kurds: An Unstable Element in the Gulf* (Boulder, CO: Westview Press, 1984), 164. What the Kurds held out for was Kirkuk to be declared part of the autonomous Kurdish area. To the author, this seemed not to make sense. Kirkuk is where Iraq's oil is; could the Ba'thists have been expected to assign such a valuable piece of property to the non-Arab Kurds? Had they done so, they would not have lasted in power a day.

47. Information on the Israeli involvement and, in general, on the details of this affair was published in *The Village Voice* of February 23, 1976, after being leaked from the *Report of the House Select Committee on Intelligence* (the Pike Report).

48. After the United States compensated the Israelis for the weapons transferred.

49. For a critique of the debacle by a Kurdish leader who participated, see Ismet Sheriff Vanly, "Kurdistan in Iraq," in *People without a Country*, Gerard Chaliand, ed. (London: Zed Books, 1980).

50. Ibid.

51. For a discussion of Barzani's war-fighting ability, see Edgar O'Ballance, *The Kurdish War* (Hamden, CT: Archon Books, 1973).

52. *New York Times* (April 1, 1975).

53. Just as Barzani always maintained a close alliance with the Soviet Union, he also had excellent relations with Nasser, and, of course, the Egyptians, as Arab nationalists, could not countenance Barzani's statements about what he would do, vis-à-vis Israel, were he to get his autonomy.

54. At this time there may have been as many as 4 million Iranian Kurds, who had been firmly suppressed by the shah's father.

55. Pelletiere, *The Kurds: An Unstable Element in the Gulf.*

56. Indeed, as part of the deal Saddam ejected Khomeini from Iraq (at the shah's behest), and in 1978, when the shah was being pressured at home, Saddam received Empress Farah in Najaf and accorded her all the respect due an empress. Terzian, *OPEC: The Inside Story*, 278.

57. According to Marion Farouk-Sluglett and Peter Sluglett, *Iraq since 1958* (London I. B. Tauris, 1987), 186f., Saddam started tightening up on the communists in 1976, and the actual purge came in 1978.

58. Some of the shah's statements about this time displayed an almost visceral hatred of the West. He said, for example, "There are people who thought—perhaps still think—I am a toy in the Americans' hands. Why would I accept to be a toy? There are reasons for our power which will make us stronger, so why would we be content to be anybody's catspaw?" Yergin, *The Prize*, 638. Another time he said, "I hope my good friends in Europe and the United States and elsewhere will finally understand that there is absolutely no difference between Iran and France, Britain and Germany. Why should you find it absolutely normal that France will spend that much money on her army, and not my country? . . . The strength that we have now in the Persian Gulf is ten times, twenty times more than the British ever had." Sampson, *The Arms Bazaar*, 249.

59. By 1980 it was estimated that there were as many as 50,000 to 60,000 U.S. citizens in Iran, most of them U.S. military personnel or U.S.-supplied arms contractors. See Rubin, *Paved with Good Intentions*, 174.

60. When worldwide inflation struck, largely due to oil price rises, this hit the Iranians hard, particularly those on fixed incomes such as civil service workers.

61. Under agreements reached between the United States and the shah, U.S. citizens accused of crimes allegedly committed in Iran could not be tried by Iranian courts. This rankled the Iranians and was seen as a throwback to the days of the capitulations.

62. Yergin, *The Prize*, 658.

63. Immediately after the OPEC takeover, the companies in the lower Gulf had to surrender 40 percent of their equity. The Saudis maintained that this would be all that they would have to forgo, which was an important concession because the American companies' taxing arrangements with the U.S. government was based on the fact that not more than 40 percent of the overseas operations could be foreign-controlled. Eventually, however, the Saudis took 100 percent control, as did the other OPEC countries.

64. Mobil bought the Montgomery Ward chain of department stores. Yergin, *The Prize*, 665.

65. It seems that the panic may have been triggered, without its meaning to, by ARAMCO, which had told the Saudis they could produce over 10 million b/d. This led the Saudis to confidently declare that they could compensate for Iranian oil going offline. However, when the Saudis attempted to do this, they badly damaged some of their most important wells and had to shut down. At that, speculators, sensing shortages, moved into the market. Also, the major oil companies held back on their oil, refusing to fulfill so-called third-party contracts, probably because they sensed that the price was going up. Terzian, *OPEC: The Inside Story*.

66. Ibid.

67. The Saudi Shia community was domiciled in the eastern province, where the oil wells are, and moreover constituted practically all of the oil workers.

68. The worst of these upheavals occurred in Bahrain, where the rebels came close to unseating the ruler. Pelletiere, *The Iran–Iraq War: Chaos in a Vacuum*.

69. The usually accepted figure is between 55 and 65 percent of the population, bearing in mind that the northern-dwelling Kurds are a distinct minority making up about 20 percent. Thus the Sunni Arab component is even more isolated. Ibid.

70. During the detente period between Saddam and the shah, the shah asked Saddam to eject Khomeini from Najaf, where the latter had taken refuge after being expelled from Iran. Saddam complied, which won him Khomeini's enmity.

71. Immediately after the Khomeini revolt, the Iranian Kurds demanded autonomy under the Kurdish leader Abdur Rahman Qasemlu. This was forcefully put down, with

much loss of life. Later, the Iranians assassinated Qasemlu in Europe. Pelletiere, *The Iran–Iraq War: Chaos in a Vacuum.*

72. This did not make sense because the Saudis, at this stage, were trying to control prices under the direction of Yamani. In fact, Yamani repeatedly accused the Western countries, in particular, the United States, of causing the run-up in prices by stockpiling (about which we have more to say later). Terzian, *OPEC: The Inside Story*, 261.

73. It's interesting how the caricatures of the oil sheikhs in the media reproduced the anti-Semitic caricatures of the Jews of the last era. The faces were the same; only the clothes were different.

74. The Kuwaitis made a similar declaration when the United States expressed such threats in 1973. See Klaus Knorr, "The Limits of Power," in Vernon, *The Oil Crisis*, 236. For a compilation of statements made during the 1979 period and chronology of what went on, see *Petroleum Imports from the Persian Gulf: Use of U.S. Armed Forces to Ensure Supplies*, Issue Brief, Congressional Research Service, Library of Congress, May 1980.

75. Adding to the hysteria was a CIA report saying that the Soviet Union was running low on oil and might have to take oil from the Gulf within a few years. Ibid.

76. This was the February 26, 1921, Friendship Treaty, mentioned earlier.

77. CENTCOM is the only command not based in area.

78. The Saudis did not subscribe to the charter, but at the same time they did not advise their fellow sheikhs to abstain, which to the author means that they approved. Pelletiere, *The Iran–Iraq War: Chaos in a Vacuum*, 30.

79. Essentially, Saddam's demands on Iran were three—return of the disputed portion of the Shatt; return to Sharjah of the three islands in the gulf seized by the shah; and a plebiscite to determine the status of the largely Arab population of Iranian Khuzistan. All three are concerned with opening Iraq's way to the Gulf.

80. Saddam also condemned the Soviet invasion of Afghanistan, which put him in the Russians' bad books with immediate, unfortunate results, as we will see.

81. Nonneman confirms this. Gerd Nonnemann, *Iraq, the Gulf States and the War* (London: Ithaca Press, 1986).

82. They later expanded that to protecting all the Arabs, hence, their claim of being the guardians of the eastern flank of the Arab world.

83. Sephir Zabeh, *The Iranian Military in Revolution and War* (London: Routlege, 1988), 117.

84. The capture of Khoramshar was no mean feat. Since 1967 no major city that was defended had fallen in the Middle East. Israel was not able to take Beirut against entrenched opposition of the militias, as we shall shortly see.

85. Abdol Hasan Bani Sadr was Iran's first president under the Islamic Republic. A noncleric, he soon ran afoul of the clerics and attempted to keep himself in power by taking personal charge of the war against Iraq. He went to the front looking for a decisive victory and, with this in mind, committed Iran's forces to an immense tank battle at Suzengard, which the Iranians lost, after which Bani Sadr fled Iran to Paris.

86. One of the stories current had the Iranians sending children in to clear minefields by detonating the mines with their bodies. Thus, they opened the way for the human wave attacks. The children were supposedly given small silver keys to paradise.

87. Although the Iraqi army comprised up to 85 percent Shias, the Ba'thist leadership was loath to trust them, fearing that they would go over en masse to the side of their coreligionists in Iran (who were almost 95 percent Shia). For a good treatment of the

differences between the Iraqi and Iranian Shias, see Yitzhak Nakash, *The Shias of Iraq* (Princeton, NJ: Princeton University Press, 1994).

88. A part of the reason for this was that in the beginning the attacks were staged at night.

89. Pelletiere, *The Iran–Iraq War*, 42.

90. Ibid.

91. The best source of the Shia origins of the Ba'th is Hanna Batatu, *The Old Social Classes and the Revolutionary Movements of Iraq* (Princeton, NJ: Princeton University Press, 1978).

92. Nakash, *The Shias of Iraq*.

93. This is a point that is often overlooked by those who claim that the Iraqi Shias will support any movement that opposes the Ba'th. In fact, these movements are generally headed by representatives of the ancien régime, those who fled the country after the 1958 revolution, and the Shias who formerly constituted the poorer classes despise them.

94. After this, Iraq's Jewish community (what was left of it after the 1967 war) decamped, and, interestingly, once they left, the Shias took over as leaders of Iraq's business community.

95. For a profile of the social origins of the early Ba'thists, see Amazia Baram's article "The Ruling Political Elite in Ba'thi Iraq, 1968–1986: The Changing Features of a Collective Profile," *Journal of Middle East Studies*, No. 21 (1989): 447–493.

96. Sluglett and Sluglett, *Iraq since 1958*, 248, for details on the security apparatus.

97. Saddam, like Baker, came from the town of Tikrit. According to Batatu, the Tikritis were extremely poor, and they gravitated into Iraq's police under the monarchy because one of their number had achieved a high post there. Later, the Tikritis used their police connection to work their way into the political leadership, and when the Ba'th took over, the Tikritis worked to supplant the Shias in control of the party. Batatu, *The Old Social Classes*.

98. Marr, *The Modern History of Iraq* (Boulder, CO: Westview, 1985), 269. The reader should be aware that before the Gulf War Iraq could be classified among group III nations with an annual GNP over $3000 per capita. See Peter Pellet, "Sanctions, Food, Nutrition, and Health in Iraq," in *Iraq Under Siege*, ed. Anthony Arnove (Cambridge, MA: South End Press, 2000).

99. Immediately after the revolution, Iran's liberals expected the clerics to hand over power to them. Mehdi Barzagan, Iran's acting prime minister, eventually quit in disgust when he could not prevail over the clerical faction.

100. The *basij* is an institution unique to the Iranian revolution. Originally, it comprised 22-man squads recruited by the clerics after the American hostages were seized and when the Iranians expected an American invasion. The *basij* units were supposed to rally to the clerics' support and fight the invader. They were institutionalized as a low-grade Revolutionary Guards corps.

101. Nonneman, *Iraq, the Gulf States and the War*, 48.

102. Battlefield casualties for this war are suspect. Neither side permitted observers at the front, and satellite reconnaissance cannot accurately assess the slain. Pelletiere, *The Iran–Iraq War*, 64.

103. "Peace Threatens Sales in the Arms Bazaar," *Le Monde* (July 26, 1998).

104. The Soviet Union cut off Iraq as soon as the war broke out and did not restore weapons supplies until the war had turned against Iraq and until Iran refused to heed

Moscow's appeals for a truce. The United States, declaring itself neutral, refused to supply either side, although, as we shall see, it soon abandoned that stance.

105. America's arms relationship with Israel goes back to 1970, when it signed a so-called Master Defense Development Data Exchange Agreement, which essentially gave Israel advanced technology so it could produce weapons on its own. During the Fourth Arab–Israeli War Nixon transferred some $2.2 billion in emergency military aid to Israel—effectively, Washington stripped its stores in the North Atlantic Treaty Organization (NATO) to resupply the Israelis. Currently, Israel receives roughly $3 billion in aid from the United States annually, distributed between economic and military. For details of how, by means of special bookkeeping accommodations, Israel effectively gets its aid free, see Donald Neff, *Fallen Pillars* (Washington, DC: Institute for Palestinian Studies, 1995); see also "Israel Has Unique Deal for U.S. Aid," *New York Times* (September 21, 1990).

106. Gaddis in *Strategies of Containment*, 93, says that economist Leon Keyserling advised Truman to treat weapons production in precisely this way to keep the economy going without letdown after World War II.

107. For details on numbers of Lebanese killed by the Israelis, see Robert Fisk, *Pity the Nation* (Oxford: Oxford University Press, 1992), 250, 323, 389, 450, 537.

108. Essentially the Israelis were deceiving the Americans. They claimed they got a so-called amber light to go ahead with the operation from then-Secretary of State Haig, but the whole deal was problematic. Haig later said that he had not actually given such encouragement. Whatever the Israelis' arrangement with Haig, it clearly would not stand up were others in the Reagan administration to weigh in against it, and that is precisely what happened.

109. In part, this perception was fostered by Haig, who seemed to be deliberately thwarting attempts to roll back the Israeli invasion, because the Israelis had convinced him that they could resolve the Palestinian problem once and for all. Also, the Arabs knew that America could have restricted the Israelis' use of American-supplied weapons by the simple expedient of invoking provisions of their aid agreement, under which the weapons were to be used only for defensive purposes, which was clearly not the case with the invasion. Seeing the Americans fail to act put the onus for the civilian deaths on Washington, in the eyes of the Arabs.

110. Bob Scheiffer, *The Acting President* (New York: E. P. Dutton, 1989), 135–138.

111. Nonneman, *Iraq, the Gulf States and the War.*

112. For details of the meeting, see Anthony Cordesman, *The Iraq–Iran War and U.S. Iraq Relations: An Iraqi Perspective* (Washington, DC: National Council on U.S.–Arab Relations, 1984).

113. This situation was fostered, in part, by the fact that, since the combatants would not allow correspondents at the front and, further, since neither side had relations with the United States (so newsmen had great difficulty traveling to the area), the journalists were almost entirely dependent on the government for information.

114. Before the United States did anything, however, it restored relations with Iraq (which had been broken by Iraq in the 1967 war). On its side Iraq forswore aiding terrorists and expelled certain groups from Baghdad.

115. For details on this whole affair, see Pelletiere, *The Iran–Iraq War*, 83–84.

116. U.S. and Russian help for Iraq was conditioned on the fact that there not be a military victory in the war.

117. Aziz makes this claim in his interview with Shultz. Cordesman, *The Iran–Iraq War and U.S. Iraq Relations.*

118. There was also some substitution of alternative forms of energy. In particular, Britain began to shift away from oil to coal.

119. Skeet, *OPEC: Twenty-Five Years of Prices and Politics*, 183.

120. If you are going to stockpile, you might as well leave it in the ground. But in the 1980s, since it was primarily the companies that were stockpiling and since the companies had lost their equity, that was not an option.

121. Alnasrawi, *Arab Nationalism, Oil, and the Political Economy of Dependency*, 138f.

122. The high absorbers were Iran, Iraq, Nigeria, Algeria, Venezuela, and Indonesia.

123. Iran consistently refused to borrow. Hence, it was living from hand-to-mouth.

124. Skeet, *OPEC: Twenty-Five Years of Prices and Politics*, 178f.

125. Steven Schneider, *The Oil Price Revolution* (Baltimore: Johns Hopkins University Press, 1983), 452.

126. Mohammad Ahrari, *OPEC: The Failing Giant* (Lexington: University of Kentucky Press, 1986), 169.

127. The best treatment of this episode is in Robinson, *Yamani: The Inside Story*, 256f.; Terzian, *OPEC: The Inside Story*, 298f.

128. For a good discussion of the terms under which the North Sea Fields were operated, see Kenneth Dam, *Oil Resources, Who Gets What, How?* (Chicago: University of Chicago Press, 1976).

129. By setting the price, Britain could affect the companies' production policies. Hence, if it was in Britain's interest to conserve its reserves, it could do that. Also, North Sea oil is light and sweet; Britain mainly needed heavy crude for heating oil. By selling oil to the companies to refine and market, the British could realize cash to buy heavy.

130. Skeet, *OPEC: Twenty-Five Years of Prices and Politics*, 178f.

131. This seems altruistic, but to put it in context, the Saudis' insistence on keeping their production up all those years had contributed to the glut.

132. Skeet, *OPEC: Twenty-Five Years of Prices and Politics*, 185.

133. Iran was producing only 1.2 m b/d, whereas under the shah it had been up to 5 m b/d. Ibid., 185.

134. Ahrari, *OPEC: The Failing Giant*, 183.

135. Skeet, *OPEC: Twenty Five Years of Prices and Politics*, 206.

136. Ibid.

137. Under the arrangement, the Saudis would not charge a set price to the refiner for their oil. Rather, the refiner would be paid on the basis of what refined prices earned in the market. The refiner, however, would be guaranteed a predetermined profit off the top, say, two dollars a barrel. He would get the two dollars, and the Saudis would get the rest, minus various costs. See Yergin, *The Prize*, 748.

138. Ibid., 750f.

139. Ibid, 755. Reagan's action backfired from another angle. There was the prospect of diminished weapons buys by the sheikhs. If the price of oil was plumbing all-time lows, the sheikhs could hardly be expected to keep up with their excessively costly purchases.

140. "Bush to Seek Saudis' Assistance in Stabilizing Plunging Oil Prices," *New York Times* (April 2, 1986).

141. Ibid.

142. "Oil Price Drop Puts Texas Deep into Revenue Hole," *Washington Post* (February 4, 1986).

143. "Possibility of Oil Price War Spells Trouble in the Southwest," *New York Times* (December 17, 1985). Bush considered himself an oilman, having relocated to Texas from Connecticut to work in the oil business.

144. "Norway to Reduce Oil Exports," *New York Times* (September 11, 1986).

145. "Thatcher Said to Back Oslo," *New York Times* (September 13, 1986).

146. "Saudis Ask to Increase Their OPEC Quota," *New York Times* (October 14, 1986).

147. "Fear of Iranian Sabotage Led Kuwait to Involve the Superpowers," *Washington Post* (July 8, 1987).

148. Ibid.

149. Nadav Safran, *Saudi Arabia: The Ceaseless Quest for Security* (Cambridge: Harvard University Press, 1985), 299.

150. Pelletiere, *The Iran–Iraq War*, 128.

151. Specifically, the Congress wanted Reagan to pledge that he would invoke the War Powers Act before committing U.S. ships.

152. This was the case. Iraq was free to go on targeting Iranian ships.

153. "Nunn, Kissinger Warn of U.S. Tilt toward Iraq," *Washington Post* (June 15, 1987).

154. Joseph Harsch, "Kuwait, the U.S. and Moscow," *Christian Science Monitor* (June 2, 1987).

155. "After Mecca: Saudi Arabia Is More Stable Than It Looks," *Washington Post* (August 9, 1987).

156. "Moslem World Criticizes Iran over Mecca Clash," *New York Times* (August 5, 1987).

157. "Iranian Officials Urge 'Uprooting' of Saudi Rulers," *New York Times* (August 3, 1987).

158. "Saudi Charges Iran Plotted to Upset Kingdom's Control over Shrines," *Washington Post* (August 26, 1987).

159. "A Mine Sends Shock Waves through U.S. Policy in Gulf," *New York Times* (July 26, 1987).

160. "U.S. Destroyers Shell Iranian Military Platform in Gulf," *Washington Post* (October 20, 1987).

CHAPTER 6

Iran-Contra and Iraq; The Media Campaign that Took America to War

In this chapter we trace the outbreak of the Gulf War to the breakdown of the international oil system. There is some evidence that we can adduce to show this, in particular, a number of actions carried out by the media at the time. Before we do that, however, we want to discuss Iran-Contra, as that has direct bearing on the occurrence of the war; it was a crucial factor in deciding the Iraqis to fight.

In regard to Iran-Contra, it is fairly clear who got that up—the Israelis. It is not possible to read the narrative version of Iran-Contra and be unconvinced of that. One of their people, David Kimche, devised it; he sold it to the National Security Council (NSC), and, when the thing would not work as originally designed, Kimche revised it to keep it going.[1]

As to why the Israelis did it—they wanted to sell weapons. They had weapons that they had acquired from various sources and they wanted to dispose of them for cash. For example, after the 1967 war they captured enormous quantities of Soviet arms supplied to the Arabs. Then, after the 1973 War, the Israelis got more weapons as the United States stripped its arsenals in Europe to resupply them. Some of these arms, we saw in Chapter 5, went to the Kurds, so they could carry on their war against the Iraqis. In the late 1970s, the Israelis started secretly supplying the Maronite Christians in Lebanon.[2]

Some of these transfers were obviously cleared through the Americans, as when the Israelis got Kissinger's approval to resupply the Kurds. But other deals—and one suspects the resupply of the Maronites fell into this category—were never vetted and hence were, under terms of the transfer agreement, illegal.

Israel had been selling arms to Iran since the start of the Iran–Iraq War.[3] This was in defiance of a U.S. Congress–imposed ban on permitting American weapons to be supplied to third countries without congressional approval. Evidently, after the blowing up of the Marine Corps' barracks, the Israelis had concerns about continuing with arms sales to Tehran, for fear of offending the Congress.

By getting the U.S. government to go along with an arms-for-hostages swap, in which Israel would provide the arms to be exchanged, Tel Aviv, in effect, would be covering itself. That seems to have been the rationale behind this.

As for the Reagan administration's reasons for agreeing to it, this seems partly to have been a matter of sentiment. The president had developed a deep concern over the plight of the hostages—it pained him that they were being held by the Lebanese Shias and that he could do nothing about it.

There may also have been fear on the president's part of the families of the hostages, who were known to be getting restive as time passed and as the United States had done nothing to secure their release.[4]

In any event, what is most interesting about the affair is the scant concern that anyone involved in it paid to the Iraqis. The Israelis were proposing to sell TOW (anti-tank) and Hawk (anti-aircraft) missiles to the Iranians. These would improve the Iranians' offensive capability, and the victim of Iranian aggression would be Iraq. Iraq, at this time, was supposed to be a U.S. ally, and Washington was supposed to be committed to ending the war by supporting UN Resolution 580; but here was Reagan authorizing arms sales to Iraq's enemy.

Even worse, the CIA, under orders from the president (and this, too, was part of the Israeli-brokered arms-for-hostages deal), passed intelligence to the Iranians. The CIA's deputy director, John McMahon, says in the Tower Report that he passed the Iraqis' order of battle and satellite photos showing Iraqi dispositions along the front.[5]

The intelligence was passed in January 1986, and just before that, in November 1985, 508 TOW missiles and an unspecified number of parts for Hawk missiles had been handed over to Iran. Then, on February 10, 1986 (i.e., immediately after the intelligence transfer), the Iraqis found themselves surprised by a successful penetration of their line. The Iranians had managed to cross the Shatt Al Arab and seize the deserted Iraqi city of Faw.

The loss of Faw was a major setback for the Iraqis. Up till then they had not suffered a significant defeat since being pushed back to the border in 1982. To be sure, Faw was deserted, but still it was an Iraqi city, and the effect on homefront morale was severe.[6] We know this because the Iraqis made strenuous efforts to recapture Faw and lost many men in the process.[7]

The loss of Faw compromised the Iraqi position strategically. They now, in effect, had to defend on three fronts. They had a smoldering guerrilla war by elements of the Kurdish community going on in the north. They had a permanent obligation to defend Basrah, which once a year the Iranians attempted to take by storm; and now they had to build a defensive perimeter to seal off Faw, keeping the Iranian penetration there contained.

One of the ironies of Iran-Contra was that it led the Iraqis in July 1986 to switch strategies. Up till then they had been fighting a war of static defense. Content merely to hold the line, they relied on the United States and Russia to bring about a negotiated cease-fire in the United Nations.[8]

After losing Faw, the Iraqi leadership called a Congress of the Ba'th in July 1986. At it, the civilian leadership agreed to a proposal by the military to abandon the defense and go over to the offense, which they would do by creating elite commando units capable of fighting such an offensive war.[9]

It is beyond the scope of this study to say how the Iraqis managed the switchover. (In fact the author has written about it elsewhere.[10]) Suffice it to say that they did succeed in stepping up recruitment to the elite Republican Guards; they were able to attract previously deferred college students to take on this commando assignment.

As of July 1986, it is unlikely that the Iraqis intended to use the reconstituted Guard detachments to do more than retake Faw. But when in November 1986 Washington's secret dealings with Iran were revealed (through reports in the American media), the Iraqis then had to confront the harsh reality of betrayal.

The civilian leadership's policy of relying on Washington to end the war was seen to be bankrupt.[11] It was probably at this point that the Iraqis decided to go all out, as it were, and try to bring about a military solution to the war on their own terms.

So, as a consequence of American's secret dealings with the Iranians (and the Israelis), the course of the war was now redirected as the Iraqis prepared to pursue a military solution, which was the last thing that Washington wanted to see them do.

INTERESTS

Why was Washington so apparently insensitive to what ought to have been seen as threats to its interests? It could only have been hurt by an Iraqi defeat in the war. Worse, it would have been grievously harmed were there to have been any disruption of operations in the Saudi oil fields, and yet, this precisely is what would have occurred had Iran defeated Iraq. It would have turned immediately south to overrun Kuwait and Saudi Arabia.

That Washington could not see this would seem to confirm what we have been saying—that the United States was indifferent to the Middle East. This despite the fact that so much was invested in the area; that the world depended on the Gulf, specifically, to remain prosperous; and that any crisis of a military nature occurring in this part of the world would certainly have necessitated the introduction of U.S. troops.

All this notwithstanding, the United States paid scant attention to events in the region. The quality of its intelligence on the Gulf was poor, the analysis of the intelligence that it did obtain was inferior, and there appears to have been little or no intelligence sharing with any of the area states. In many respects, this last is the most puzzling part of all.

In the last chapter we speculated on the condition of the oil system after the demise of the oil cartel. We suggested that it would have been hard for the system to carry on once the cartel had expired. The events of 1986 would seem to prove that the system was moribund; there was not a single influential group in the United States interceding for the Gulf with the Reagan (or, as we shall see, the Bush) administration.

The CIA, which was supposed to be watching over the area under Casey was tainted; indeed, in involving itself with the Iran-Contra affair, it made what was already a bad situation worse. One wonders why Reagan did not call in military experts. They could have told him of the risks that he was running.

We bring this up because Iraq's strategic situation—or perhaps we should say its strategic vulnerability—was key to everything. We mentioned earlier that Iraq had no strategic depth. This can be seen by looking at a map—all its major cities are right on the border. Hence, once Iranian forces had pushed to the border, Iraq's major population centers were exposed.

We saw what occurred when Faw was taken. Faw was deserted, which somewhat mitigated the loss; nonetheless, the effect on the people's morale was distinctly adverse. Practically all analysts of the war agreed (at the time) that, were Iraq to lose Basrah, it would cease to exist as an integrated nation-state.

Despite this, the United States was supplying Iran with sophisticated weapons to assist in the taking of Basrah. It was also (as mentioned earlier) supplying intelligence to subvert the Iraqis' defense. How could the Reagan administration do this?

The whole thing is particularly odd, because Reagan had thoughout this whole period been faced with one oil-related crisis after another. In the last chapter we detailed a whole slew of disasters, all related to the Third Oil Shock, when the Saudis ran the oil price practically into the ground. Then, as we saw, hard on the heels of that came the 1987 reflagging episode. In other words, Reagan had plenty of examples of how dangerous it was, in a manner of speaking, to play around with oil, and yet he did it.

The author has an explanation for this curious behavior—America's view that the Gulf was vital was based on the *negative* perception that the area might fall into Soviet hands. Once Moscow began to recede as a threat (and this had already begun to be apparent by this time), the United States stopped being much concerned with the region.

It never occurred to the Reagan administration that any other state—in particular, Iran—could take over the Gulf. Americans seem pretty routinely to disparage the capabilities of states other than their rival superpowers—the Soviet Union and China. To use a colloquialism, after these two, all other threats, to America, are chump change.

This line of analysis becomes important when we turn to examine the drift toward war of Iraq and the United States. There have been two theories advanced as to how the Americans could have allowed this drift to happen.

One theory (widely credited in the Middle East) holds that Washington trapped the Iraqis, that it misled them into believing that the Gulf was not important to it. America did this because it wanted to crush Baghdad, the theory goes.[12]

The evidence cited for this is the interview of (U.S. ambassador to Iraq) April Glaspie with Saddam. Supposedly, therein she deliberately misled the Iraqi into believing that America was not particularly interested in Kuwait, and so Iraq could invade, which is what Saddam was threatening at the time.

The other theory is that Washington was, in some vague, undefined way, colluding with the Iraqi leader—not to the extent of sanctioning his takeover but rather supporting Saddam's perception of himself as the head of a significant power that had claims to leadership both in the Gulf and in the wider area of the Arab world.[13]

Under this interpretation, only later—after Margaret Thatcher intervened—was Bush induced to take a more assertive stand, at which point Washington put together the broad coalition that took the world to war.

Based on what we have seen with Iran-Contra, the author would argue that neither of these theories is correct (and the latter one is absolute nonsense). In fact, Washington simply was not involved with Iraq or with the Gulf—it was indifferent. It did not believe that Iraq could take Kuwait as it was threatening to do.

If the administration was indifferent to the Gulf, there were plenty of others, who, for their own reasons, were quick to interfere. There were the Cold Warriors, men like Casey. Casey apparently was eager to "win one back from the communists" (as if Iran were ever caught up with communism in the first place).

Also there were the so-called neo-conservatives, who saw in Iraq's rise a threat to Israel. These two interests were very strong. Also allied with them were the arms dealers.

Actually, viewed objectively, that's what Iran-Contra was all about—selling arms. There are differing opinions on why Iran-Contra ever developed. Some maintain that it was about getting the hostages back; others claim that it represented an American tilt toward Iran in the war; others say that it was meant to place America in a position to influence the succession in Iran. However, when one looks at the facts of the matter (and they exist in profusion), one has to conclude that it was, basically, a commercial enterprise.

Consider for a moment the modus operandi of the business—is it not the case that the arrangements worked out by the Israelis *always* broke down? The idea was that the arms were *not* to be turned over to the Iranians until *all* of the hostages had been released.[14]

In every case (and the operation was repeated several times) the plan worked *up to the point* where the exchange was to be effected, and then the Iranians balked at handing over the hostages, *but the arms were passed anyway.*

So over a period of months thousands of weapons (not counting spare parts), each worth between $10,000 and $12,000, were transferred to Iran, and only three hostages were released (and as soon as they were released Hizbollah, the Lebanese hostage-takers, grabbed three more, to make up for the loss, presumably).[15]

Does this make sense? It does if one assumes that the hostage exchange was a pretext, that is, that the Israelis were interested only in unloading the weapons. Once they were in the hands of the Iranians, the Israelis had accomplished their purpose.

But there were Americans who took over the operations from the Israelis, and they behaved in the same way. How explain that?

Practically all the agents involved in the affair were arms dealers—not just on the Israeli side (Ghorbanifar, Schwimmer, Nimrodi), but on the American side as well (Secord and Hakim); and, for these people, the handover was crucial because only then could they claim their commissions.

So what is the point? It is this—the transfer of arms had by 1986 become big business in the Middle East. In the frantic pursuit of markets, arms dealers did not think in geopolitical terms—how will this affect the interests of the United States or even of Israel? All that was important was to move the weapons.

The arms dealers put interests that could be described as vital (both to the United States and to Israel) at risk. One could argue that Israel was fulfilling *its* interests, since it was working against the interests of an Arab state. If Iraq lost the war, that was one less enemy for Israel to worry about.

Had it been possible for Iraq to lose and the damage to be contained, that is, if there were no chance of Iran's following up with a strike into the Saudi peninsula, then one could say, yes, this is probably correct. But Israel, which depended on the United States for its financial well-being, could hardly have benefited from having its patron's control over Gulf oil disrupted.

But would the situation have been any better had Iraq won the war? The author believes that it would have been. Saddam Hussein was disposed to be accommodating, much more so than the Iranians, who were zealously trying to export a revolution.

Saddam—accommodating? Yes indeed, and we will soon show how that could be.

THE END

In 1987 the Iraqis defeated the biggest offensive that the Iranians had mounted to date.[16] In fact, the Iranians had billed the attack as "the battle of destiny," the single engagement that would decide the war. Iran had amassed over a million men (it claimed) to confront Iraq outside Basrah. It orchestrated a campaign consisting of three major battles—Karbalas IV, V, and VI. The Iraqis met each attack and not only withstood it but effectively lured the attackers into so-called killing zones where they massacred them.

At the end of Karbala V, the war was essentially over. The Iranians fought several more battles and throughout maintained that the momentum of the campaign was not yet spent. In fact, this was not true. Iran's failure to break through in the Karbala V battle—after having expended so many lives—meant that, for them, the fight was finished.[17]

The actual end, however, did not come until the following year. In 1988 the newly organized Iraqi army took the offensive in the so-called Tawakalna ala Allah (in God We Trust) campaign and, in the space of a few weeks, fought five major battles, besting the Iranians in every one.[18] Then, on July 18, 1988, the Iranians sued for peace; Khomeini was forced to "drink from the poisoned cup," as he put it.

One of the interesting sidelights (and an extremely revealing one, at that) on the war's ending was the refusal of U.S. intelligence to concede that the Iraqis had won it fair and square, so to speak. Both the intelligence and the media (which were getting their slant from intelligence sources) maintained that Iraq won only because it used gas.[19] We will have more to say about chemical warfare later. Here it's enough to state that gas might have been used in one of the five battles of the campaign (although it is not at all certain that it was in that one). It certainly was not used to retake Faw.

It is not true (as also was claimed) that Iran ended the war because it was anxious to move on to other things; this is silly.[20] The Iranians surrendered because their units were dissolving at the front. The Iraqis carted away tons of captured equipment, which filled acres of parks outside Baghdad (after the war the Iraqis actually gave the stuff away).[21]

So the war was over. Now what? Well, from the standpoint of Washington this was clearly an embarrassment. This was not at all what Washington had wanted to see. Washington had hoped for a war with no clear victor. Barring that, it would have been just as pleased to see the thing drag on, become another "hundred years' war," as the diplomats jokingly referred to it.

As long as these two, Iran and Iraq, were at each other's throats, Washington was relieved of having to worry about them. For example, in 1981, when Washington cobbled together the GCC, Iraq was not invited to join, and, as it was then taken up with fighting, it had to accept exclusion.

Again, during the war, the Saudis were successful in keeping oil prices down, and Iraq went along with this, even though normally—as a high-absorption country—it would have sided with Iran and Algeria and the rest of the hawks, arguing for significant price rises.

What would the Iraqis do, now that they were out from under, so to speak? They did not have to be beholden to anyone, since they had won the war on their own. What stand, in particular, would they take on Gulf security? These were all matters with which the United States was going to have to concern itself, on very short notice.

There was another factor, and must have worried the oilmen—late in the war, Iraq had gotten the Saudis to agree to Iraq's tapping into Petroline, the major oil pipeline carrying Saudi oil from Dharan to the Red Sea. In doing that, Iraq had a large degree solved its problem of achieving access to the world market.

As long as Iraq was restricted to moving its production over a single line through Turkey it was vulnerable. But, by gaining access to an oil route through the Saudi desert it was, in effect, making itself more difficult to control.

Clearly at fault here were the Western intelligence agencies that had agreed among themselves that Iraq's military lacked the skills to force a defeat upon its enemy.

What the intelligence agencies had missed was the change that overcame the Iraqi army after the loss of Faw. After the Ba'thist Congress of 1986 intense preparations were made to change the army's style of war fighting, and some of this activity was apparently known to the Americans, but they failed to evaluate it correctly.[22]

So the intelligence failure was real and of profound significance. What was the Americans' reaction to it? Initially, it was to make excuses, to try to explain the reverse away by claiming (falsely) that the Iraqis had relied on chemical weapons.[23]

This was in the nature of an alibi, a way of saying that anything was possible with an outfit like this; in other words, there was no way of predicting with an enemy so depraved that it would use gas.

IRAQI DISCOMFORT

The United States was not alone in being caught short by the end of the war; the Iraqis themselves appear to have been surprised by it. Whatever they hoped to accomplish with Tawakalna ala Allah, it was not that the war would end so quickly. They wanted to drive the Iranians off Iraqi territory—specifically, off Faw and Majnoon, the site of a major Iraqi oil field. But once the Iraqis perceived Iran's front to be crumbling, they pressed ahead. Then, when Khomeini sued for peace, the world demanded that Iraq accept.[24]

Unfortunately, Iraq had changed its mind. Where previously it would have welcomed an end to hostilities, this was no longer the case. Iraq felt it must first consolidate its gains. To have stopped in place as of July 18, 1988, would have been of no advantage to it, as then it would have nothing to show for eight years of suffering. The Shatt al Arab was still half in Iranian hands; Iraq's access to the Gulf still could be challenged by an active Iranian naval presence; and, perhaps worst, Kurdish rebels remained under arms in the north. At the very least, the Kurdish revolt—anathema to Iraqi nationalists—must be ended.

So Saddam Hussein temporized. He rebuffed the overtures of the United Nations, anxious to send a peace delegation to the area. He received representatives from the Gulf sheikhs, who also pressed him for a cease-fire; but he put them off as well.[25]

The Americans, too, he rebuffed. As the days stretched into weeks, and the appeals from interested parties multiplied, the Iraqi leader evidently felt backed into a corner. He perhaps thought to obtain a respite by demanding, as a condition for calling a halt, that the Iranians agree to face-to-face negotiations, which Saddam almost certainly believed they would not do.[26]

The Iranian leadership was claiming to its people that it had been forced to sue for peace by the world community. The leaders were claiming that they retained the will to fight, but pressure, not only from the West but from the Soviet Union, was forcing them to negotiate.

By agreeing to conduct negotiations through the United Nations but not face-to-face, the clerics hoped to maintain the myth of their still being autonomous agents, and, at the same time, they could go on refusing to recognize the regime in Baghdad.

At any rate, this was the situation as of the summer of 1988, as the two sides fenced over the terms of resolution. Then on September 9, 1988, the United States effectively inserted itself into the affair.

We are now ready to discuss what perhaps is the most controversial aspect of the developing U.S.–Iraq rivalry—the allegation of Iraq's using gas against its Kurdish community.

GAS

Iraq had since at least 1983 been using gas against the Iranians.[27] The Iraqis used it in discrete instances, all known to the world community—although the Iraqis, until late in the war, did not own to the fact that they were doing so. Still, knowing that the world knew did not seem to faze them. As Tariq Aziz expressed it, gas was a weapon that worked for them; why should they not use it?[28]

The Iraqis felt keenly the disparity in population between themselves and their enemy. Iran outnumbered Iraq three to one, and out of Iraq's total population a large percentage was hors de combat. This was due to the fact of the college students' being exempt (until 1986) and the Kurds' (who make up 20 percent of the population) by and large refusing to fight.[29] Consequently, the war was carried on by those Iraqis who could not secure exemption. Thus, the burden of suffering fell on a limited cadre, which posed great morale problems.

At the same time, the Iraqis were advantaged in that the Iranians, having opted to gut their regular military at the start of the war, were unable to mount the sorts of operations that would have ensured victory.[30]

Relying on paramilitary forces whose competence was limited, the Iranians were restricted to launching human wave attacks, and, most expediently, these could be overcome with gas. By laying down a wall of mustard gas—a persistent agent—the Iraqis could break up the charges, which they learned to do with increasing success as the war wore on.

The world community might profess outrage, declaiming that, since gas was outlawed under international law, Iraq must desist from using it. But the Iraqis were not persuaded. As long as gas was effective to break up the head long charges of the Revolutionary Guards, gas would continue to be employed.

Thus, a paradox obtained—the United States (and most of the world, it seemed)—wanted to see Iraq hold out in the war, but it also wanted it to stop using chemical weapons. The Iraqis knew that if they abandoned gas, their chances of holding on to Basrah would be seriously impaired.

HALABJA

On March 16, 1988, at Halabja, an Iraqi Kurdish city near Baghdad, the Iraqis *and the Iranians both* used gas. The Iranians, it seemed, had come to see the advantages of chemical warfare under circumstances advantageous to them—not mustard gas, the persistent agent that the Iraqis used, but non-persistent forms that disorient the enemy but then are quickly dissipated, allowing the human wave attacks to pour through.[31]

At Halabja the action developed like this. The rebel Kurdish leader, Jalal Talabani, facilitated the introduction of Iranian forces into Halabja by night so that the Iraqi commander was unaware of the penetration. In the morning, the Iranians burst from hiding, overwhelmed the Iraqi garrison, and drove it from the city.

The Iraqi commander, in an attempt to regain possession, called in a chemical barrage (of mustard gas). This had the effect of disconcerting the Iranians, which allowed the Iraqis to regain possession. The Iranians now sprang their surprise, as they dumped a blood agent on the reoccupying Iraqis.[32]

Mustard gas from the Iraqi side, cyanide-based gas from the Iranian side—and the citizens of Halabja caught in the middle. Several hundred Kurdish civilians were killed during these successive attacks.[33]

However, when the Iranians took back the city, they photographed the dead Kurds and subsequently publicized the deaths, making out that Iraqi gas had killed the civilians and denying that they had used gas as well.[34]

Reporters let into the city to inspect the devastation noted, however, that most of the dead Kurds were blue in their extremities, implying that they had been killed by a blood agent, a chemical that Iraq did not use and, at this time, lacked the capacity to produce. This fact was noted in the press accounts and also by officials of several nongovernmental agencies called to inspect the scene.[35]

Later, the U.S. government confirmed the fact that both sides had used gas and averred that, in all likelihood, Iranian gas killed the Kurds; however, this new information was not revealed until 1990, so the impression remained in the public mind that the Iraqis alone were responsible for the gassings.

SHULTZ'S MOVE

We go forward now to the period immediately after the end of the war, when the Iranians had agreed to cease fighting and when the two sides remained at odds over how to bring the war to a close. As stated earlier, the Iraqis were reluctant to call off their attack, given that they did not trust the Iranians to make concessions. Hence, even though by August 20 Saddam had been pressured into agreeing to enter into negotiations, the Iraqi army remained poised to resume the offensive. UN delegations went out to the area; talks were set up in Geneva. There was a plan to shift the venue of the talks to New York—but all this was like pulling teeth, since the Iraqis fought every move to advance the process.

Then, on September 7, 1988, America's secretary of state George Shultz invited Iraq's junior foreign minister, Sadoun Hammadi, to Foggy Bottom, ostensibly to discuss how the negotiations could be speeded up. Hammadi appeared on September 8, unaware that he was about to be ambushed. For, in a routine press briefing before television cameras, Shultz, without warning, leveled the charge that, once again (as at Halabja) Iraq was using gas against its Kurdish citizens.[36]

In fact, the Iraqis were at the moment carrying out operations to recapture the north from rebel Kurds (concentrated in an area called Amadiyah, close to the Turkish border). However, the Iraqi minister denied, vehemently, that gas was being used. He demanded that Shultz reveal his evidence, and Shultz said that he was not at liberty to do that, as this would compromise intelligence sources.[37]

Well, then, said Hammadi, where are the victims?

Here was a problem. *Where were the victims?* Rebel Kurds were pouring across the borders into Turkey and Iran, desperate to escape the Iraqi onslaught. *Pesh mergas* were everywhere in evidence, but reporters who rushed to interview them all reported they were seemingly fit; there was not a sign of gassing.[38]

Indeed, Turkish doctors asked by the reporters to confirm that Kurds had been victimized denied this to be the case, or at least they said that they could not confirm that any such attacks had occurred because they had not seen any gassing victims. The UN High Commission for Refugees (UNHCR), which also had representatives in the area, confirmed this view, as did the Red Cross and the Red Crescent Societies and a doctor from Medicins du Monde.[39]

Momentarily, it appeared that the Iraqis were exonerated. It was not to be, however, because of what happened next.

THE SENATE STAFFERS

If the ambush interview arranged by Shultz caused controversy, what followed certainly augmented it. Within 24 hours after Shultz's public accusation of Iraq, the Senate voted sanctions on the basis of his charges. The vote was nearly unanimous, and, as the *Washington Post* reported, it put a heavy burden on the Iraqis, since they would now have enormous difficulties trying to roll over their $69 billion debt (more about that later).[40]

To be sure, the Senate's action was not the final word on the matter; the

House had yet to act. But in the meantime, the Senate Foreign Relations Committee sent two of its staffers to the region to report personally on what might have occurred.

Within a week the two were back, claiming that the Iraqis had gassed not only the rebel guerrillas but some hundreds of thousands of other Kurds, killing in the process possibly as many as a 100,000.[41]

The Iraqis were naturally upset by this allegation. When newsmen confronted their defense minister, he denied that this had occurred and further claimed that Iraq had no need of gas. Indeed, in that terrain, he said, gas would have been a liability.[42]

This essentially is correct. Gas is an extremely tricky weapon to use and, except under certain circumstances, is not particularly lethal. It is interesting that although this feature of chemical warfare is well known throughout the military community, no one in the Western media (to the author's knowledge) ever confirmed it.[43]

As the controversy escalated, the Iraqis became as incensed as the Americans. They demanded that the Arab League take a stand, and the league did, branding the outcry against Iraq as contrived. Like the Iraqis, the league asserted that the Americans lacked proof of their allegations.[44]

The Senate staffers claimed to have "overwhelming" proof that the attacks had occurred. However, this turned out to be anecdotal evidence—the Kurds *told* them that they had been gassed. The staffers also claimed to have seen obvious gassing victims and to have taken photographs of them. But no photographs were ever produced, and the alleged victims never were identified. As for the claim of 100,000 dead, this would appear to have been speculation. At the same time, however, it was quite a serious charge, implying "genocide."[45]

The whole affair is disturbing, inasmuch as 10 years after the event no victims of the alleged attack have ever been produced, and the United States has never revealed what led it to claim that the attack occurred.[46] Either this was a rush to judgment—that is, that the U.S. State Department and Senate moved in haste and made charges that could not be supported later on—or the whole thing was deliberately contrived.

In the former case, one would have supposed that the claimants would later have set the record straight. Instead, the matter has been left hanging, as it were.

Shultz leveled his charges at the tail end of the Reagan administration. Perhaps awareness that power soon would change hands (since Reagan could not serve another four years) caused the affair to subside, because it did for a time die down.

Also helping to avert a crisis was the fact that, when the Congress attempted to get its sanctions proposal enacted into law, it failed on a technicality.[47] In the meantime, some sectors of the nation, which rather looked forward to improved commercial relations with Iraq, had begun to mobilize against the sanctions, speaking out against them.[48]

But then in March 1990 everything started up again, as a series of Iraqi-related exposés began appearing in the American and British press.

THE EXPOSÉS

The first of these exposés was the so-called Bazoft affair, in which the Iraqis were censured for having executed a British journalist whom they claimed was a spy; at least, it was alleged that he was a journalist and British.[49]

Before the Iraqis hanged Bazoft, Margaret Thatcher appealed for clemency. The *New York Times* and *Washington Post* editorialized in his behalf, and several writers' associations in the West also made appeals.[50]

The carrying out of the sentence touched off a wave of protests against Iraq worldwide. Thatcher condemned the hanging as "barbaric."[51]

Almost immediately, however, the campaign against Iraq was undercut when it was brought out that Bazoft was a common criminal and an Iranian, to boot.[52]

It appeared that he had immigrated to Britain from Iran to get away from Khomeiniism. He had enrolled in school in London. However, he seems to have attended classes only occasionally, and, in fact, he lived in a high style on regular donations supplied by his parents.

At a certain point, however, the parental support dried up, and Bazoft sought to supplement his income by bank robbing.[53]

He was caught, sent to jail, and eventually released into the custody of MI6. After that he disappeared, only to resurface as a journalist accredited to the *London Observer*. His first (and last) assignment was to go to Iraq, where the previous August a mysterious explosion had occurred.[54] Disguised as a doctor, Bazoft gained access to the blast area (declared off-limits by the Iraqis) and was caught gathering soil samples.

So it would appear that, Margaret Thatcher and the writers' unions notwithstanding, Bazoft was a spy.

The second exposé surfaced on March 29, 1990. It involved an alleged attempt by the Iraqis to illegally acquire so-called capacitors, which, it was claimed, were triggers for atomic bombs (A-bombs).[55] As in the Bazoft affair, the case first broke in Britain, where the Iraqis had been arrested, caught in the act of transporting the capacitors out of the country by British customs.

Along with the Iraqis, two employees of the British firm supplying the capacitors were implicated and brought to trial. Subsequently, government experts testified that the devices could be used only in connection with A-bombs. The Iraqis maintained that this was nonsense, that they were standard equipment, with purely civilian applications. They did not even, the Iraqis claimed, require export licenses.[56]

It took three years before the case worked its way through the British courts (the employees of the firm had sued). In the end, the judges decided against the Crown and for the defendants (and, by extension, for the Iraqis).[57] It seemed that the expert witnesses, who claimed the capacitors were specially designed for atomic weapons, were shamming. The devices were, as the defendants had alleged, routine items; they had no connection with atomic weaponry.[58]

Moreover, it was brought out in the investigation that MI6, at the behest of American intelligence, had entrapped the defendants, that is, that the British deliberately set them up for arrest, evidently hoping to exploit the case through the media. It was also brought out that Margaret Thatcher knew of, and approved, the sting in advance.[59]

Next, on April 5, 1990, came the affair of the Big Gun. Here, it was claimed that the Iraqis were seeking to produce the largest cannon ever, capable of propelling a missile 1,240 miles.[60] This would qualify it as a strategic weapon. The casings for this "cannon" were intercepted by British customs. The British outfit that produced the parts denied that they had any military application, and the Iraqis claimed that they were oil piping.[61]

What sensationalized the case was the assassination, as the story broke, of the designer of the putative Big Gun, Gerald Bull, allegedly by agents of Mossad.[62] As in the capacitor story, once the case got to court, it fizzled. The government dropped charges.[63]

All of these stories originated in Britain. One other cropped up in Sacramento, California. This involved an alleged attempt by Iraqis to assassinate an Iraqi expatriate living in Sacramento.[64] In this one federal authorities allowed the alleged hit man to escape, and the supposed victim claimed that he knew nothing of the affair other than what was told him by the Federal Bureau of Investigation. However, an Iraqi diplomat in Washington was asked to leave the country.[65]

WAS ALL THIS A PLOT?

In trying to answer this question, we start with Shultz. As far as his contribution to the business is concerned, an explanation suggests itself. The Iraqis, as pointed out earlier, had won a decisive victory over Iran, something that the U.S. State Department claimed was beyond their capability. When, in fact, they did it, this compromised America's position in the Gulf. The United States really had no well worked-out policy for the area. To be sure, in 1987, as discussed, it went to Kuwait's aid by reflagging its tankers. In doing so, it seemed to be claiming the area as a sphere of interest, but this was by no means an established position.

Iraq, as we said in Chapter 5, before the outbreak of the Iran–Iraq War, had taken a stand opposing an American presence in the Gulf. As long as the war dragged on, Iraq was in no position to insist on its demand, but now that the war had ended, this was set to become an issue.

One can argue that Shultz, with his gassing allegation, was signaling to Iraq not to take the United States for granted. Washington had interests in the region that it intended to uphold (Shultz could have been telling the Iraqis). By raising the issue, Washington could also be said to have been tilting toward Iran. Indeed, there is some evidence of this. Almost immediately after the war ended, the Americans began putting out feelers to the Iranians to reconcile.[66]

Or there might have been a more immediate aim—to try to preserve the Kurdish resistance. Along with his condemnation of Iraq, Shultz asked the Iraqis to permit a UN team to enter the north to investigate the supposed gassings. Had the Iraqis acquiesced, this would have had the effect of freezing operations on the ground; Iraq would have been unable to regain control of its territory, and, by dragging the matter out in the United Nations, the United States might have hoped to save the guerrillas.

The Iraqis did not agree to a UN investigation, although they did say that one could be made after the area was secured. It is interesting that once they took this stand, Shultz seems to have lost interest in the Kurds, which would appear to indicate that this had been a tactical maneuver on his part.[67]

If we accept the preceding explanation of Shultz's behavior, we then can set down the Americans' performance to real politik. Having failed to anticipate the end of the war and having been badly caught off-guard by the way it turned out, they were trying to regain leverage over the principals—Iraq, mainly, but also Iran.

This said, we still have to explain the Senate's performance, and this is more troubling; a number of questions arise over it. For example, was the Senate's decision to send staffers to the area coordinated with Shultz at the State Department? It would almost seem that it would have had to be. The Senate committee moved so quickly not only to push the sanctions through but to get staffers out to the area that it must have been forewarned of the action to be taken (i.e., the accusation that Iraq had used gas).

It also is noteworthy that the Senate's action was practically unanimous; this is not a body known for such behavior. In this case, the senators managed to secure a vote on sanctions with virtually no opposition within a matter of hours after Shultz had acted. That had to have entailed organization by individuals who knew what they were doing.

The sanctions business needs further consideration, and we return to it later. Now we want to take up the exposés (the Bazoft case and the other three). All of these stories surfaced in March and April 1990, at just the time when the Senate was essaying to reintroduce the sanctions measure (which had already failed once on a technacality). Thus, it would appear that the exposés were meant to influence public opinion, that is, to develop sentiment against Iraq so that the sanctions would not be obstructed.

As it happened, there was opposition—President Bush came out against the move to penalize Iraq.[68] He sent Senator Bob Dole and a delegation of other senators to Baghdad to meet with Saddam in what appears to have been an attempt to conciliate the Iraqi.[69] Further, the U.S. ambassador to Iraq, April Glaspie, in her famous interview with Saddam (which we look at later), renounces, on the part of the administration, any complicity in the media campaign against Iraq.[70]

In light of all of this activity on the president's part, it is remarkable that the sanctions effort was not abandoned. The anti-Iraq publicity not only kept up but intensified with an explosion of op-ed pieces, television documentaries, and commentary in the public affairs journals. This hostile commentary really never died down until the outbreak of the war the following year. Also the sanctions were eventually passed, although in a diluted form.[71]

IF IT WAS A PLOT, THEN . . . ?

Since there seems to be justification for presuming that this was a plot, the question we need to address is, Who was behind it? We already, in large part, have absolved the Bush administration. As we said, the new president disassociated himself from the anti-Iraq furor, and, as the transcript of the Glaspie interview (see later) suggests, this actually seems to have ingratiated Bush with the Iraqis.

There is the possibility that the Israelis were involved. All of the congressional activity was carried on by strong supporters of Israel. This is not necessarily proof, but it is suggestive.[72]

The Israelis were certainly disturbed by the sudden advance of Iraq in the military arena. Iraq's military went from being something of a joke, to a real menace, if we take the Israelis' assessments seriously.[73] It is indisputable that the Iraqis' win over their traditional enemy, Iran, shifted the balance of power in the region.

What about the British? Three of the four exposés originated with them. But, in at least one (according to British court testimony), American intelligence figured. American security services also appeared in the Sacramento case, according to the California papers, not just the U.S. Justice Department and the Federal Bureau of Investigation (FBI) but also the Customs Service.

If we focus on this angle (of there being official U.S. involvement), what do we find? Those who were most deeply implicated were elements of the intelligence community. What did they have against Iraq?

SETTING THE RECORD STRAIGHT

Go back to the point made earlier of the failure to predict the outcome of the war and the trouble that this caused for the State Department. The CIA was as much damaged by this lapse as was State.

If anything, the CIA was even more culpable. Iraq's victory over Iran was not a fluke. Before Baghdad could defeat its enemy, it had practically to reinvent itself, so to speak. The Ba'thists had to remake their entire system, not only the military but the political as well.[74] This was not something that could have been accomplished overnight. It took years to effect basic changes in the way that Iraq did things, any one of which could have tipped Langley to what was going on; but the agency missed out all along the line (and not just the CIA did this, but MI6 and Mossad as well).

When civil servants let down the side in such a high-profile fashion (and especially when they do it in an area crucial to national security), there is a desire on the bureaucrats' part to, as they say, "set the record straight," and the principal means whereby they do this is by leaking material favorable to themselves to the press.[75]

We suggest that, in regard to the exposés, this is what was going on. The bureaucrats were trying to salvage a policy line about which doubts had now been raised.

The "wrong" side had won the war. For analysts there is nothing worse, as they now have to fear that the administration will rethink its approach; after all, it is normal to want to side with a winner. What if an attempt were made by Bush and his people to co-opt the Ba'thists?[76] That could compromise a lot of careers at the agency.

To head off such a development, it would have made sense to defame the Iraqis, to promote the idea that they had won a sneak victory (using gas) and were now covertly trying to capitalize on that development by doing something really horrendous.

Like what? Like building an atom bomb and then manufacturing a bizarre piece of artillery by which to deliver it. All of the exposés, with the exception of the Sacramento affair, are tied to atom bomb production.

In effect, the bureaucrats seem to have been saying, we may have failed to predict the end of the war, but our overall analysis on Iraq was correct—the Iraqis *are* threats to the world community. There should be no change in policy toward them; they should continue to be isolated, for they are rogues.

In other words, a lot of this anti-Iraq activity can be set down to bureaucratic defensiveness, an attempt at career maintenance.

Now let's look at the sanctions end of the business. That operation was indisputably malign. Who was behind that, and why did they persist in trying to get the sanctions through, even after the president had signaled his opposition?

A COVEY OF INTERESTS

Certain interested parties were watching and waiting to see how the Iraqis would conduct themselves after having won the war. After a year had passed, it was clear that Baghdad would not accept a subordinate role in the Gulf; it had no intention of becoming a foil for the West. Rather, Baghdad sought to secure the strongest position possible, one that would be, if not unassailable, then exceedingly difficult to overcome.

So, then, it is the author's view that the maneuvering in the Congress (toward passage of sanctions) was a form of public diplomacy, an attempt to cow the Iraqis into exercising self-restraint. When Iraq did not respond, the tempo only increased.[77]

Who specifically was doing this? It's not possible to say, precisely. However, clues can be gleaned from studying the op-ed pieces, the commentary in the international news supplements, and the exchanges on the Sunday talk shows.

Iraq undertook a number of ventures after the war that, to many, must have seemed threatening. For example, on February 17, 1989, the *New York Times* reported that the Iraqis, Jordanians, Egyptians, and Yemenis were forming the so-called Arab Cooperation Council (ACC). This was a regional trading bloc that intended to enact tariffs to promote native industry. Something like this would have militated against the concept of a New World Order.

On October 23, 1989, the *Washington Post* reported, "4 Arab States Seen in Position to Reclaim World Oil Control." Three of those states—Saudi Arabia, Kuwait, and the UAE—were known entities. But the fourth was Iraq. Having Iraq in a position to control oil prices would have been extremely disquieting to a whole host of interests.[78]

And *The International Defense Review* in June 1989 interviewed an Iraqi general in charge of defense production who outlined Iraq's plans to build an Arab arms industry in cooperation with Saudi Arabia and Egypt. The Arabs are the leading buyers of American weapons, so this was a move that threatened the powerful arms lobby.

Any one of these projects, to Western eyes, might have appeared provocative. To be sure, the Iraqis maintained that they were only trying to rehabilitate themselves after the war. But, based on the tone of the articles appearing in the media, this defense was not credited. Iraq was made out to be a deliberate spoiler, a bully on the block, someone looking for a fight.

The tendentious coverage was most evident in the press' treatment of Saddam's statement about "incinerating half of Israel."[79] That outburst was not as belligerent as it was made to appear. Israel had just lofted a spy satellite, with which it hoped to get real-time intelligence, and several Israeli officials stated that this would enable them to take out Saddam's weapons plants, in other words, a repeat of Osirik. Saddam was telling the Israelis that this was not an option, at least not one that could be undertaken with impunity.

So, in answer to the question posed initially, was this all a plot? Probably it was. There could not have been that much anti-Iraq publicity appearing in so concentrated a time frame, and it not have been a plot.

Moreover, it was malign one. How do we know? Because of the persistent effort to legislate sanctions, a way of stigmatizing Iraq before the world, so that it could not get the loans that it needed to revive its economy.

At the same time, however, it was not a plot directed by a cabal (as the Middle Eastern conspiracy theorists would have us believe). It was rather a case where a lot of different interests, each for its own purpose, sought to harm the Iraqis, and they all pretty much acted independently of each other. The end result *gave the appearance of being* a classic plot, but it was not such.

We now look at how the thing affected the Iraqis.

ACTION/REACTION

During 1989 and 1990, when all of this was going on, the Ba'thists were trying to reschedule payments on their war loans. The scare headlines, the critical op-ed pieces, the television pundits castigating Iraq's alleged irresponsibility—all this had the effect of intimidating the banks; in other words, no rescheduling. At that point Saddam, who was under tremendous pressure throughout this whole period, began to show signs of real paranoia.

The Iraqi's outraged reaction to statements by Israelis (in connection with the spy satellite launching) is evidence of this.[80] With that one outburst Saddam ratcheted up the tension level enormously. It suddenly did appear that the world was moving toward war.

But was Saddam's reaction (to the statements of the Israelis) so out of line? When we consider what had gone on in Iran-Contra? There, Reagan apparently had signed off on a nine-point program, one point of which was that Saddam would have to be overthrown. Saddam knew this because it had come out in the American media.[81]

If the Iraqi leader was paranoid, perhaps he had a right to be. His fear of the mounting anti-Iraq campaign was based on experience. He thought that the media were creating an environment in which Israel could with impunity attack him.[82]

But what about Kuwait? After all, that was what eventually precipitated the war; in the end it was not Israel that Iraq went to war against, but Kuwait. Why Kuwait?

In Chapter 4, we discussed Qasim's ham-handed attempt to annex Kuwait, which only compounded his problems and probably hastened his downfall.

We have no intention of rehashing the history of Kuwait–Iraqi relations. We say only this: the British created Kuwait as a means of sealing off the area then known as Mesopotamia from the Persian Gulf because, as pointed out in Chapter 2, the Germans were building a Berlin-to-Basrah railway that would terminate in the Gulf. Kuwait was meant to be a gate that the British could shut against attempts to gain access to the waterway from the north.[83]

The reader will recall that Iraq originally went to war with Iran to regain unfettered access to the Gulf through the Shatt al Arab. When the war ended, Iran took the position that it would not discuss the Shatt until the United Nations first branded Iraq as an aggressor. Since the Iraqis could not overcome this stance, they had to concede all hope of opening the country to seagoing traffic any time soon.

Thus, Baghdad began pressuring the Al Sabaghs (Kuwait's rulers), demanding that they cede Bubiyan and Warbah Islands to it (see map).[84] Possession of these two islands would have given Iraq access to the Khor Abdullah channel, which it could then have dredged so large-draft vessels could reach Iraq from the Gulf without passing through the Shatt.

The Kuwaitis supposedly offended the Iraqis by offering to lease the islands for several years for billions of dollars (when the Iraqis obviously were expecting them to deed the islands to them gratis for having defended them in the war).[85] At that, the talks apparently turned nasty, with the Iraqis supposedly locking the Kuwaiti delegation in a conference room and hectoring them for hours about their base ingratitude.

In any event, the port issue is important because Iraq, badly in need of material with which to rebuild, did not have adequate facilities to receive imports. So, in the most fundamental way, its recovery was blocked. Even if it had the money to buy the things it needed, it could not get them physically into the country.

Perhaps if Kuwait had made concessions on Bubiyan and Warbah, Iraq would have backed away from confrontation. But Kuwait did not do that. And then it compounded the difficulty by cheating on its oil quota. It was not at all wise for the Kuwaitis to cross the Iraqis in that particular way.

As we said earlier, Iraq desperately needed money, and the only way it could get it was by selling oil. The UAE was cheating on its quota (the UAE always cheated on its quota, which it had never accepted, not from the first when OPEC set it). Now, Kuwait started cheating, and the logical result of that was that prices started going down, *way down*.

In 1990, when all of this was occurring, oil was selling for around $15 a barrel.[86] It was estimated that Iraq had over $80 billion in war debts. Of this figure, $37 billion was owed to the Arabs, mostly the GCC states, and another $10 billion to Kuwait alone. Iraq's annual debt service just on the money owed the Europeans was $23 billion. It was to the point that Iraq could not service the debt with revenues from oil sales, all that it really had to count on. The country obviously was in trouble.[87]

Moreover, the action of the Kuwaitis in cheating on their quota was blatant; it constituted a direct challenge. Indeed, it was an escalation—Iraq would threaten Kuwait over Bubiyan; well, two could play at that game.

Saddam Hussein, who (as we know) is inordinately sensitive to points of honor, was thus presented with what he must have seen as a personal affront. Moreover, coming, as it did, just after he had won this great victory over Iran, he was hardly likely to let it pass.

In addition, Kuwait's action did not end with mere cheating on its quota. It ultimately announced that all of the money given to Iraq during the war was a loan; in other words, it would have to be repaid.

This aid had always been understood to be in the form of grants, never loans. Indeed, the Saudis, who had also been subsidizing the Iraqis, had so construed it; they never demanded repayment.

The Kuwaiti demand is mystifying. They must have known that Saddam would be driven to exasperation over this. It is inconceivable that the Kuwaitis would have run such a risk had they had not had assurances of protection from someone on whom they could rely.

The result of all this was that the banks stiffened their resistance; the chances of rescheduling were doomed. What else could one expect? Was it likely that the banks would loan to Iraq, when, as it now appeared, it owed billions more dollars than anyone had realized?

When all of these influences converged on the Iraqi ruler (the media campaign, the Kuwaiti demands, the collapse in oil prices), he called in America's ambassador in Baghdad for a frank exchange of views.

AN APPEAL FROM THE HEART

The April Glaspie interview was a unique occurrence. Saddam never gave personal interviews to accredited foreign representatives. Now here he was, on July 25, 1990, summoning Glaspie to the Presidential Palace, where he informed her that he was close to the end of his rope (this was the thrust of what he told her).[88]

Saddam ran briefly through the state of Iraq's finances (the most sensational admission being that he could not pay the pensions of Iraq's war widows), and after tying the distressed condition of the country's economy to the expenses incurred in wartime, he appealed to Washington for help.

In the conventional wisdom view of the exchange, Saddam's aim was to get the Kuwaitis and the UAE to stop cheating on their oil quotas so that prices could rise, and supposedly he believed that he could bring this about by getting Washington to pressure the sheikhs.

That certainly was a part of what he was aiming for, but clearly, he was also asking for help in ending the media campaign. It is remarkable how much of the interview was taken up with Saddam's complaints about the media, even to the point of his singling out specific journalists and news agencies for censure.

Glaspie told him that, although she sympathized, there was nothing that she could do, and she made plain that she was speaking on behalf of Bush. This, she said, is part of living in a democracy, where the press is allowed freedom from government control.

To be sure, what Glaspie was saying is, for the most part, true, but it seems to us that, in answering so, she was not being forthcoming with the Iraqi leader. She must have known that, as long as the campaign in the media went on, Iraq's chances of getting relief financially were hopeless.

What the media were doing was similar to talking down a stock, that is, reinforcing the popular perception that Iraq was a bad risk.[89]

That being the case, Glaspie should have known that, if there was to be some hope of settling the dispute without violence, action would have to be taken by the president to offset the campaign.

It would appear that the Americans were ducking the issue. It seems hard to conceive that they did not perceive what was being asked of them. If the Bush administration decided not to respond to Saddam's appeals, it was most certainly because it did not feel compelled to do so.

Bush did not perceive that inactivity would cost him anything; that is, he did not believe that Iraq could do anything to Kuwait. Here, then, we encounter yet another intelligence failure. Recall, American intelligence had never abandoned its insistence that Baghdad had won the Iran–Iraq War by using gas. It had never conceded that the Iraqi military had transformed itself into a competent force, and so it continued to advise the president that Iraq was incapable of performing such a maneuver (as taking over Kuwait).

Along with that, anything that Bush might have done in the way of supporting Saddam would have furthered the Iraqi's effort to discipline OPEC members.

That would have opened the way for OPEC to return to the status of a cartel, something that it had been between 1928 and 1973 and briefly in 1983 but that it stopped being as soon as Saudi Arabia abandoned the role of swing producer and opted for market share.

Bush was not about to hand over that kind of power to the oil producers, and certainly he would have been unwilling to assist Iraq to become head of OPEC (which certainly it would have become, if it were the instrument whereby members were disciplined). Nor would the special interests in the United States, which were active in the campaign against Iraq, have permitted him to do this. Thus, (for the president) the simplest thing was to pretend helplessness. In effect, that is the stance that Glaspie adopted. Later on, she absorbed considerable criticism for this. She is supposed to have given Saddam a green light to invade.

To argue thus is to miss the point. By saying that the United States would not intervene, Glaspie was telling Saddam that he must get on as best he could. For Saddam that was not an answer.

ECONOMIC WAR

Conventional wisdom views Saddam's move into Kuwait as a miscalculation; he is supposed to have believed that he could invade and get away with it.

As we have just argued, he most certainly believed no such thing—he felt himself forced to do what he did. The alternative to not seeking a showdown, as one Iraqi figure (perhaps Ramadan) put it, was to be left slowly twisting in the wind.

Saddam expressed a sentiment similar to this when he told Glaspie that the United States and the sheikhs were waging economic war against him.[90]

So, then, the Iraqis knew what they were getting into. Was this, then, a suicidal gesture, a way of causing harm to one's adversary even at the cost of inflicting hurt on oneself?

It's possible to speculate that Saddam believed that he might be able to wriggle out, provided it never came to a shooting war. If Iraq took over Kuwait and then allowed itself to be talked into relinquishing possession in return for concessions on the debt rescheduling, the move might have made sense.

That way the Iraqis would have come out ahead, because while war clouds lowered, the markets would have destabilized, oil prices would have risen, and this could have been expected to exert pressure on the United States to compromise.

But the market fears only uncertainty. Once the administration made it clear that it was going to fight and that it was going to employ the Dugan strategy, all uncertainty disappeared.[91] America, with its enormous edge in airpower, could, by standing off and bombing the Iraqis from the air, compel them to surrender; and the outcome need never be in doubt because it would be only at the very close that ground troops would engage.

Thus, we could say that, to the extent that he did not understand the economic system, to that degree Saddam miscalculated. But he made a worse miscalculation by failing to perceive how his enemies (and some of those whom he probably counted as friends) would exploit his position. Not just the Israelis and the British but elements of the Arab community pushed Bush to go to war.[92]

Once the issue between Bush and Saddam was fairly joined (and it was, as soon as the Iraqi army entered Kuwait), war was inevitable. This is why we say that the war came about because the international oil system had broken down. It's hard to imagine this happening had there been powerful interests in the United States concerned to maintain the stability of the Gulf, entities like the cartel companies (pre-Nixon era).

Because there was no such entity, the aggressive forces, which thought to exploit what to them must have appeared as a windfall, went into action. It always is so whenever a system that has been long in place breaks down; any pushy individual or group can discover means of exploiting the temporary confusion.

One could argue that the international security system should have acted to prevent the war from occurring. But the Cold War was about to end. The Berlin Wall had just come down. In that sense, the confusion was absolute.

The year 1990 was a repeat of 1973, only worse. In 1973 the oil company executives were tipped to the coming crisis by the Saudi king, and they tried to warn Nixon. In 1990 no one warned Bush as to what would happen were Saddam's plea to be spurned.

Instead, outside agitators, we might call them, misrepresented the situation. The record of their essays, obtainable through perusal of the media of the day, indicts the whole process. The war was a media coup.

Given the great destruction of people and property that came out of the war, it is inexcusable what happened. Not only were Kuwait's oil facilities gutted (when the retreating Iraqis put them to the torch), but unknown numbers of Iraqi civilians died in the aerial bombings, which went on for 45 days. (More tonnage was dropped on Iraq in those 45 days than was delivered to targets in Germany during the whole of World War II.)

Additional Iraqi soldiers died when the fighting commenced, many perishing in the brutal Highway of Death episode, where a column of Iraqi troops was trapped on the last days of the war and systematically destroyed by air attacks.

After the war the Coalition presented the bill to the Gulf sheikhs—$40 billion at least (some say the real figure was as high as $86 billion). One could argue that Kuwait would have been better off letting Iraq have Bubiyan and Warbah.

We now—by way of ending the study—want to look at where America has come in regard to the Gulf.

DUAL CONTAINMENT

Not until 1993 was an attempt made by the United States to craft a system to control oil prices. This was the Dual Containment Policy of Martin Indyk.[93]

Basically, it reassigned the quotas of Iraq and Iran to the countries of the lower Gulf. Thus, it compensated the sheikhs for the expense of having subsidized the Gulf War.

From 1993 until almost the end of the decade the price of oil stayed down and would have remained so, as this suited the United States; Europe was content, and, obviously, there was no complaint from Third World countries.

What disturbed the arrangement was the Asian Meltdown. Oil sales fell so precipitously that the producers (non-OPEC as well as OPEC) could barely cope.

In 1999 OPEC embarked on a new course of driving prices back up. One senses that the election of a populist government in Venezuela opened the way for this.[94]

At any rate, the United States was constrained to suffer this alteration in a setup that was working fine for it. It did so probably believing that OPEC could not hold out, that, once again, the members would cheat, thus bringing about a price downturn.

Cheating did not occur. Even the sheikhs, who ordinarily could be counted on for this, held firm. It is not easy to say why this happened, but it would appear that the Saudis had something to do with it.

The Saudis want OPEC to remain a force in world politics. They count on it as a vehicle of their national policy. Unless OPEC can respond to emergencies, such as the Meltdown, it cannot survive. That means from time to time it must change direction, even at the risk of displeasing the United States.

With discipline holding in OPEC ranks, the oil price kept on rising, until by the year 2000 it had reached over $30 a barrel. Then the United States began to suffer, as certain segments of American society felt the pinch.

The winter of 1999–2000 was intermittently quite cold, which pushed up heating bills in the Northeast. This brought protests from homeowners. The independent truckers mobilized and "marched" on Washington, demanding that the government open up the strategic oil reserves.

This demand, which is almost always political, is heard every time there is a price rise. It is the prelude to an anti-OPEC, anti-Arab campaign.

At the same time, the U.S. energy secretary traveled to the OPEC countries and to the non-OPEC ones as well, trying to jawbone down the price. Refusing to open the strategic reserves, the Clinton administration instead appropriated money to help those who were having difficulty paying their heating bills.

This is where we are as of this writing.

WHAT'S TO COME?

The problem is that Americans have become used to having cheap oil. The price of $25 a barrel, which Saddam wanted (in his interview with Glaspie) is not inordinate. Even $30 a barrel (which we are seeing now) is not a lot.

But Americans cannot give in on this. The fault seems to lie with the business leaders, who have incorporated the low price of oil into their strategizing. Whole industries have grown up whose maintenance depends on oil prices remaining low. For example, producing sport utility vehicles (SUVs).

Also, take the case of the independent truckers. This component of the national transportation industry feels itself aggrieved. Has it a right to feel so?[95]

Or look at home building. How many homes in the Northeast are built to efficiently cope with winter weather? Are they adequately insulated?

Why are housing developments being located farther and farther from the centers of the great metropolises, where people work?

In other words, is it not the case that the oil producers are being asked to subsidize the wasteful, inefficient lifestyles of the Americans?

Another aspect of this problem is bothersome. The new system worked out by the United States (i.e., Dual Containment) is devoted as much to developing the arms industry as protecting the oil sheikhs. The United States expects the sheikhs to keep up their arms purchases, and indeed Secretary Cohen's arms-brokering tours through the Gulf have now become regularly scheduled events.[96]

This is essential to the well-being of the United States, as the purchases fund jobs in California and Washington in the West and Texas in the South, all highly populated states that pay a crucial part in national politics.

The problem is that the weapons systems, as discussed earlier, are superinflationary. To be able to afford them, the sheikhs must maximize income from oil sales. Effectively, if this goes on long enough, the countries that are now low absorbers will become high ones. Eventually, OPEC will become a body in which all of the members are agreed on oil pricing, and the interests of all are antithetical to those of the United States.

It would appear that at some point the United States is going to have to work out a modus vivendi with *all* of the oil producers. It cannot hope to keep on as it is, dominating the system through its special relationship with just the sheikhs.[97]

America's policy is dog in the manger, no different from the policy practiced by the British against Iran and Iraq in the 1950s. We retard the development of these two countries so that the system, which currently is functioning to our satisfaction, does not have to undergo change. One could argue that the great push of Iraq at the end of the Iran–Iraq War to turn itself into a first-rate power was a rejection of precisely this hampering arrangement.

Had Iraq been able to proceed along the lines that it set for itself, it would likely have founded a coalition of high absorbers, which then would have overhauled OPEC along more nationalistic lines. Interestingly, just before the Gulf War broke out, OPEC seemed to be moving toward this. Iraq and Iran had lined up to push for higher oil prices.[98] Even as the two were refusing to discuss peace, they were nonetheless cooperating on a common oil policy. Even more interesting, there were signs that in this endeavor, they had the support of the Saudis.[99]

Ten years after the end of the Gulf War, the U.S. State Department continues to devise policy toward Iraq as if it were a criminal society, which now we can see that it is not. It is time for the United States, in effect, to put up. If it has evidence that Saddam Hussein gassed his own people, then it should present it to the world. If, as the author believes, the famous gassing incident was all a hoax—or perhaps we should say a nonevent—then it should admit it and lift the sanctions, as there is no justification to keep on with this harsh punishment.[100]

The fact that the discredited policy is maintained *against reason* raises the possibility that self-delusion, far from being something to be abjured, is being cultivated.

Is the leadership in the United States deliberately perpetuating this sham of an irremediably vicious Iraq because it serves its purpose so to do? Since the deception has been going on for almost 10 years now, it would appear to be the case.

Why should it be?

The United States, as we have tried to point out in this book, has never really conceded that it is dependent on the Gulf. For years after oil was discovered there, it maintained the stance of the Gulf's being of no consequence to it. Supposedly, America had all the oil that it needed.

Had America's leaders reckoned aright, they would have seen that, in the way that the oil industry is structured, Gulf oil is important irrespective of whether America has its own or not. Prices cannot be regulated unless Gulf oil production is controlled.[101]

American leaders ought to have grasped this fact after the Third Oil Shock. However, no sooner was that crisis ended than they went back to ignoring the Gulf and thus missed the end of the Iran–Iraq War and the emergence of Baghdad as a potential regional superpower.

After the war, Iraq indicated that it wanted a say in managing Gulf security. America evidently felt that it could not allow that. But rather than enter into talks with Iraq to attempt to sort it out, Washington behaved as if Iraq's victory over Iran had changed nothing; that the balance of power regionally had not been disturbed; that things would go back to being as they were before the Iran–Iraq War erupted.

We saw how that worked out. There was another war, a brutal, destructive one that not only crippled Iraq but ruined the economies of the sheikhs. Saudi Arabia, Kuwait, the UAE—all ended up deeply in debt. Kuwait ended worst of all, since the Iraqis in a final gesture of defiance set fire to its wells.

Still, the United States refuses to confront what has come out of this. It insists on believing that the Iraqis will eventually overthrow the "hated" regime of the Ba'thists and that this action, once taken, will set things right. But the Iraqis have proved strangely derelict in this regard. Could it be that they reject the program that Washington has worked out for them?

Be that as it may, Washington is now funding an Iraqi opposition that, it hopes, will do the job, although how this is to be accomplished no one seems able to tell.

In the meantime, the sanctions go on and on. The United Nations has published statistics on infant mortality in Iraq that are extremely disturbing. The rate has doubled since the embargo was imposed.[102] This is solely due to America's policy; it cannot be blamed on anything else. The claim of America's leaders that this is Saddam's fault is obscene.[103]

America seems incapable of devising an acceptable solution to the impasse that it finds itself in. It will not allow the two northern Gulf states to recover, knowing that they would immediately seek to build up new production facilities to rival Saudi Arabia's. This refusal on America's part is most apparent in the case of Iraq, where it blocks any attempt by Baghdad to import oil field equipment with which to refurbish its deteriorating plant.[104]

Both Iraq and Iran (although Iran to a lesser degree) have the reserves to challenge the Saudis' leadership role in OPEC; what they lack are production facilities. In the case of Iran, those facilities that the AIOC (BP) built up and the shah improved upon were destroyed after the Khomeini revolution, a process of destruction furthered by the Iran–Iraq War.

The IPC never provided the Iraqis with much infrastructure to begin with. Under the republic, the country strove to supply itself, but the accumulation process was interrupted by the Iran–Iraq War, and, of course, since the Gulf War Iraq has lost what little plant it had.

That retarding the accumulation process for these two is the true aim of Dual Containment, Washington will not admit. At the same time, however, few believe the rationale for the policy that America professes. An alternative would be to confess to the public that it is acting for purely economic motives—Iraq and Iran must be held down if the oil price is to remain low. But this would invite Americans to reconsider the problem of oil, and, as we have stressed in the study, whenever this occurs, the results are problematic. Americans usually do not want to have anything to do with the oil industry.

As a consequence, Washington is forced to keep up this monumental deception—that the present *stasis*, which it is expending enormous resources to perpetuate, is actually *movement* toward a better condition for all the peoples of the region, including—and especially—those who are being most oppressed by America's policy, the Iraqis and Iranians.

How long can America keep on with this? Who knows, maybe for years. The British managed to keep control in the Gulf for 40 years. America should be able to tie that record.

Still, as pointed out earlier, it is not just Iraq and Iran that America is having to repress; it is also Algeria, Venezuela, Indonesia, Nigeria—in other words, all of the high-absorption countries.

The United States justifies its stance by describing oil as a public good, and most certainly all of the OECD states go along with this. But it is hardly that to the producers, all of which have need to derive as much return from its production and sale as they can.

So, in the end we come down to discussing systems. The international oil system started out as a setup to control a *commodity*, oil. Over the years and most recently under the direction of the United States, that has metamorphosed into a form of *people* control.

In 1993 Washington, evidently thinking that the status quo was not a half-bad arrangement, declared the Dual Containment Policy. This appears to be as far as the policymakers can go toward devising a long-term solution to oil regulation in the new millennium. Americans evidently think that they can make Dual Containment work over time. The author doesn't believe it for a minute.

THE AFRICAN PIPELINE SCHEME

After this was written, a story surfaced of American support for a $3.7 billion oil pipeline to run from the Kingdom of Chad to the Cameroons in Africa.[105] This new development, it seemed to the author, is pregnant with possibilities, and it has a direct bearing on the thesis we have been developing throughout the book, namely, the great power of the international oil system, and its ability to rise Phoenix-like from the ashes to carry on, even after it has been presumed dead.

The details of the pipeline story are these.

The Clinton administration has thrown its support behind a World Bank proposal to essentially subsidize the construction of a 659-mile pipeline that would allow Exxon-Mobil and Chevron to develop oil fields in Chad, guaranteeing them a cheap, dependable means of conveying the oil out of the landlocked kingdom.[106]

Clinton supports this project despite the objections of various non-governmental organizations. The NGOs are unhappy because construction of the line would have serious deleterious effects on the ecology of Central Africa, and part of the the money would go to subsidize what the NGOs consider corrupt governments in the affected countries.

The Clinton administration professes to have taken such objections into account, and here is where—to use a colloquialism—the beauty part comes in.

Washington wants to escrow the profits from the oil development that would accrue to the African regimes, stipulating how the money could be spent, supposedly just on worthwile projects.

But, a government that does not have control over revenue derived from its chief natural resource is a protectorate! In other words, this whole thing has the smell of a typical international oil system operation. Indeed, it appears to carry us right back to the end of World War I and the mandates arangement, whereby the Allies took over tutelage of undeveloped states, and in the process (according to local nationalists) raped them of their natural resources.

This latter interpretation seems partially to be confirmed by the quote of one of the NGO representatives (printed in the *New York Times*), "You make the World Bank a shareholder in the project, and no government is ever going to nationalize it."

The author believes this may signal the revival of the international oil system in a new phase, as it were. Consider, with the Iraqis and Iranians refusing to submit to America's Dual Containment policy, what better way for Washington to get its way than this—shift the center of gravity of the oil industry yet one more time, away from the troublesome Persian Gulf to presumably stable Central Africa?

The governments in the Central Africa region are probably as developed as were the Middle Easterners back in the 1930s, when the last such gravity shift occurred. Hence, they should be tractable, for some time anyway. The whole operation is too new to be analyzed definitively, but this certainly does appear to be worth watching.

NOTES

1. For the involvement of Israel and, individually, of Kimche in Iran-Contra, see *The Tower Commission Report* (New York: Bantam Books, 1987), 23, 83, 111, 137, 150f.

2. For data on Israeli arms sales to markets outside the ambit of the U.S. arms industry, see "U.S. Officials Suspect Israelis Sent Ethiopia Cluster Bombs, *New York Times* (January 21, 1990); "Noreiga 'Advisor' Mike Harari Interviewed," *Foreign Broadcast Information Service*, January 6, 1990, TA0601212590; "An Israeli in Panama: Whose Broker?," *New York Times* (January 11, 1990); "Israeli Tied to Suspect Colonel Is Discovered Slain in Miami," *New York Times* (January 24, 1990); "Ethiopian Army Stops Rebel Advance," *Washington Post* (February 10, 1990); "Two Columbians Arrested in Scheme to Buy Missiles," *Washington Post* (May 8, 1990); "Israeli Arms, Ticketed to Antigua, Now in a Colombian Drug Arsenal," *New York Times* (May 6, 1990); "United States Troops Seize Israeli Regarded as Top Noreiga Advisor," *New York Times* (December 28, 1989); "Israelis Aided China on Missiles," *Washington Post* (May 23, 1988); "Israeli Consultants Should Be More Careful," *Washington Post Outlook* (September 3, 1989); "Israeli Hired Guns," *New York Times* (September 8, 1989).

3. *The Tower Commission Report*, 23.

4. Ibid., 261.

5. On U.S. provision of intelligence on Iraq to Iran, see ibid., 40, 218, 240.

6. Stephen Pelletiere, *The Iran–Iraq War: Chaos in a Vacuum* (Westport, CT: Praeger, 1992), 93f.

7. Ibid.

8. In testimony before the Congress, Secretary Weinberger stated, "I certainly did not have the view that Iraq was winning [the war] or anything of that kind. Quite to the contrary. As a matter of fact, it was basically Iraqi military strategy not to pursue any kind of decisive military end." *Report of the Congressional Committees Investigating the Iran-Contra Affair* (Washington, DC: Government Printing office, 1987), 209.

9. See Pelletiere, *The Iran–Iraq War*, 105.

10. Ibid.

11. The fact that the Iraqi military could dictate to the civilian leadership was extraordinary. Prior to this, the military was suppressed by the civilians. The names of prominent generals were never played up in the press. When victories were achieved, the generals thanked Saddam and the Ba'th leadership for them, never the other way around. Obviously, a part of what was operating here was civilian fear of the military, in particular, of having any one general gain a popular following.

12. "Conspiracy Theories and the Gulf War," *Middle East Insight* (July 19, 1996).

13. "Observer Details U.S.–Iraqi 'Oil Plot,' " *Foreign Broadcast Information Service*, LD2110075590, *London Observer* (October 21, 1990).

14. *Report of the Congressional Committees Investigating the Iran-Contra Affair*, 175.

15. *The Tower Commission Report*, 421.

16. For a discussion of the military activity in that year, in particular, of the fateful Karbala V battle, see Pelletiere, *The Iran–Iraq War*, 117f.

17. Iran may have lost as many as 70,000 to Iraq's 10,000.

18. Pelletiere, *The Iran–Iraq War*.

19. "Iraq Launches Offensive on Faw Peninsula," *Washington Post* (April 18, 1988).

20. For example, Pilip Hiro, *The Longest War* (New York: Routledge, 1991), 238, suggests the Iranians and Iraqis had brokered a truce before Iraq commenced its final offensive, under terms of which Iran agreed not to contest further.

21. They gave it to the Egyptians and Jordanians, and also to Lebanon's General Aoun of Lebanon, which certainly was done to devil the Syrians, Aoun's enemy.

22. U.S. intelligence had evidence, via satellite photographs, that the Iraqis were rehearsing the recapture of Faw by running troops through a set-piece operation in an area in which crucial sections of the Faw sector were roughed out on terrain mock-ups. See "Iraq's Dark Victory," *New York Times Magazine* (September 25, 1988).

23. Western intelligence mistakenly assumed that the Iranian garrison on Faw was five times larger than it was. After the 1987 debacle at Basrah, the clerics could not mobilize an effective force for a repeat offensive in 1988. Hence they drew off troops from Faw to bolster other areas of the front. When the Iraqis attacked, the few Iranians manning Faw fled after only a token resistance. This they could do because the Iraqis left one bridge standing over the Shatt. Western intelligence could not comprehend how the seemingly well defended Faw garrison could be so speedily overcome. They therefore claimed that Iraq had used gas. The answer was that the Iranians gave up without a fight, knowing they were hopelessly outnumbered.

24. "Gulf Peace Talks Said to Inch Ahead," *New York Times* (October 4, 1988); "Iraq, Assailing Iran's Truce Terms, Says It Must Press War in Gulf," *New York Times* (July 20, 1988); "U.N. Council Asks End to Hostilities in Gulf," *New York Times* (July 29, 1988); "U.N. to Send a Peace Mission to the Gulf," *New York Times* (July 21, 1988); "Iraq Takes Hard Line as Talks Open," *Washington Post* (July 31, 1988).

25. "Ceasefire Plan of U.N. Leader Rejected by Iraq," *New York Times* (August 3, 1988).

26. "U.N. Chief Moves for Quick Gulf Cease-Fire," *Washington Post* (July 21, 1988).

27. The first known and fairly well credited use of gas by the Iraqis was at Haj Umran in 1983. There, the Iranians, with the cooperation of the Barzani Kurds, had invaded the northern Kurdish territories, and the Iraqis, to dislodge them, used gas. The attempt was a fiasco, as the Iraqis dropped the gas on peaks held by the Kurds and the Iranians only to have it drift down into the valleys, where the Iraqi forces were set up, which disoriented Iraq's attack.

28. Iraq acknowledged use of gas on July 2, 1988, at which time Aziz said that every nation has the right to choose the means for its defense. "Iraq Acknowledges Its Use of Gas, but Says Iran Introduced It in War," *New York Times* (July 1, 1988).

29. The Kurds technically were combatants, but their activity was restricted by rules governing their participation, which the Kurds themselves had worked out. The Kurds

assented to join militias set up in the Kurdish north, and there they fought against rebel Kurds, the Barzanis, and Talabanis. The Baghdad government could not order them to leave the Kurdish areas to fight in the south.

30. The Iranians did this because the imperial army had been the bastion of support for the shah and was deemed by the clerics to be disloyal.

31. See Stephen Pelletiere, Douglas Johnson, and Lief Rosenberger, *Iraqi Power and U.S. Security in the Middle East* (Carlisle, PA: Strategic Studies Institute, U.S. Army War College, 1990); and Stephen Pelletiere and Douglas Johnson, *Lessons Learned: The Iran-Iraq War* (Carlisle, PA: Strategic Studies Institute, U.S. Army War College, 1991). Both studies have appendixes on gas. Also "Both Sides Gassed Kurds, U.S. Analysis Finds," *Washington Post* (May 3, 1990).

32. Good accounts of the battle appeared in the Western press at the time. "Poison Gas Attack Kills Hundreds," *Washington Post* (March 24, 1988).

33. Reporters ushered by the Iranians into the city after the battle reported seeing scores, at most hundreds of dead. The number of claimed victims has subsequently swollen until it has reached impossible proportions, upward of 10,000. "Poison Gas Attack Kills Hundreds," *Washington Post* (March 24, 1988).

34. Publicizing of the attack was quite slick. Of particular interest is a glossy booklet that appeared shortly after. Widely circulated, it carried color photos of the dead Kurds, with accompanying text indicting the Iraqis. *The Proliferation of Chemical Warfare: The Holocaust at Halabja* (Washington, DC: People for a Just Peace, 1987).

35. "Both Iraq and Iran Gassed Kurds in War, U.S. Analysis Finds," *Washington Post* (May 3, 1990).

36. "U.S. Charges Iraq Used Gas on Kurds," *Washington Post* (September 9, 1988).

37. Ibid.

38. *See* "Turkey Reports Kurdish Refugees Showed No Signs of Gassing," *New York Times* (September 10, 1988); "Fleeing Assault by Iraqis, Kurds Tell of Poison Gas and Lives Lost," *New York Times* (September 5, 1988); "Kurds' Symptoms: Gas or Poor Diet?," *New York Times* (September 12, 1988).

39. Ibid.

40. "Senate Votes Sanctions against Iraq," *Washington Post* (September 19, 1988).

41. These claims are contained in the staffers' report, *Chemical Weapons Use in Kurdistan: Iraq's Final Offensive*, September 21, 1988.

42. "Iraq Denies Using Chemical Weapons on Kurds," *Washington Post* (September 16, 1988).

43. One would have expected military correspondents on the major dailies to have raised this consideration. Among U.S. Army officers, it is fairly accepted that gas is not a weapon of mass destruction, and this is because of its extreme volatility; the effects cannot be easily controlled, nor can they be focused to achieve a really lethal result. "Survival Rate Stressed in Gas Warfare," *Washington Post* (October 29, 1990); "U.S. Experts Doubt Power of Poison Gas," *Washington Post* (December 13, 1990); also Stephen Pelletiere, Douglas Johnson, and Lief Rosenberger, *Iraqi Power and U.S. Interests in the Middle East* (Carlisle, PA: Stratgic Studies Institute, U.S. Army War College, 1990); Pelletiere and Johnson, *Lessons Learned: The Iran-Iraq War*.

44. "Why Do They Lie about Iraq?," *New York Times* (May 4, 1990).

45. *Chemical Weapons Use in Kurdistan*; also, "Senate Inquiry Finds Strong Evidence That Iraqis Gassed Kurds," *Washington Post* (September 22, 1988).

46. Investigations published by two organizations, Middle East Watch and Human

Rights Watch, purport to clear up these matters. However, in the author's view they raise more questions than they resolve. They are almost entirely based on anecdotal testimony. One of the reports is by a team of forensic specialists who went out to Iraqi Kurdistan to dig up remains. The team spent a week in the area and seems at most to have uncovered 15 victims. Nothing in the report indicates that these 15 were, in fact, killed by the Iraqis other than claims by the Kurds that this was the case. In any event, 15 victims is hardly genocide. The reader might want to consult two of the reports—Middle East Watch and Physicians for Human Rights, *Iraq's Crime of Genocide* (New Haven, CT: Yale University Press, 1995); Middle East Watch and Physicians for Human Rights, *Unquiet Graves: The Search for the Disappeared in Iraqi Kurdistan* (New York: Human Rights Watch and Physicians for Human Rights, 1992, 1993).

47. "Senate Votes Compromise on Iraq Sanctions," *Washington Post*, October 12, 1988.

48. "Senate Votes Compromise on Iraq Sanctions."

49. "Executed Reporter's Record of Crime Clouds Spying Case," *Washington Post* (March 17, 1990).

50. Ibid.

51. Ibid.

52. Ibid.

53. Ibid.

54. "Hundreds Reported to Have Died in Iraqi Explosion," *New York Times* (September 7, 1989).

55. "Bomb Parts Seized on Way to Iraq," *Washington Post* (March 29, 1990); also two special treatments in the newsmagazines: "The Big Sting," *Time Magazine*, April 9, 1990; "Public Enemy No. 1," *Newsweek*, April 9, 1990. These latter articles were obviously derived from intelligence sources, as can be seen from even a superficial reading.

56. "Iraq Denies Smuggling Charge," *Washington Post* (April 17, 1990).

57. "Convictions Quashed over Military Use," *Independent* (June 7, 1994).

58. "Jailed Arms-to-Iraq Pair Cleared," *Times* (May 24, 1994).

59. Ibid.

60. "Slain Specialist Worked for Iraq," *Washington Post* (April 6, 1990).

61. "Britain Blocks Shipment of Metal Tubes to Iraq," *Washington Post* (April 13, 1990).

62. "Slain Arms Maker Linked to Tube Shipment," *Washington Post* (April 17, 1990).

63. "Charges Dropped over Supergun Exports to Iraq," *Financial Times* (November 16, 1990).

64. "U.S. Alleges Plot to Kill by Iraqis," *Washington Post* (April 7, 1990).

65. This, in many respects, is the most puzzling story of the lot. It is quite clearly a nonevent, as can be seen from perusing the *Post*'s account. Yet the *Post* played it in the number two spot on page 1.

66. "U.S. Welcomes Move by Tehran," *New York Times*, July 17, 1988.

67. Iraq did allow journalists to tour the affected area. "Kurds Disappoint Iraqi PR Effort," *Washington Post*, September, 18, 1988.

68. "Administration Seeks to Defer Decision on Iraq Sanctions," *Washington Post* (April 27, 1990); "Bush Aide Opposes Sanctions on Iraq," *New York Times* (June 15, 1990).

69. "U.S. Maligns Him, Iraqi Tells Senators," *Washington Post* (April 13, 1990).

70. "Excerpts from Iraqi Transcript of Meeting with U.S. Envoy," *New York Times* (September 23, 1990). This transcript was released by the Iraqis; the author considers it authentic.

71. "Stopping Saddam's Drive for Dominance," *Washington Post Outlook* (August 5, 1990); "Iraq's Criminal Credit Line," *New York Times* (October 26, 1989); "Israeli Defences against Arab Gas Attacks," *Manchester Guardian* (March 12, 1989); "Iraq Said Developing A-Weapons," *Washington Post* (March 31, 1989); "The Middle East's Awful Arms Race: Greater Threats from Lesser Powers," *New York Times* (April 8, 1990); "Iraq's Arsenal of Horrors," *Washington Post* (April 8, 1990); "Why Are We Helping the Third World Go Nuclear?," *Washington Post Outlook* (April, 1990); "Arab Weapons Challenge Israel's Role in the Region," *Washington Post* (April 4, 1990); "Iraq Said to Build Launchers for Its 400-mile Missile," *New York Times* (March 30, 1990); "To Combat the Growing Iraqi Threat," *New York Times* (May 30, 1990); "Israel Looks Around and Finds New Causes to Worry," *New York Times* (May 27, 1990); "Turning a Blind Eye to Baghdad," *Washington Post* (July 5, 1990); "Must the U.S. Give Brazil and Iraq the Bomb?," *New York Times* (July 20, 1990). It is also interesting that, even though in 10 years no victims of the alleged gassing attack on the Kurds have been produced, the media go on treating the incident as an established fact. "Germs, Atoms and Poison Gas: The Iraqi Shell Game," *New York Times* (December 20, 1998); "Lessons from Halbaja," *Washington Post* (August 20, 1999).

72. For example, Senator Alphonse D'Amato (R–NY), Senator Claiborne Pell (D–RI), and Representative Howard Berman (D–CA).

73. "Israel Worries That Iraqi War Machine Poses Threat," *Christian Science Monitor* (July 20, 1988).

74. As pointed out earlier until 1986 Saddam micromanaged the war. The generals took orders from the civilian leadership. To achieve the success of the Tawakalna Ala Allah campaign, Saddam and his fellow RCC members had to step back and allow the generals to take charge. For a totalitarian government such as Iraq's, this was a fundamental shift.

75. Someone who was well known for this sort of behavior was J. Edgar Hoover. Hoover regularly fed exposés, showing off the prowess of the FBI to the press. Indeed, the FBI cooperated with Hollywood in producing films like *The House on 92nd Street*, puffs for the FBI. Also Hoover was relentless in targeting civil rights leaders in various sting operations.

76. There were some moves to do this. An Iraqi-American Business Council was formed. Senators in the Midwest were active promoting farm aid, and there was even a move to bring an Iraqi officer to the U.S. Army War College.

77. The author assumes that the interests worked through the Congress. Given how lobbyists came to dominate the American political system in the 1990s, that seems a legitimate assumption.

78. Especially if Iraq were to supplant Saudi Arabia as the leader of OPEC, given that Iraq was a high-absorption state.

79. In April 1990 Saddam threatened to incinerate half of Israel if it moved against him. His blast was occasioned by Israel's announcement that it would loft a spy satellite that would give it real-time intelligence, and then, Israel officials hinted, Israel would go after Iraq's weapons plants. In other words, a repeat of Osirik. "Iraqi Warns of Using Poison Gas," *Washington Post* (April 3, 1990); "A New Spy in the Sky," *Time Magazine* (April 2, 1990).

80. Ibid.

81. *The Tower Commission Report*, 49f.

82. Which was done by the Israelis before the Osirik attack.

83. For the origins of the Iraq–Kuwait dispute, see H. Rahman, *The Making of the Gulf War* (Reading, England: Ithaca Press, 1997); and Majid Khadduri and Edmund Ghareeb, *War in the Gulf* (New York: Oxford University Press, 1997).

84. "Sluggish Iran–Iraq Talks Worry Kuwait," *New York Times* (March 25, 1989).

85. Ibid.

86. "OPEC Meets Today; Talks Are Clouded by Iraq's Threat to Kuwait," *New York Times* (July 25, 1990).

87. Rick Francona, *Ally to Adversary* (Annapolis, MD: Naval Institute Press, 1999). 40.

88. Transcript reprinted in *New York Times*, September 23, 1990.

89. Another analogy would be red-lining, when banks refuse to loan to businesses and homes in a neighborhood to force them to sell out, so that the neighborhood can be gentrified.

90. Transcript of the Glaspis interview, *New York Times*, September 23, 1990.

91. "If Mideast War Erupts, Air Power Will Hold Key to U.S. Casualties," *Wall Street Journal* (November 15, 1990). U.S. Air Force General Michael Dugan believed the Iraqis could be bombed into submission and no ground troops would have to be used.

92. The behavior of both Egypt and Saudi Arabia is particularly suspect. Arab League actions up to this point were supposed to be taken unanimously. However, when Iraq brought its case against Kuwait to the League, the Saudis asked for a change so that a simple majority rather than unanimity would be sufficient for any voting procedure. Egypt was instrumental in getting this change approved, and this is the way that Iraq lost out.

93. Indyk delivered his talk "The Clinton Administration's Approach to the Middle East" as a keynote address at a dinner put on by the Washington Institute for Near East Policy, a pro-Israeli think tank in Washington, D.C. The date was May 18, 1993.

94. "Venezuela President's Oil Bet Pays Off," *Wall Street Journal* (August 16, 1999).

95. When one considers the enormous amount of public money that goes to subsidizing this industry, it's hard to take the truckers' part. They destroy the roads with their huge rigs, not to mention wrecking the small towns that they necessarily pass through.

96. "Cohen Seeks Defense Help," *Harrisburg Patriot-News* (April 9, 2000).

97. Essentially, the trade-off is that the sheikhs, who are anachronisms in the twenty-first century, get protection in return for paying tribute (arms purchases) to the United States.

98. "OPEC Meets Today; Talks Are Clouded by Iraq's Threat to Kuwait," *New York Times* (July 25, 1990).

99. Ibid. The Saudis' action is difficult to fathom. The author believes Riyadh attempts to balance its moves with OPEC—Riyadh can resist opposition from one strong state, e.g., Iran, but a lineup of Iran and Iraq or Iran and Venezuela is, for the Saudis, problematic.

100. The only satisfactory procedure for the United States would be either to say where the 100,000 alleged gassing victims repose (which it should be able to do with all of its satellite and infrared imaging equipment) or to give a convincing explanation of how the Iraqis could have gassed 100,000 people in a two-week period and disposed of them without a trace.

101. In any event, the United States is no longer self-sufficient in oil, or at least it cannot be so without conservation. "U.S. Reliance on Imported Oil Is at Record High," *New York Times* (February 16, 1990).

102. "Iraq Sanctions Kill Children, U.N. Reports," *New York Times* (December 1, 1995).

103. Albright's statement that half a million infant deaths is something Americans are prepared to accept certainly is that. "Albright's Tiny Coffins," *Counter Punch* 16, Vol. 6 (September 16–30, 1999). For additional details on civilian deaths in Iraq due to the embargo, see "A Re-examination of U.S. Policy on Iraq," *AAUG Monitor* 1, Vol. 15 (Spring 2000).

104. "U.N. Chief Faults U.S., Britain for Iraqi Supply Delay," *Washington Post* (March 14, 2000).

105. "$3.5 Billion Africa Pipeline Expected to Pass," *New York Times* (June 6, 2000).

106. Exxon and Mobil merged in 1999; BP and Amoco, the former Standard of Indiana, merged the same year to form BP Amoco PLC.

Index

STEPHEN PELLETIÈRE is a Professor of National Security Affairs at the U.S. Army War College. He is a specialist in Middle East politics. As an intelligence officer since 1982, he has covered the Iran-Iraq War and the subsequent Gulf conflict. Prior to that, he was a Professor of Political Science and a foreign correspondent in the Middle East. He has written several books on the Middle East, including *The Iran-Iraq War: Chaos in a Vacuum* (Praeger, 1992).